GLIMPSES OF DEVĀYAṆA

प्र मे पन्था देवयाना अदृश्रन्नमर्धन्तो वसुभिरिष्कृतास ।
अभूदु केतुरुषसः पुरस्तात्प्रतीच्यागादधि हर्म्येभ्यः ॥ Rig. VII.76.2.

The result of this birth of divine vision is that man's path manifests itself to him and those journeys of the Gods or to the Gods "Devayana" which lead to the infinite wideness of the Divine Existence. Before me the paths of the journeyings of the Gods have become visible, journeyings that violate not, whose movement was formed by the Vasus. The eye of the Dawn has come into being in front and she has come towards us over our houses.

Sri Aurobindo, On the Vedas, p. 209

GLIMPSES OF
DEVĀYAṆA

A Short Synopsis
of
The Third Epic of India

BY
DR. HAJARI

Editor
Amita Nathwani

New Age Books

ISBN: 978-81-7822-284-4

First Edition: Delhi, 2007

Published by
NEW AGE BOOKS
A-44 Naraina Industrial Area Phase-I
New Delhi-110 028 (INDIA)
Email: nab@vsnl.in
Website: www.newagebooksindia.com

Printed in India
at Shri Jainendra Press
A-45 Naraina Phase-I, New Delhi-110 028

FEELINGS

Feeling the sunrise
Feeling the sunset,
Our minds trickle
With the passion of the wise

Feeling the good
Feeling the evil,
Our souls are absorbed
By what we trust
Sometimes leading to happiness
Sometimes leading to disgust

Feeling the heat
Feeling the cold,
Our spirits burn
With the desire for gold

Feeling the future
Feeling the past
I finally wonder;
What is going to last?

—Nishin Nathwani
(12 Years)

Significance of the Cover Page (Designed by Sonal & Radhika)

The red ball signifies the massive divine dawn appearing from the East.

The grey contour over the red ball signifies the transient present time that is full of doubt, despair and disapproval. The world has still to accept the Devāyaṇa.

The golden (yellow) light represents the Golden Age of full Divine Light that will inevitably come for a long period. This is wonderfully described in the Epic Devāyaṇa.

The monkey being a victorious power represents divine victory over the vital and the physical plane. The two lotuses symbolize divine consciousness and divine conscious power.

In action, this power establishes divine consciousness and power on the vital and physical plane through its indomitable heroism.

CONTENTS

In Gratitude xiii
Editor's Note xv
To My Motherland xix
Foreword xxi

1. Descent of the Devāyaṇa 1
- The Beginning
- Structure and Contents of The Epic

2. Creation, Manifestation and Evolution 5
- On Creation
- On Manifestation
- On Evolution

3. Early Days of Man 19
- Ancient History of Man
- Aryan and Non-Aryan

4. Startling Crystallization of Thoughts 23
- Birth and Death
- Death and After Death
- On Time
- Relation Between Time, Rebirth and Māyā
- Dharma and Peace
- Varṇa (Caste) and Chanda (Metre)

5. Battling the Asuric Forces 33
- World Peace and Unity
- Influence of Hostile Forces on Unity
- Invocation of the Supreme Truth
- An Adoration of Divine Indra

6. Retaliation of the Hostile Forces 39
- Asuric Influence on the Divine Kingdom
- Manifestation of the Divine Mother
- Opposition of the Demon Mother

7. Division of Time 43
- Ascertainment of the Ages
- The Arrangement

- Birth of the Ages
- Trita Yuga
- Dvita Yuga

8. The Iron Age Appears **59**

- Baleful Influence of Kali
- Iron Age and Its Functions
- The Material Consciousness
- The Life Energy
- The Mental Creation
- Knowledge and Ignorance
- Discovery of Supermind
- Reality of the Supramental Plane
- The Destiny

9. Efforts of the Immortals **93**

- Memories of the Past
- A Moment of Peril
- The Spiritual Cataclysm
- The Future Vision

10. Appearance of the Devāyaṇa **143**

- The Controversy
- In the Course of Manifestation

11. Transit to The Golden Age **155**

- Adventure of Dawn Towards Night
- Release of "Rātri", The Night
- The World Soul (Viśvadeva–Jagat Sūrya)
- Pure Vital Existence (Taranta)
- Existence of Pure Joy (Bhagadevatā)
- Existence of Divine Beauty and Immunity
- Transformation and Divine Victory
- Why the Divine Victory is Variable?
- Opening the Wide Gate of Immortality
- Sacrifice of Simplicity and Sincerity

12. Advent of the Golden Age **177**

- Divine Birth in the Human Ignorance
- Conqueror of Ignorance
- A Transitional Period

13. The Golden Age **183**

- Coronation of Vasukra
- Golden Age Manifested
- Kingdom of the Vasus and Perfection of Devāyaṇa
- Exchange of Vasu Race

- A Transmutation, Kingdom of Traiaruna
- Curse of Saci, Appearance of Arbuda
- The Supreme Errand

14. End of the Golden Age—A Transitional Period **197**

- Beginning of Efforts in Nature
- Commencement of Fight in Nature
- Conqueror of Demons
- Conclusion

APPENDICES

I. Short Summary of The Epic Devāyaṇa **207**

- Chronology of the Four Ages

II. Cantos 1–4 of The Devāyaṇa—A Concise Description **235**

- The Dream and The Vision
- Om and Its Significance
- Goddess Gāyatrī and the Gāyatrī Mantra
- Creation of Other Metres
- The Epic Devāyaṇa
- Method of Manifesting The Epic

III. Tables of Contents **247**

- Volume I
  - ♦ Deva Maṇḍala
  - ♦ Ṛṣi Maṇḍala
  - ♦ Yajña Maṇḍala
  - ♦ Biti Maṇḍala
  - ♦ Pragaṭha Maṇḍala
- Volume II
  - ♦ Trita Maṇḍala
  - ♦ Rāma Maṇḍala
- Volume III
  - ♦ Rāma Maṇḍala (Contd.)
- Volume IV
  - ♦ Bhṛgu Maṇḍala
  - ♦ Rājarsi Maṇḍala
  - ♦ Sāvitri Maṇḍala
  - ♦ Dvita Maṇḍala
- Volume V
  - ♦ Dvita Maṇḍala (Contd.)
  - ♦ Bharata Maṇḍala
  - ♦ Bhārata Maṇḍala
- Volume VI

- ♦ Bhārata Maṇḍala (Contd.)
- Volume VII
  - ♦ Bhārata Maṇḍala (Contd.)
  - ♦ Parīkṣit Maṇḍala
- Volume VIII
  - ♦ Kṛṣṇa Maṇḍala
  - ♦ Ahi Maṇḍala
- Volume IX
  - ♦ Kali Maṇḍala
  - ♦ Arbuda Maṇḍala
  - ♦ Laya Maṇḍala
- Volume X
  - ♦ Pratiṣthā Maṇḍala
  - ♦ Aptya Maṇḍala
  - ♦ Kasyapa Maṇḍala
  - ♦ Aditi Maṇḍala
  - ♦ Udyama Maṇḍala
- Volume XI
  - ♦ Udyama Maṇḍala
  - ♦ Uṣā Maṇḍala
  - ♦ Ākhyana Maṇḍala
  - ♦ Bhaga Maṇḍala
- Volume XII
  - ♦ Indra Maṇḍala
  - ♦ Vasu Maṇḍala
  - ♦ Vrṣṇu Maṇḍala
  - ♦ Sohana Maṇḍala

Glossary **289**

Mantras to be Chanted to Prepare Oneself to Welcome the Golden Age **307**

End Notes **309**

First Four Cantos of Devāyaṇa in Original Bengali **313**

First Four Cantos of Devāyaṇa in Devanāgarī **323**

Charts **333**

- Chart A – Three Creations of Parabrahman
- Chart B – Kaśyapa's Creation of Devas and Asuras
- Chart C – Creation of Brahmā, Viṣṇu, Maheśvara
- Chart D – Three Creations of Kaśyapa
- Chart E – Creations of Satyadeva and Nakta

IN GRATITUDE

Whoever hopes to publish Devāyaṇa, has waged a war with family, friends, society and public life for it is a poetic work of a colossal bulk. It is expected that one who works for this mammoth task has no time for anything but for Devāyaṇa. One is compelled to live totally in its spirituality, feelings, thoughts, language and rhythms that combine the movements of the whole history of mankind, repeating again and again in its four cycles of evolution. When I told my family that I am going to rewrite the original synopsis—everyone in the family just responded with a big silence.

When the time came, the same family stood by me, and supported me, much above my expectations.

My heartfelt gratitude to my mother who introduced me to the Devāyaṇa.

My deep appreciation to my children Niraj, Sonal and Suraj—who helped me in jumping over many hurdles.

With heartfelt thanks and appreciation to my brother Rakesh and his wife Geetika who always provided their unstinted support.

My profound thanks to my nephew Nishin who luckily came from Toronto to spend a summer vacation in the beautiful city of Vienna. He helped me by solving minor and major problems of my computer. He made the charts printed in this book and wrote the poem "Feelings".

My husband, like all husbands, is exactly opposite to my nature. He, who never agrees with me on anything, to my surprise never even once showed opposition though we did not see eye to eye on a common working method. Much against his nature, he kept patience and silence and let me work in my own way. In silence, he wrote letters for me and carried my computer to repairs without being grumpy whenever it broke down. This was quite often. That was indeed an immense help. I thank him from the bottom of my heart for always being there.

Above all, my love to my grandson Amit, who stood by me smiling, not knowing what I was doing, and to my grandson, Shivam, who arrived in this world while this work was being prepared for publication. Also a big thanks to Radhika, who has recently joined our family.

My sincere thanks to Prashant Khanna who agreed to edit this synopsis when everyone else shook their heads.

Above all, my deepest gratitude and prayers to Dr. Hajari who always remained with me in spirit, to help me and guide me, whenever I wished. With Dr. Hajari's name I may appropriately close the insights into the mystical third epic of India. Devāyaṇa is a mission for the spiritual life's inner transformation. This endeavour keeps alive the deepest rhythms of our quest for inner beauty and eternal joy. May this joy infuse all who read this short account, inspiring them to turn to the original Devāyaṇa.

Amita Nathwani

EDITOR'S NOTE

Devāyaṇa, the third epic of India, narrates the complete human cycle lasting for 26,000 years covering the Golden, the Silver, the Bronze and the Iron Ages. It consists of twelve volumes, each having a thousand pages, in the Anuṣṭubh chanda—the classical Indian epic metre. The Anuṣṭubh metre is four-footed, each foot consisting of eight letters, with the fifth letter short, the sixth long and the seventh short. In addition, there are some two hundred seventy different metres utilised for the thousands of closing couplets at the end of each saṁvarga as well as in the innumerable hymns and prayers to the Gods.

With its mighty poetic rendering, invincible in its approach in all aspects, this epic unveils a new era that puts us in the midst of a new civilisation, a new consciousness in which we find the activities of the Vedic Godheads in their manifestation in the human form. For the first time, we find the description of the Golden Age that will divinise the earth lasting for 13,000 years. This Age commences with the descent of Lord Viṣṇu in his Avatāra as Kalki, signalling the beginning of the Satyayuga. In this Age, Lord Indra together with the eight Vasus will reign supreme and the entire creation will experience unimaginable joy and bliss.

Devāyaṇa predicts that the present materialism in the world would soon wither away and mankind will regain its spirituality. This epic has such an immense magnitude that it is difficult for us mortals to grasp its true importance. This reminds me of two powerful stanzas from an eloquent short poem of Sri Aurobindo called *In the Moonlight.*

It comes at last, the day foreseen of old,
What John in Patmos saw, what Shelley dreamed,

Vision and vain imagination deemed,
The City of Delight, the Age of Gold.

The Iron Age is ended. Only now
The last fierce spasms of the dying past
Shall shake the nations, and when that has passed,
Earth washed of ills shall raise a fairer brow.

—*Sri Aurobindo*

I first met the author of Devāyaṇa, Dr. Hajari, in the early 70's. He described to me the contents of Devāyaṇa that was written by him in Bengali. Since then, I developed a keen desire to know the details about this immense epic, penned down by him. At that time, I did not think that this curiosity would later on become a raging passion with me. Since I read the synopsis, it became a continuous obsession. This changed the course of my life. I decided to take an early retirement and to dedicate my life to study and to work on the epic. I learnt Bengali at the age of fifty-five to read it in the original. Undoubtedly there would be many other curious and interested individuals in the world. This synopsis is to draw their attention to Devāyaṇa. It would give them an introduction to the epic with its great plan for humanity. This may lead them to read the epic in the original.

Bengali, the original language of Devāyaṇa is very near to Sanskrit. I am at present transcribing this epic in the Devanāgarī script to make it available to a wider public. The result is Devāyaṇa in a language that is perhaps the Sanskrit of tomorrow—a readable amalgam of Sanskrit, Hindi and Bengali. All the languages of the world are going through this process, where new forms of expression are emerging, despite the opposition of conservative Pundits. This change is inevitable in the development of a language. Eventually, the classical Sanskrit will also revive in a new form and become a modern language of communication in India and the entire world. Then Devāyaṇa will play the role of a milestone in this direction. I honestly hope that this synopsis will lead the aspirants of Truth to the original Devāyaṇa now being published in Devanāgarī volume by volume.

To give a taste of the epic to the reader, the first four

cantos are provided here in the original Bengali and in Devanāgarī (transcribed from the highly Sanskritised Bengali) with their translation in English. Three volumes of the epic have already been published and can be obtained from the publishers Motilal Banarsidass of Delhi.

A companion volume to this present one, called *The Voice of the Ṛṣis* (also originally written by Dr. Hajari), is under preparation, to provide the authenticity of Devāyaṇa with references from the Vedas. This will substantiate the story of Devāyaṇa with further visions of the Vedic Ṛṣis.

Originally, this Synopsis was written and published in four parts by Dr. Hajari from 1957 to 1960 in English, and translated into French, Bengali, Malayalam and Tamil. At that time, the daily newspapers in India, The Hindu, The Sunday Standard and Indian Express commented on the epic when Devāyaṇa existed only as a manuscript. The present edition is a revised version of the synopsis keeping, as far as possible, to the terminology of the author.

I am more than convinced that no synopsis can really do justice to the original Devāyaṇa. One would require a much larger treatise to elucidate the beauty of the epic. However, a much deeper analysis will defeat its own purpose as modern readers, except researchers, have little time. With this short synopsis, we hope to draw the attention of some researchers, seekers of Truth, and lovers of literature to this much-neglected vast world literature. We earnestly wish to stimulate their curiosity about the original epic. Its close study will surely enrich them. The world cannot afford to overlook this great treasure trove.

It is absolutely essential, especially now, that humanity prepares itself to welcome the Golden Age, the much desired Satyayuga. For this, Dr. Hajari had prepared a number of mantras which needed to be chanted daily. To facilitate this mediation, we are enclosing a CD entitled—Welcome to the Golden Age—with the necessary mantras set to music. These may help us to prepare for the advent of the Golden Age.

Amita Nathwani

TO MY MOTHERLAND[1]

To remember a birthday is mainly to welcome the advent of a soul. To celebrate the birthday means to glorify the cause and reason of the soul's coming to this earth.

O My Motherland! You are presently full of sorrows, in complete disarray and in torment. Only few manifestations on your sacred soil have been for your happiness and liberation from the nefarious influence of hostile and sinister forces. Aeons before, you were fully liberated from these dark influences. You were filled with divine *Ananda* and bliss to welcome the Divine Manifestation before Thee. You were the chosen place where the divine kingdom had established itself and where the Gods remained busy in their divine play. This was at the end of the Silver and the Bronze Ages.

O Divine Brooding Motherland! We remember and worship with Thee, the 21st February, the day of advent of the Divine Mother who opened the celestial path, to facilitate the play of Gods on your soil. We remember and worship with Thee the ninth new moon day at the end of spring and the eighth full moon day at the beginning of autumn.

O Prithivī! The twenty-first February has been the day decided by you as the most auspicious day. On this day, we adore and pray to the Divine Mother thus—"O Mother Divine! Thy presence in me is my divinity. With Thy embrace, I obtain my divine nature and consciousness. O All-Puissant Mother! I adore Thy eighty years of presence

1. This prayer was included in the original synopsis of Devāyaṇa. This was blessed and signed personally by The Mother on her eightieth birthday.

in my innermost being. I bow down a hundred times at Thy Lotus Feet."

O Mother Divine, at this auspicious moment, I prostrate before Thee and offer the synopsis of the Devāyaṇa at Thy Lotus Feet.

blessings

Hajari

FOREWORD

THE MOTHER DIVINE

When a new light breaks in the human mind, a new awareness engulfs the human consciousness. Then, a new creation is seen by the eyes, a new voice echoes in the ears, and a new taste and touch is experienced by humanity. An epic manifests.

An epic cannot be visualised by the human mind nor can it be constructed by the imagination. When the time comes, the Supreme Will manifests the epic directly in the world through a human channel. A future creation takes shape through words. And a new age epic takes a concrete form to increase our awareness of this new manifestation.

Neither mental endeavour can create an epic, nor human efforts achieve it. The Supreme Will alone chooses the time and place to manifest the epic. At first the Supreme Power decides within itself; then brings down the light, divine joy *ananda*, peace and consciousness through the human mind, and slowly wakes it up to a greater life.

All my thoughts, efforts and time were used by the force of the Divine Mother to realise the Supreme Will in the form of the Divine Play "Devāyaṇa". This is to be seen as her homage to the Lord.

I became the witness of the Supreme Mother's action. I remained a spectator. I noticed how She was using my mind, life and body to bring about a divine creation through the words of Devāyaṇa.

It was on Her will that I acted. With joy at the completion of this divine work, I bow down my head again and again at the Mother's lotus feet.

Hajari

Chapter 1

DESCENT OF THE DEVĀYAṆA

The compiler of the epic Devāyaṇa, Dr Hajari, suddenly woke up from a profound sleep towards the end of one deep dark night. All was quiet around him. He heard the sound of the creation *OM*, coming from his navel centre. He experienced the divine grace pouring over him and felt that he was drenched in heavenly ambrosia. In this way, he became an instrument of the divine will and witnessed a magnificent vision in the form of words and images that poured down on him from above. This he penned down.

THE BEGINNING

His daily encounter with the Divine Truth continued as the Supreme Creator, Piṅgala Maheśvara and his own Gúru, Sri Aurobindo, were with him. He knew that Sri Aurobindo's power of meditation and tapasyā, his grace and influence had made him an instrument through which the great Epic could manifest.

He realised the significance of OM, the primal universal sound; OM, as the Akṣarabrahman and the source of all creation. He realised that OM was the beginning from where the worlds of the Divine Trinity, Brahmā, Viṣṇu and Maheśvara manifested: Brahmā as the Creator, Viṣṇu as the protector, and Maheśvara as the destroyer of the Universe. Sri Aurobindo has said this very poetically in his epic poem-

There in a hidden chamber closed and mute
Are kept the record graphs of the cosmic scribe,
And there the tables of the sacred Law,
There is the Book of Being's index page,
The text and glossary of the Vedic Truth

Are there; the rhythms and metres of the stars
Significant of the movements of our fate:

Savitri, Book One-Canto Five
Sri Aurobindo

Subsequently, the Gāyatrī and six other metres of poetry (Uṣṇik, Anuṣṭubh, Bṛhatī, Pankti, Triṣṭubh and Jagati) manifested. He saw the four Vedas come out from the four mouths of Brahmā in four different directions—north, south, east, and west.

He observed the Divine Poet Piṅgala Maheśvara—who appeared before him with his matted hair, to raise humanity from an animal to the Life Divine. He heard the deep voice of Piṅgala speaking to Kaśyapa, the Creator of Gods, who observed him with astonished eyes.

Piṅgala said—"This is the right place, O Great Creator. I have decided that the Epic should manifest here and with it a new creation. Please bestow the power of your long penance to your devotee, Dr. Hajari, so that he may increase his ability to bear the immense force of the flow of this Epic."

On hearing the powerful voice of the Supreme Poet, in the Anuṣṭubh metre, the three worlds trembled and a vast epic manifested.

This new creation in the Anuṣṭubh metre signals the beginning of a new human cycle—consisting of the four Ages, the Golden, Silver, Bronze and Iron Ages, lasting for 26,000 years. With the ending of the Iron Age, the Golden Age recommences. This is the constant turning of the Time Wheel resulting in the change of Ages.

The Creator invoked Ganapati, the elephant God, who removes obstacles and provides perfection to facilitate the work of manifestation.

Dr. Hajari, with his inner eyes, saw the Divine Luminous Being—Piṅgala Maheśvara—with Kaśyapa, the Creator of Gods, and Gaṇeśa, the beloved son of Śiva and Pārvatī. When he heard their divine voices and powerful conversation, he felt exalted and his entire being vibrated with joy.

Just as a connoisseur gathers gold and jewels, that are rare and extremely precious, he started to collect and compile the divine words flowing down from above as he heard them hour after hour, every single day.

Days passed into months and years. He heard the divine voices with an increasing wonder and without any fatigue. His heart was blessed and he was swept along with the flow of the descending words. He compiled and collected this epic and remained just a medium.

Extracts from Devāyaṇa, 1-2 cantos

STRUCTURE AND CONTENTS OF THE EPIC

The Supreme Poet said to the Creator Kaśyapa – "Behold, 0 Supreme Creator! The Divine Epic, manifesting the Truth, is haloed with a brilliant light. I name this new epic – Devāyaṇa. It moves from one Golden Age to the next, unfolding the secrets of the creation. O Creator of Gods, this epic has manifested here as the result of your efforts to bring down the Golden Age, a divine life and a supramental race upon the earth. This epic is very significant for mankind."

"It is divided in twelve volumes, each volume having a thousand pages—containing innumerable ślokas. Everything that had happened in the four aeons is recorded here in its entirety in the order of its occurence.

"Look at the Devāyaṇa in the eternal sky. See the four Vedas flanking its four sides, Ṛgveda from the east, Yajurveda from the west, Sàmaveda from the north, and Atharvaveda from the south. O Great Creator, in the dark sky, the Sun and Moon are the brightest. There, Devāyaṇa shines like a bright star. In the divine blaze, observe the divine incarnation of Viṣṇu, descending on the earth as King Rāma of the Solar Dynasty. This is described in the epic Rāmāyaṇa. Śrī Rāma was a famous warrior and became uniquely victorious in the three worlds by overpowering the demonic forces."

"On the other side, you can observe the glorious life of Lord Kṛṣṇa from the Lunar Dynasty as in the epic

Mahābhārata. Lord Kṛṣṇa descended from Janārdana (Viṣṇu). He is famous for his deeds through his incomparable intellect and knowledge. There are thousands of other glorious characters, each glowing with divine power and knowledge."

See the passing of the four Ages, like day and night, in Devāyaṇa. The Golden Age is radiant like a bright day, where Sūrya as the Lord of Truth and the Divine Mother with her children manifest. The Iron Age is pitch dark like the night, where Kali, the Lord of the Iron Age, and the demonic forces dominate. Between these two ages, Time is divided further. Trita is like the dusk and Dvitā the first part of the night. Then the Truth Sun manifests."

Chapter 2

CREATION, MANIFESTATION AND EVOLUTION

A Mystery's process is the universe.
At first was laid a strange anomalous base,
A void, a cipher of some secret Whole,
Where a zero held infinity in its sum
And All and Nothing were a single term,
An eternal negative, a matrix Nought:

Sir Aurobindo:
Savitri, Book Two/Canto One

ON CREATION

Nothing existed in the beginning, before the creation of the universe, no life, not even light or darkness. There was only a vast void, like the sky, spread out as the one omnipresent, unthinkable and unmanifested cosmos. The cosmic consciousness Parabrahman as indicated by the Vedas had a three-fold will for the creation.[2] The first wish of the unmanifested Supreme was to manifest. This wish, known as the conscious force of Parabrahman, is called Juhū.

Juhū drew the Parabrahman in herself and manifested a creation with an incalculable ecstasy. This creation, full of delight—*ānanda,* manifested nine-fold. The Veda called them Pataṅga, Prajaban, Yajña, Vimada, Viṣṇu, Sāmvaraṇa, Hiraṇyagarbha, Yakṣmanāśana and Dakṣiṇā, being the daughter.

The **second wish** of the Parabrahman was to multiply and to increase. With this wish, a huge area of light (the Marīci-

2. Refer to Chart A Three Creations of Parabrahman. (see p. 333)

Maṇḍala) manifested. Within this light appeared the seven creators—Kaśyapa, Aṅgirā, Atri, Bharadvāja, Gautama, Kaṇva and Mitra-Vasiṣṭha. Kaśyapa was the first-manifested and the eldest of the creators. He asked the Parabrahman why he was called into existence in the midst of a vast void. The answer came for the multiple manifestation of the One. How can these be acquired, Kaśyapa asked. The Parabrahman replied that this could be done through intense meditation.

Kaśyapa started meditating on the Supreme Consciousness. His deep and intense meditation lasted twenty-six thousand years. As a result of this intense effort, all that was pure and good in his body manifested as a radiantly beautiful figure, possessing great power, and scattering a vast brilliant light all around. She is known as Aditi in the Veda. She is the Goddess of the infinite being and the mother of Gods.

All that was impure and dark in Kaśyapa's body also manifested as a figure possessing great power. She was Diti. Thus, through his intense efforts Kaśyapa, the Creator, brought into existence both light and its antithesis, darkness. Both Aditi and Diti became creative powers, and gave form to their own worlds with Kaśyapa's help[3].

Aditi created the Godheads (suras) and the plane of Gods (suraloka). The Transcendent Mother, Aditi has created the Gods as the permanent manifestations of the Divine. Gods are the offspring of her intense Light. Their duty is to fortify man, pouring in him light from the higher planes, and the heavens, in abundance, and making him aware of the Divine Truth. Gods build up Divine worlds in the entire creation as well as in the individual being. They shield him from all anti-Divine attacks and lead him to divine *ānanda.*

At the same time, Diti, the antithesis of the Divine Mother, has diametrically conflicting goals. She created the world of the Devils so that she could oppose the Divine descent. The Devils created by her are immensely powerful vital beings in nature whose main aim is to oppose the Gods. They love to

3. Please refer to Chart B—Kaśyapás Creations of Devas and Asuras. (see p. 334)

divide and rule. They are the ones who delude the immortal soul of a human being by suggesting that he is mortal, and that many things are beyond his reach. They receive pleasure and satisfaction in tearing him down, devouring him, and convincing him that he is powerless, imperfect and inadequate. These powers work constantly against the inborn will of a being that wishes to turn towards the Divine. Thus, the Creator himself created the principle of duality, or thesis and antithesis, which we see prevailing all around us.

These luminous and sombre forces exist on the higher supramental plane (the Maharloka). The supramental plane is the dwelling place for both Gods and Devils at the same time.

Aditi created the seven great Godheads—Indra, Candra, Sūrya, Vāyu, Bṛhaspati, Agni and Mitra-Varuṇa. These seven Godheads formed the heaven and dwelt therein (svargaloka or suraloka).

Diti created two very powerful Devils, Vṛtra and Paṇi. From the beginning of creation, there were bitter and prolonged fights between the Gods and the Devils. Indra managed to defeat and destroy Vṛtra after a long and protracted struggle. Paṇi remained alone and created hell (Asuraloka). Paṇi and his creations are called Paṇis, the Devils. One of them was the famous Śukrācārya, the renowned teacher of the Devils.

The Āindras[4], sons of Lord Indra, the sons of the other Godheads and the Paṇis existed in a plane called the greater heaven. The grandsons of the great Godheads lived in a plane called the lower heaven or little heaven.

The **third wish** of the Supreme Consciousness, the Parabrahman, was "to act"[5]. A huge commotion began through the will of the Supreme Consciousness. This caused

4. Indra's creations—Jaya, Laba, Vasukra, Vimada, Vṛṣakapi, Sarbahari, Apratiratha.
Candra's creations—Mangala and Buddha
Surya's creations—Abhitapa, Dharma, Cakṣu, Vibhrat.
Vayu's creations—Anila, Oula
Brihaspati creations—No son, only two daughters—Lakṣmī and Dākṣayanī.
Agni's creations—Cākṣuśa, Tapasa, Pavaka, Barhaspatya, Sauchiki, Vaishvanara.
Varuna's creations—Bhrigu, Satyadhriti.
5. Please see Chart C—Creations of Brahmā—Viṣṇu—Mahesvara. (see p. 335)

the coming into existence of Vācya (Brahmā), the Creator; Parameṣṭhī (Viṣṇu) the Protector; and Rudra (Śiva), the Destroyer as the Divine Trinity. The Purāṇas describe in detail the activities of Brahmā, Viṣṇu and Maheśvara. Vācya is the Viriñci Brahmā. Parameṣṭhī, Hiraṇyagarbha or Sarasvān is Viṣṇu. Viṣṇu remains on the water as a protector of the ocean, Brahma-Sindhu, and is portrayed as seated on the thousand-headed snake. Rudra, the destroyer, is called Maheśvara. Brahmā is by his very nature the Creator. By the word and the cry he expresses and creates all beings and starts existence and a movement in life as knowledge begins to evolve. This brings out eventual forms of beings from the darkness that evolve out of the Inconscient. Rudra, the Violent and Merciful, the Mighty One, takes control of the struggle of life to establish himself as the divine power. He is fully equipped with arms, is furious and still a beneficent powerful expression of God. He pushes the creation higher, destroys all that opposes him, scourges all on the wrong path. He restores all that is wounded, suffering and complaining. Viṣṇu of the immense pervading motion holds all these worlds in his triple stride. Only with him we ascend to the highest position in creation where we find waiting for us a Friend, a Beloved, and the Serene Godhead.

Vācya, made a tremendous commotion waving his four heads. As a result, the four Vedas came out from his four mouths–Ṛg, Sāma, Yajur and the Atharva Veda. A huge light emanated with it. This was the formation of the Āditya Maṇḍala.

The coming into existence of the four Vedas was accompanied by a huge upheaval in the Universe. Vācya continued shouting. This disturbed Rudra, the Destroyer, who was in his deep meditation. He went after Vācya to silence him and not upset the creation. However, when the Destroyer wakes up from his meditation he destroys everything around him, both good and evil. At that time, Parameṣṭhī, the Protector, came in front of Rudra to save the Vedas and the creation. He exercised his will on Rudra to quieten him down.

Rudra calmed down and took the form of Śiva. In the immense effort to save the Universe and the Vedas, Rudra, the destroyer, succeeded in becoming Śiva, but became exhausted and he perspired.

This huge flow of perspiration formed a great ocean and was named the Brahma-Sindhu as mentioned in the Purāṇas. From the Brahma-Sindhu, three beings were born, named Dakṣa, Sarasvāna and Tvaṣṭā.

From all creations of Kaśyapa, Bṛhaspati is the most intelligent. Bṛhaspati gives the word of knowledge, the rhythm of expression to the superconscient. Parabrahman was very pleased with Bṛhaspati and gave him Dakṣiṇā, his daughter. Through this marriage, two daughters were born, Lakṣmī and Dākṣāyaṇī. Lakṣmī married Lord Viṣṇu and Dākṣāyaṇī was given to Dakṣa. Dakṣa and Dākṣāyaṇī had hundred daughters. They married various Godheads.

Tvaṣṭā remained as the Artist of the Universe.

The Supreme Godheads were happy to see the vast enlightened ocean. They asked their father, Kaśyapa, why the water was ablaze with such a dazzling light? Kaśyapa's answer fascinated them. He told them that the ocean contained immense treasures and vast riches. They could possess these if they succeeded in extracting them from the ocean. The Gods and the Devils were both very tempted. They asked their father how could they acquire these riches from the depth of the ocean. Kaśyapa said that through an intense churning of the ocean, the riches would come out. Thus, both the Gods and the Devils started churning the ocean. Both wanted to acquire the riches so as to possess immense power. By churning the ocean, incalculable treasures were found that included the Vedas, the Divine knowledge and *amṛta* or ambrosia, the nectar of immortality. All these riches, however, preferred to belong to the Devas and to avoid the Asuras. The Asuras or the Devils felt cheated, as they did not receive even half of the riches. They became furious and violent. They fought with the Gods, as they felt betrayed. Above all, they wished to obtain the nectar of immortality, *amṛta*. The Gods swallowed the whole bowl of the nectar before it fell in the hands of the Devils. The Devils also tried to possess the Vedas, the universal knowledge. These were given to the creators, who swallowed them to protect them from the Devils.

With the manifestation of the four Vedas, a vast light emanated from the four mouths of the Vācya-Brahmā. Tvaṣṭā was busy as an artist. He created an illuminated male being—a Puruṣa—called the Āditya Chanda (metre), the personification of the metre. Tvaṣṭā undertook a great spiritual austerity to create—Satya (the Truth), Nakta (the Falsehood) and a Divine power named Gāyatrī. She is the goddess of the Divine chants and metres. Goddess Gāyatrī brought into existence, six chandas (metres)—, Uṣṇik, Anuṣṭubh, Bṛhatī, Paṅkti, Triṣṭubh and Jagatī. From these six metres were formed fourteen secondary metres. The Āditya Chandas was also called the Akṣarabrahman, the primordial sound that created the universe. The ocean, Akṣarapa, where Sarasvān (Viṣṇu) has his seat, remained illumined by Akṣarabrahman.

The Ṛṣis worshipped the Akṣarabrahman and prayed to the Lord of Akṣarapa to protect and save the Vedas. The Ṛṣis came into existence from the four dynamic powers (Māheśvarī, Mahākāli, Mahālakṣmī and Sarasvatī), and the creators, Kaśyapa, together with the seven creators—Aṅgirā, Atri, Kaṇva, Gautama, Bharadvāja, Vasiṣṭha and Mitra. The names of these Ṛṣis are in **Endnote 1.**

To bring back the Vedas, the Ṛṣis were illumined with the power and light of the Vedic knowledge. The Ṛṣis maintained the knowledge of the Vedas by chanting them for the Devas as well as for the Akṣarabrahman and Akṣarapa. The four Vedas—Ṛg, Sāma, Yajur and Atharva Veda—appeared before them. The Ṛṣis then asked Satyadeva (the Lord of Truth) to guard the Vedas and to keep them safely for future generations. Satyadeva held the four Vedas in his four hands and was called by the Ṛṣis as "Puruṣa Vedamaya" (The Male Being with the Vedas).

Parameṣṭhī created another creation through his Will—similar to Āditya Chandas—called the Sūrya Vivasvān. Under the influence of Satyadeva and through his own meditation (tapasyā), he increased his own power and light and created an area around him called the Savitṛi Maṇḍala. Vivasvān was advised by Parameṣṭhī to create, so he together with his power Savitṛ-Sūrya created Vivasvatas—Manu, Sūrya-Vivasvat and Jagat-Sūrya or Viśvadeva. The higher heaven extends up to the Vivasvān.

As mentioned earier, Kaśyapa, the Divine Creator, brought into existence the seven great Gods as well as powerful Devils with his two powers, Aditi and Diti. He engaged himself further in intense meditation for several years[6]. As a result of his powerful efforts in this direction, two more powers appeared from his body named Yākṣāyanī and Rākṣāyaṇī. Yāksāyanī created Viśvāvasu and Rākṣāyaṇī gave birth to Kālkeya. Furthermore, Viśvāvasu created Yakṣaloka or Gandharvaloka (where the semi-Divine beings lived) and Kālkeya the Rākṣasaloka (where the Demons lived).

Again, Kaśyapa engaged in a long and protracted meditation and from his body two further powers emanated called Vinatā and Kadrū. Vinatā had two sons, Sampāti and Garuḍa. Kadrū had hundred sons—Ananta, Vāsuki, Seṣa, and Arbuda etc. These were the three creations manifested by Kaśyapa, the Divine Creator. Parameṣṭhī, Vācya and other creators also formed other creations. Parameṣṭhī created through his will—the splendid Puruṣa—Āptya and the powerful Prakṛti—Ambhrinī. They grew up and were educated by the Āditya Chandas. The Puruṣa—Āptya and Prakṛti—Ambhrinī became united. Āditya Chandas became angry at their marriage and cursed them. As an effect of this curse, Dvita, their eldest son was born a weakling, his body half burnt. Trita, their second son was handicapped, he was lame. The Creator Āptya shaped the three worlds, Bhūr[7] Bhuvar[8] and Svar[9] and a daughter Vāk. Āptya offered his daughter Vāk to Satyadeva (the Lord of Truth) for the

6. Please see Chart D– Three Creations of Kaśyapa. (see p. 336)
7. World
8. Hell
9. Heaven

manifestation of Truth. His sons controlled the three Bhuvanas, the three different planes of existence at certain periods in the human cycle.

The Svar Bhuvana is the plane that we see from the earth and call it heaven. There the Sun—the Jagat Sūrya or Viśvadeva—remains shining. When Vivasvān ordered the Bhuvanas to further the creation, Gāyatrī Devī gave her daughter Jagatī to them. Svar Bhuvana and Jagatī created two sons, Sādhana and Viśvakarmā. Moreover, Jagatī created with Bhuvar Bhuvana a son Pitṛvya and with Bhūr Bhuvana a daughter Mahī, the earth.

Vāk, daughter of Āptya and Ambhriṇī, was given to Satyadeva for the creation of Truth. However, Nakta (the dark force) kidnapped Vāk and forced his will on her. When the Creator came to know that Nakta had captured Vāk, he became furious and roared for him. Nakta, on hearing the Creator's powerful voice, was frightened. He fled and tried to hide himself, leaving Vāk. The Creator found Vāk, and discovered that she was pregnant. He was extremely offended and asked her to abort the child. She aborted and a half developed child came into existence. That obnoxious birth was a being with an oblique shape, having the body of a serpent, wings of a bird and head of a horse. It had the circular movement of a wheel.

Aptya, the Creator, gave him the name Kālacakra (the Time Wheel). He ordered the Kālacakra to direct the three worlds. In this manner, he became the holder of the three worlds.

After giving birth to Kālacakra, his mother Vāk liberated herself from the influence of Nakta, by undergoing a prolonged purification process to remove all traces of evil from herself. She was absorbed in a trance for a long period. With the touch of Satyadeva, she was purified.

Together with the Sun, the Jagat Sūrya, Sādhana and Viśvakarmā, the Vasus and Ṛbhus were also staying at the Svar-Bhuvana. The seven Vasus came from the Aindra-Vasukra and were as follows: Vasukrid, son of Vasukra; Vasukarṇa, son of Vasukrid; Vaṣurociṣa, son of Vasukarṇa; Vasuyuva, son of Vasurociṣa; Vasuśruta, son of Vasuyuva; Vasuna, son of Vasuśruta; and Vasumāna, son of Vasuna. These Vasus reigned on the earth during the Golden Age.

Gāyatrī's son Paṅkti had a son called Virāja. He in his turn had a son named Ribhava-vairāja. The son of Ribhava was called Ṛbhu and then there were many Ṛbhus. These Ṛbhus are the builders of immortality on the earth. They are in the form of human beings who have arrived at the state of Godhead by the power of their knowledge and perfection. The Ṛbhus help Indra in the evolution of man towards that level of divine light and bliss that they themselves have reached.

The Ṛṣis chanted mantras to invoke Satyadeva, the Lord of Truth in the Svar-Bhuvana. In response, Satyadeva, the Lord of Truth, manifested[10]. He took birth as the son of Abhivarta-Aṅgiras and played like a boy. While playing, the Lord of Truth began to transform everything he touched. He was asked to hold the Time Wheel, and to guide the three worlds with the power of Truth. The Ṛṣis requested Satyadeva to unite with Vītihotra, the psychic being. Their union brought into existence Uṣā-Saṅgana (the Divine Dawn) and Pūṣa (the Power of Truth) whose help would be essential to bring about the Golden Age. Satyadeva gave Uṣā-Saṅgana to Jagat Sūrya for the creation of the Bhuvanas. Jagat Sūrya married Uṣā-Saṅgana, the daughter of Satyadeva.

Nakta, who had disappeared from the creation, did not like the influence of Truth on the three worlds. He undertook a great penance for a spouse. Through his tapasyā, the power Vibhāvarī appeared from his body. She became his wife. Nakta and Vibhāvarī gave birth to a daughter, Sandhyā-Chāyā.

At the same time, Jagat Sūrya and Uṣā-Saṅgana gave birth to a son, Vaivasvata Yama and a daughter, Yamī. The Puraṇas narrate that when the Sūrya or Viśvadeva became a creator, the brightness, light and power emanating from him was absolutely unbearable for Usā-Saṅgana. After the birth of

10. Please refer to chart E—Creations of Satyadeva and Nakta. (see p. 337)

Yama and Yamī, the mother became extremely frightened. She fled from the Svar-Bhuvana and hid herself in the deep sea. At that time, Nakta instructed his daughter, Sandhyā-Chāyā, to take the form of Uṣā-Saṅgana, and remain with Jagat Sūrya in her place during her absence. So he created with Sandhyā-Chāyā, another twin birth. These were Śani (Saturn), the son and Mṛtyu (death), the daughter.

After some time, an acrimonious and bitter quarrel began between Śani and Yama as well as between Mṛtyu and Yamī. Yama and Yamī saw their mother giving constant preference to Śani and Mṛtyu. Seeing this partiality, Yama started doubting his own mother and complained to his father Sūrya. The Purāṇas say that Yama is Dharma.

When Jagat Sūrya became conscious about this deception, he asked Sandhyā-Chāyā about the whereabouts of Uṣā-Saṅgana. She was frightened and trembled on hearing the question. She could not give any reply. So Sūrya went to look for Uṣā-Saṅgana. He entered the ocean in the shape of a horse and found Uṣā-Saṅgana hiding there as a mare under water. They met each other in the water, became joyful, and created twin sons, called the Aśvinī Kumāras. They emerged from the sea by rejecting their horse shapes. When Uṣā-Saṅgana came to her own place, there was a great quarrel with Sandhyā-Chāyā.

To avoid further altercations, Sūrya kept them in two separate worlds. Uṣā–Saṅgana stayed with Yama, Yamī and the Aśvinī Kumāras in the pure heaven (śuci-svarga). Sandhyā-Chāyā remained with Śani (Saturn) and Mṛtyu (death) in hell.

For the creation of the pure heaven, Yama married eleven daughters of Dakṣa—Lakṣmī (Goddess of fortune, prosperity and beauty), Lajjā (modesty), Dhṛti (satisfaction), Kṣamā (forgiveness), Dayā (sympathy), Puṣṭi (good health), Tuṣṭi (contentment), Smṛti (good memory), Kānti (brightness), Medhā (intellect), and Prīti (love). With these eleven wives, Yama created seven sons (Dharmeyas) and one daughter. They were Aurdhva-Kṛṣṇa, Kumāra, Damana, Devaśrava, Mathita, Śaṅka, Saṅkusuka and a daughter Śānti-Yamāyani.

For the creation of hell, Śani created eighty-four Narakas (hells) with Mohinī-Māyā and these Narakas created innumerable diseases.

The creations of Dharmeyas and Narakas influenced Pitṛloka. Pitṛloka is the place where Pitṛvyas (the departed spirits) stay just after death. Pitṛvya created two sons, Dyuma and Antarikṣa. Taranta, son of Uṣā-Sūrya also stayed there as a Sun of that plane. Taranta married Śaśīyasī, the daughter of Vāyudeva and had two sons called Vaidadaśmi and Purumilha. They influenced the Bhūr Bhuvana. In these three planes, (Bhūr, Bhuvar, Svar) there are also other Godheads and Ṛṣis. These are mentioned in the **Endnote 2.**

In the Bhuvarloka, the being (jīva) has six enemies, which are—passion, anger, greed, attachment, ego and jealousy (kāma, krodha, lobha, moha, mada, mātsarya). Three necessities make a deep impact on all beings—hunger, thirst and sleep. These were created by Manu, the Creator of the world.

ON MANIFESTATION

The seven Creators created a world for themselves. Each was divided in two sub-worlds. Hence, fourteen worlds were created and inhabited by Gods and Goddesses, Ṛṣis and Ṛṣikas, Gandharvas and Gandharvīs, Vasus, Ṛbhus, Pitṛvyas (departed spirits), and Vihaṅgama (birds), Asuras (devils), Rakṣāsas (demons), Naktas (dark forces), Narakas (hells), Pretas (spirits) and Bhujaṅgamas (snakes) living in them. The names of these planes were given according to the beings inhabiting there. Devaloka was for the Gods and Goddesses. Ṛṣiloka was for the Ṛṣis or sages, Gandharvaloka, the plane of absolute beauty for the demi-gods—the singers, musicians and artists. In Vasuloka—the eight deities or Vasus, who were custodians of wealth, lived there. The Ṛbhuloka, world of the Ṛbhus, was created for them, Pitṛloka—for the spirits of the ancestors, Vihaṅgaloka—for the birds, Asuraloka—for the devils, Rākṣasaloka—for the demons, Tāmasaloka—for the forces of darkness, Adharmaloka—for the beings who do not live according to the rules of right conduct, Narakaloka—hell, Pretaloka—for the spirits, and Nāgaloka—for the snakes.

These are the fourteen planes of existence. Seven are above the earth—constituting the higher regions, and seven beneath the earth that are the nether regions. The beings in these various worlds asked their Creators what the purpose of their existence was and what aim they should pursue. The response was that they should manifest further through their own efforts.

The beings of the Mahar world, which is just above the earth level, started their activity through intense worship. Viśvakarmā, with an immense effort, took the lead as an artist towards giving a shape to his manifestation. The Gods chose Manu for the manifestation.

Before starting the creative effort, Manu engaged in a long meditation. Through his yogic austerity, the evolutionary force (Śatarūpā) appeared from his body. This was the Śakti or the female creative power of Manu and she had a radiant body. With the evolutionary power, Śatarūpā, Manu started the manifestation. A huge light emanated from Śatarūpā's physical body and spread out in the sky. This light was given an artistic shape and was arraṇged throughout the sky by Viśvakarmā, as the sun, the stars and the planets. As Sri Aurobindo has so well said in his Savitri,

A gas belched out from some invisible Fire
Of its dense rings were formed these million stars
Upon earth's newborn soil God's tread was heard.

Savitri- Book Two/Canto One

Śatarūpā became apprehensive of Manu's immense power of manifestation, as the light appeared in the sky. As Manu advanced towards her, she wanted to escape and then to flee. Manu used his creative will on Śatarūpā's fast movement that resulted in a vast spread of water. In order to escape further efforts, she hid herself in the water. Manu went searching for her in the water and applied his creative will on her. As a result, she created soil in the water. That huge quantity of soil delivered with the help of Sādhana was shaped by Viśvakarmā and thus land was formed under water. With the creation of soil, Śatarūpā had nowhere left to flee. She walked on the land and Manu followed her there. His creative will formed an upward movement inside the earth. Viśvakarmā caused the formation of mountains and trees on earth. To avoid further creation, Śatarūpā took refuge in an atomic body. Manu gave his creative light in her atomic body. This was the beginning of the process of evolution on earth with the help of intense meditation.

ON EVOLUTION

Śatarūpā started to evolve from the atomic to the molecular form and delivered a world of bacilli. Viśvakarmā gave different shapes to them. Manu, on seeing that huge bacilli creation, gave his creative light in the molecular body of Śatarūpā, and thus started the process of evolution with the help of Sādhana. From a molecular body, she evolved into the form of a small reptile. After that, she delivered an immense number of reptiles. The reptile then evolved into a small insect that resulted in a large assortment of insects. Manu, then, gave his creative light in the insect body and through evolution the insect body developed into a big reptile. There were huge numbers of big reptiles. From big reptiles, the evolution progressed on to fishes, and further through various types of fish. The fish evolved into an animal body and then the evolutionary force progressed through different types of animals. Until this stage, the evolutionary process remained still under water.

Innumerable varieties of life remained under water. The creators asked the Godheads to bring the creation out of the water. Through the effort of the Gods, part of the creation came out of the water and manifested as our earth. On the land that emerged from the water, there were mountains, trees, bacillii, insects, reptiles, and animals. Many of them became extinct in the process of evolution, as they did not survive the direct sunlight. Still, a large number of animals adapted themselves to the new earthly conditions. They changed their colours, shapes, and sizes by coming into contact with the sun and evolved into different forms. The lower Godheads, up to the Bhūvar Bhuvana (vital plane) saw these beings and were impressed by the animals, birds and others. They made their abode in these vital bodies.

The higher Godheads did not like the shapes of the existing beings. They asked the creators, how they could manifest. The Creator ordered Manu to continue with the evolution. To please the higher Godheads, he started creation of a higher order on land with the help of Śatarūpā. With Manu's creative light in Śatarupā's animal body, she achieved the shape of a cow. Then, there were a large number of cows. The cows were shown to the Godheads, but they did not like making their abode in a cow's body. Evolution continued further and the form of a horse was fashioned. The Godheads did not like the horse as well. Manu continued with the next stage that was a being, which was half-animal, and half-man. Śatarūpā delivered the form of a monkey but still this did not meet with the complete approval of the Gods. Manu once again gave his creative force, in Śatarūpā's monkey body. She started to evolve and passed through many kinds and shapes of monkeys. At last, the shape of a woman was created. Manu gave his creative light in her human body. She delivered a man-child. On seeing the shape of the woman and the first-born man, the Godheads expressed joy and agreed to make their abode therein. Manu was content and he stopped Śatarūpā from evolving further. He finished his work of manifestation and Śatarūpā, the evolutionary force, retired from the woman's body. Thus, the process of evolution reached the stage of completion.

Chapter 3

EARLY DAYS OF MAN

Mircea Eliade said that man is essentially homo religious—a being who craves the transcendent. This inherent craving is most evident in the elaborate myths and rites of initiation through which archaic man understood and organised his world. Objects such as a mountain, a stone, water or a tree were assigned a sacramental character, which revealed the sacred without, at the same time, erasing their profane identities. For Eliade the history of religion is the study of the sacred and its manifold manifestation.

A Scholar's Sacred Quest – Newsweek
July 15,1985

With the completion of the work of manifestation and evolution by Manu, a great step forward was taken in the grand plan. Gods were then asked to enter into the human body, which they did gladly. As the Aitareya Upaniṣad says: Agni (Lord of Fire) entered into the mouth as voice, Vāyu (Lord of the Wind) entered into the nose as the life force of a man, Sūrya (Sun God) came into the eyes as sight, Rudra (Lord Śiva) in the ear as hearing. Vanaspati (Lord of Vegetation) entered into the skin as touch, Candra (Moon God) entered in the heart as mind, Mṛtyu (Goddess of Death) entered into the navel centre and Varuṇa (Lord of the Ocean) entered into the lower abdomen as semen.

ANCIENT HISTORY OF MAN

The first man who manifested on the earth was left to himself amidst huge populations of insects, reptiles, animals, birds and monkeys. The Godheads were an intrinsic part of the man to protect him from other beings. The Veda named him "Kardama"[11]. He realised that he was very different from other creations as it was the Gods, existing in him, who influenced him. He started to become aware of himself. As he became increasingly conscious, he saw the creators and Gods residing in himself. He gained knowledge about his own birth and his innate powers. He remained in long meditation and from him manifested Ivā[12], his female creative power. She was needed for furthering the human race on the earth. On observing the skeleton body that was initially left by Satarūpā, Ivā entered that body and brought it to life. She came before Kardama. The creators instructed Kardama to create and to expand the human race. They also told him that he would receive this knowledge through the meditation of Brahmā. Kardama, together with Ivā, meditated on Brahmā. Then Saṁvaraṇa, the creative power, appeared before them. Through that power, Kardama created a son in the womb of Ivā—who was called Mānava—Saṁvaraṇa. Again, Kardama meditated on Indra, and Sarvahari appeared, who influenced the womb of Ivā and a child named Śaryāti–Mānava was born. Then he meditated on the sun and there appeared Sūrya-Cākṣuṣa. With his influence, a child was born named Cākṣuṣa Mānava. After that Kardama came under the influence of anti-divine forces. He created hundred sons and daughters. After a large number of sons and daughters were born, the creation process ceased.

ARYAN AND NON-ARYAN

Human beings, born under the divine influence, were worshippers of Gods and created a distinguished culture of their own. Others, who were born under the demonic influence, had no inborn culture and were brought up in different human environments. In families having good karma, where the divine was worshipped, Gods and Ṛṣis were

11. Note how this coincides with Adam of the West.
12. Eva of Western thought.

born during different times. They used to cultivate land and build their houses. They developed art, and further advanced their technique in agriculture. They were able to domesticate cows, horses, elephants etc., and used them to make their life more comfortable. Laws were developed to avoid clashes and misconduct in the society. They established a kingdom, where the king was the leader of the country. Divine power was also attributed to his person. These people called themselves Aryan. Aryan in Sanskrit means dignified, noble or chaste.

The Aryan is noble as he works hard and fights valiantly to improve himself and to propel upwards towards the Truth. He is neither lazy nor a coward. He is not afraid of efforts in the mental or physical plane to seek and serve the Supreme. Problems do not deter him. He does not give up due to fatigue. In the struggle to achieve the realisation of the divine kingdom within himself and in the world he is not ready to accept any compromise. Such are the warriors of Truth.

However, the others, who lived nearby and were not worshippers of higher Godheads, developed no culture. They used to live in the mountain caves and under the trees. They did not cultivate land. They managed to still their hunger by eating half-burnt animals and birds, plucking fruits from trees and digging out roots of plants. They were the non-Aryans.

Thus in the beginning, as even today, two different kinds of people populated this world, the Aryans and the non-Aryans. There were those who pursued spiritual and intellectual goals in life and others whose aim in life was for more power and riches.

The Aryans did not respect the non-Aryans as they found them wild and uncivilised, having no culture. The non-Aryans led their lives without any rules. The Aryans continued to push them into a corner, to defeat them and to kidnap their beautiful girls for marriage. The non-Aryans became very violent and began to fight with the Aryans. In this, the devilish forces influenced them. The non-Aryans discovered newer and more powerful weapons to win in their constant battles.

This caused an increasing number of deaths on both sides. Death became dominant and a greater part of the population died.

The Aryans concentrated on finding solutions to problems facing them and they gained deep insights into themselves. They examined problems which are confronting us even today and they came up with solutions which continue to surprise us.

Chapter 4

STARTLING CRYSTALLIZATION OF THOUGHTS

The Aryans concentrated on finding solutions to problems facing them and they gained deep insights into themselves. They examined problems which are confronting us even today and came up with solutions which continue to surprise us.

BIRTH AND DEATH

Then, the Aryans began looking for ways to defeat death. They tried to find the reasons for death. They discovered ways to avoid death and follow the path of immortality. They sang the songs of amṛta (ambrosia) and everlasting youth. They started an esoteric enquiry into the origins of humanity. They discovered the micro universe within themselves through meditation. They acquired this knowledge through the Vedas. To defeat the non-Aryans, they also discovered powerful divine weapons. There arose many fierce battles between these two groups, which became extremely bloody and violent. After many years of continuous warfare, the Aryans lost their inborn energy and became tired. Through fatigue, diseases started to affect their health. These diseases strengthened the power of death, which affected them increasingly. At the same time, negative feelings of passion, greed, anger, stupidity, ego and jealousy entered into all human beings. The Aryans continued to win battles and the non-Aryans became fearful and fled to the forests to hide themselves. Many of them died.

The dark forces of death, as well as disease, passion, greed, anger, stupidity, ego, jealousy, sorrow and repentance influenced the Aryans, with the result, that they lost their everlasting youth and health. The non-Aryans tried to solve the problem of death by producing more children, so that the struggle with the Aryans could continue.

DEATH AND AFTER DEATH

After defeating the non-Aryans, the Aryans successfully drove them out of their inhabited area into the wildernesses of the forests. They started a discussion on the problems that plagued them constantly. A large number of deaths had occurred in the fights. This caused them agony and despair. They understood that death was the ultimate cause of all disharmonies in their lives. Banishing death would lead to a never-ending happiness. A solution to death was to be found in the micro universe inside them.

The quest to achieve immortality commenced. They began to contemplate and to meditate. In deep meditation, they entered into an absolute trance where they did not even breathe, and their heartbeats came to a standstill. This state was called samādhi, a condition very similar to physical death. They discovered the inner soul. In the deep trance, they learnt how human beings leave their body after death. With the knowledge of death, they also discovered that the life force in a human body is due to the fire element called the soul and that it is immortal. They saw the soul attached to the body with a physical formation. This attachment of the soul to the body was mainly because of the destined life span of one person. It was also due to attachment to the world as well as the love and sympathy that destiny had in store for the person. So began the theory of Karma. In this attachment of the body to the soul, the death force makes a fissure and the life of a person ends, allowing the soul to quit the body. The soul escapes from the mortal body, just as a bird escapes an open door cage. Death is caused by diseases, epidemics, accidents etc. When the soul leaves this body, the sheath of the subtle body still remains. The soul remains for a further two days on the earth, two days in the water, two days in the air, two days in the fire and one day in the ether. Within one week, the remaining components of the body dissolve in their particular domains.

The path of the soul is described in the Piṇḍa Upaniṣad. Leaving the physical body, the soul or jivātman remains for ten days in the physical plane. In the next step, it passes to the vital plane and remains there as long as necessary for its development. The duration of the stay in the pitṛvya loka (vital plane) depends upon the actions and karma of the person during his life on the earth. His anguish or delight in this plane depends upon the nature of his activities, positive or negative, during his lifetime. At the end of his stay in the vital plane, the soul remains in attachment for two days, in desire of life for two days, in the movement of life for two days, in the effort of life for two days, and finally in the inanity of life for a day. If a person has not made any spiritual efforts in his lifetime, he does not proceed higher than this plane, but comes back with his former mental body back to the plane of his father and forefathers. His new life begins at the point he left his last body. The process of evolution begins at the point he had left before.

All the spiritual development or worship of Gods in the former life is as a spiritual credit to the spirit. It allows the spirit to go to higher planes. He goes directly to the plane of the Gods he had worshipped in his lifetime. If he was a worshipper of Brahmā, he goes to the plane of Brahmā. If he was a worshipper of Viṣṇu, he goes to the plane of Viṣṇu with the four hands. The worshipper of Indra goes to the plane where Indra with his thousand eyes is supreme. In this way, the devotees go to the planes of the Gods they worshipped during their lifetime. Their stay in that plane lasts only as long as the credit they have earned during their stay on the earth allows them. During that time, with their mental shape, the devotees can stay and enjoy the same divine life as the Godheads. When the time is over he is bound to leave that mental body. He gains a new mental body according to his desires and the help from the Gods. They push the spirit towards the plane of the earth (pitṛvya). With the help of his forefathers, he takes another vital sheath. The spirit moves towards the physical plane to enter into his mortal father. First, he enters into the mind of the mortal father, then to the life and afterwards to the blood. From the father's blood, he enters into the mother's womb. This is well described in the Garbha Upaniṣad.

It narrates that on the first day of the sperms' entry into the womb, the spirit causes blood density, in seven days it takes the shape of an egg. By two weeks, the foetus has increased to the size of a cricket ball, by a month to the size of a coconut. The further development of the new soul is as follows: by two months the head forms, by three months the two legs expand, by four months the two hands, feet, belly, stomach and waist build up. By five months, the baby gets his back bone, by six months his nose, eyes and ears, by seven months his life and all the senses. By eight months, the body is completely developed and by nine months the baby is ready to be born. The birth of a baby on the earth takes a little more than nine months. Our present science confirms the findings of the Garbha Upaniṣad.

ON TIME

The Aryans discovered the way to achieve immortality, the secrets of birth and death, what happens after death, as well as the subsequent rebirth. They realised that there was a great impact of time (Kāla) on all these. All activities of Gods and mortals are largely influenced and controlled by time. Nothing takes place, divine or demonic, without the influence of time. Time is an all-powerful force that stands between human and divine existence. All activities depend upon the movement of time. They discovered that time has two conflicting movements. One is to help the divine forces to enlighten the earth and the human beings. The other is to be of assistance to the hostile or devilish forces in further spreading darkness on earth to the detriment of human beings.

This important discovery was of great significance for all time. The Aryans divided time in two categories, good and evil. They observed that while the time of Truth was full of divine activities, the time of falsehood was full of negative or anti-divine activities. Hence, they divided the human cycle into a Day and Night of creation. The Day was under the influence of the Lord of Truth (Satyadeva) and was called the Golden Age or Satya Yuga. The Night, under the influence of the dark forces of Kali, was known as the Kaliyuga (Iron Age). In between the Golden and the Iron Ages, they recognised two periods to protect the achievements and the memory of Truth, namely the Silver and the Bronze Ages. During these ages, help was sought from the Ṛṣis who had gained the knowledge of Time. They provided aid to preserve Truth and further divine activities. These ages were called the Dvita and the Trita Yuga.

The Aryans knew that time was controlled by Rudra, the Creator and the Destroyer. For this reason, they called him Mahākāla. His power, Maheśvarī, acts as the mother of all. She is the Mother Durgā. She is also Mahākāli acting in different times of manifestation. She battles ruthlessly against the haters of the Divine.

RELATION BETWEEN TIME, REBIRTH AND MĀYĀ

The rebirth of the soul depends upon the influence of time. This influence is pronounced during the time of death and rebirth. When the soul decides to take rebirth, it comes back to the earth or rises to higher levels. This power of time is called Mahāmāyā, the cause of all attachment. This attachment could be to the world, to life, to material goods or to duty. The power of Durgā, Mahāmāyā, Maheśvarī influences the entire creation. Through her influence, human beings remain attached to life, to the world or to worldly events.

To release themselves from the cycle of rebirth, the Aryans meditated on Māyā and Rudra, Time. They realised that if human beings are not free from the influence of time and attachment (māyā), they are bound to revolve continuously through the wheel of birth and death. In this condition, they are bound to remain in the cycle of rebirth. One cannot be liberated from life and the world without worshipping Time and Māyā. Therefore, the Aryans worshipped Time (Mahākāla—Rudra) and Māyā (Mahāmāyā Durgā). They sang hymns to Durgā and Rudra so that humanity achieves liberation from the cycle of life and rebirth. Their mantras helped to achieve release from attachment to life and rebirth. One rises above birth and death, pleasure and pain, sufferings and enjoyment.

DHARMA AND PEACE

The Aryans achieved the knowledge of immortality by freeing themselves from the influence of time and attachment. They achieved liberation from the wheel of birth and death, by avoiding rebirth through complete detachment from worldly enjoyment. They entered into trance and through this way they tried to achieve immortality. However, this path did not appeal to everyone. Some tried to enjoy the world. They wished to discover how to enjoy the world and life. Through their efforts, they discovered that there were two kinds of influences on human beings. First the divine influence, the Dharma-Yama. Second the antidivine influence, the Adharma-Śani. Both are sons of the Sun God, but they are from different mothers. They observed that the influence of Dharma (Code of Right Conduct) helped the human beings to form a connection between life and soul. The soul is beyond hunger and thirst, pleasure and pain. Dharma influences the soul with his eleven powers to bring peace. To know Dharma and to become conscious of it is to attain peace. He, whose life follows the rules of Dharma, obtains peace in this world and after leaving this body enters into heaven where he enjoys immortality. They observed that the influence of Śani is a barrier between life and soul. Falsehood makes a human being insincere and leaves him open to attack from diseases, pain and sorrows.

The power of Dharma promotes truthfulness, sincerity, simplicity and steadiness in work. The powers behind Dharma are Lakṣmī (Goddess of fortune, prosperity and beauty), Lajjā (modesty), Dhṛti (satisfaction), Kṣamā (forgiveness), Dayā (sympathy), Puṣṭi (good health), Tuṣṭi (contentment), Smṛti (good memory), Kānti (brightness), Medhā (intellect), and Prīti (love). Thus, one who is happy to work is influenced by Lakṣmī, one who refrains from doing wrong or from committing mistakes is influenced by Lajjā, one who demonstrates steadiness in work is under the influence of Dhṛti, one who does not criticise other's faults has Kṣamā, one who sympathises with everyone is under the influence of Dayā, one who has sound health is influenced by Puṣṭi, one who remains ever content has the blessings of Tuṣṭi, who has love for all has Prīti, one who can remember his past has Smṛti, one who has good health has Kānti, and finally one who can memorise and utter whatever he hears is influenced by Medhā. This is how Dharma with his eleven powers establishes peace.

Crookedness, insincerity, unwillingness to work, penchant for falsehood, inclination to invite sorrows, diseases, sufferings, jealousy, anger etc. all lead us to hell.

VARṆA (CASTE) AND CHANDA (METRE)

The Aryans discovered that the difference between achieving heaven or hell depended upon their own choice. i.e. their deeds, their karma. They decided to develop a peaceful human society by following the path of dharma—right conduct to create a world without sorrows, sufferings, diseases, and disharmony. They knew that by following the rules of dharma, humanity would find everlasting peace. To establish peace, they analysed and divided the nature of work. By their analysis, they saw three different streams of activities, which affected human nature in various ways. These were the three Guṇas (constituents of nature) namely *sattva, rajas* and *tamas* which affect all human beings in various ways. The quiet movement—*sattva*—furthers knowledge, spiritual austerity, penance (tapasyā) and study. The vigorous movement—*rajas*—furthers the wish to earn wealth and property, to establish supremacy, and to become more active. The movement of lethargy (*tamas*) induces one to become lazy, inactive, unwilling to work, stupid, always sleepy. Tamas is the opposite movement of knowledge. When the Aryans discovered these three movements in the human nature, they divided humanity into four groups. These are the four castes or varṇas—Vipras or Brāhmaṇas—the learned ones, Kṣatriyas or the warriors, the Vaiśyas or the business peoples and the Śūdras or the workers. The Vipras or the Brāhmaṇas are there to further spiritual study, tapasyā and the realisation of Truth etc, the Kṣatriyas to rule the earth, to engage in warfare and pay attention to managing the human society. The Vaiśyas are responsible for the development of society, to increase the number of domestic animals and birds, to cultivate the land and to further trade and business including export and import. The Śūdras are the workers who assist the other three and work under them. In this way, the peoples of the earth were divided into four groups and they harmonised their individual activities always following the rules of dharma. This promoted peace in the human society.

However, problems arose in maintaining peace for a longer period of time. Human language is an instrument for individual expression and assists in communication. At times with the devilish influence, peace was disturbed through the words of an individual. The Aryans studied the spoken words to recognise the force guiding the sound, the formation of letters and words through an individual's speech. After a long and intense study, they found three different influences at the root.

First they saw Vāgdevī Sarasvatī, who is guiding letters to form words—a line to speak the language with the Mantras (divine couplets) in a harmonious way. They thus invoked Sarasvatī with many and varying hymns to control the clash and disharmony in the society.

Then they saw the harmonious power, the metre (chandas) and the Divine Gāyatrī, the mother of all metres. They recognised that she is the source of all metres. She guides the other six metres with divine harmony. These are Uṣṇik, Anuṣṭubh, Bṛhatī, Paṅkti, Triṣṭubh, Jagatī. From these, Anuṣṭubh was worshipped by the great poets such as Vālmīki, Vyāsa and others. The other five metres and Gayatri were worshipped only by the Vedic Ṛṣis. From the ancient times the Aryans have opened the road of rhythm for the earth—that is the Anuṣṭubh. This rhythm was selected by them for their divine Epics.

The Aryans in their pursuit of world peace and unity and in their struggle against the asuric forces, looked for assistance from the divine sources.

Chapter 5

BATTLING THE ASURIC FORCES

The Aryans in their pursuit of world peace and unity and in their struggle against the asuric forces, looked for assistance from the divine sources.

First, they invoked Gāyatrī and composed many hymns for world unity to bring harmony into human society. Then, they synchronised sound with this rhythm through the worship of Gāyatrī, the origin of all metres and the power behind all sounds.

Finally, they discovered the power of Time that influences all sounds—he is Heramba, son of Mahākāla (Time)—he is Siddhidātā, he is Ganapati, and he is Brahamaṇaspati. He is the Democrat God, who influences the individual being. He is the conqueror of the evil forces. Thus, the Aryans worshipped the Democrat God Heramba for world unity and peace.

WORLD PEACE AND UNITY

The Aryans worshipped Dharma, with his powers for peace in the human society. They invoked the democrat God Heramba to conquer the devilish forces. They called down as well the Chanda, the Gāyatrī and also Vāgdevī Sarasvatī. This was not however, enough to establish world peace and unity. The reason was that the men of earth were worshipping various Gods and Goddesses and forming different groups and parties. They had varied and conflicting mental ideas and views regarding the purpose of life. This caused conflicts and gave rise to opposition between the different groups. To unite all the groupings and parties, and to achieve perfect peace in human society, the Aryans tried to discover the root cause of discord and dissension and the part played by mental thoughts, construction and imagination. They saw that the twin Godhead, Mitra—Varuṇa, influenced the vital plane. Varuṇa is the soul of vastness and purity, Mitra that of love, light and harmony. Varuna has creative wisdom, unlimited in its scope that radiates a light of bliss and joy. Mitra arranges and organises, in the liberated nature, the luminous expansions and the serene expressions of the Truth. They also observed that Mitra and Varuna had a strong influence over the entire human life. They saw Varuna ruling over the democrat God Heramba and the social God Dharma and Mitra, while maintaining the Chandas and activity of Vāgdevī like an all—powerful, all—conquering, all—creating master. On finding this, they worshipped the divinely ruled kingdom of Varuna on the earth and to reinforce this they also invoked Mitra at the same time. Thus there are many hymns dedicated to Mitra-Varuna invoking their powers to promote a united and peaceful reign upon the earth.

INFLUENCE OF HOSTILE FORCES ON UNITY

When the Aryans conquered the negative forces with the help of Heramba, they established peace with the help of Dharma and brought into existence a kingdom, which had no adversary. There all human beings enjoyed life, remained ever youthful and lead a beautiful harmonious divine life with the help and assistance of Vāgdevī Sarasvatī, as well as the influence of Chanda, particularly the mother of Chanda, Gāyatrī. This divine kingdom was blessed by Mitra-Varuṇa with unity and love. Thus, the Aryans lead an ever-joyful life, with a cadenced movement. Their faces and eyes were lit up with a lovely smile. They worked as if they were dancing, talked as if they were singing. The human beings became like celestial musicians, the Gandharvas, and enjoyed happiness that only the immortals experience.

But this immortal happiness, enjoyed by mortal men with unity and peace, was disturbed through demonic forces which gave rise to pride, greed and unsatisfied hunger or unlimited hankering for the beauty of health, joy of life and satisfaction of mind. The hostile forces are real and conscious beings. These forces amuse themselves at the cost of mankind and cause numerous difficulties. They disturbed human unity and banished peace. On observing that the whole humanity had become immersed in this negative lower force; the Aryans, the Seekers of Truth, started to meditate on this problem. They saw that the forces, which had formerly promoted happiness and peace, had become inactive and were controlled by the devilish forces.

To remove these negative forces they invoked a more powerful Godhead, who was Marut—Lord of the Wind, the Supreme Commander of the Divine Military. The Maruts are powers of will and vital force that have attained to the light of thought and the voice of self-expression. They are behind all our thoughts and lead us towards the Light, Truth and Bliss of the Supreme Consciousness. The Aryans composed many hymns to the Lord of the Wind. Through these hymns, they gained more power and were able to conquer the devilish forces. With the help of Marut—Lord of the Wind, they re-established peace and unity in the human society as before.

INVOCATION OF THE SUPREME TRUTH

When the Seekers of Truth saw the power of the all-conquering Marut Lord of the Wind, the one who had conquered the devilish force and re-established world peace and unity, they were eager to know more about his powers and activities. To make constant communication with this most powerful Godhead, they invoked the Supreme Truth. First they recognised the connection of Marut—Lord of the Wind to the Supreme Truth. They wished to reach to the Supreme Truth with the help of Marut, Lord of the Wind, who was coming from the higher Truth. That is why the Seekers of Truth started on their journey to the Supreme Truth along the path of the Lord of the Wind. When they came to the end of this plane or Bhuvana, they saw a big gulf between the two worlds, existing between this Creation and the Supreme Truth. Then they saw an aspirant light, climbing straight towards the Supreme Truth without any help from outside. When they observed the ascent of fire towards eternity, they invoked Agni, the Lord of Fire, for assistance. They heard a voice arise from the Fire "What is thy desire, O mortal man?" These human beings replied, "We are seekers of Truth, O Fire! We have tried to find Truth with our intellect and with our own efforts, but we see that we have come only to the end of the creation of the world. Before us, we see a vast space. Now we invoke thee—O Fire! Thou who art climbing alone towards eternity without any help, assist us also to ascend towards the Supreme."

Again they heard a voice arising from the Fire, "Sacrifice thy intellect, thy effort and thy desire for the Truth. I will bear thy prayer and invocation to the Supreme Truth, and I shall bring back His message for all of you." After hearing this voice, they sacrificed their intellect, their personal efforts, and their desire for Truth into the fire. After the completion of their sacrifice, Agni, the Lord of Fire, manifested and asked the Seekers of Truth, "Pray what is your wish, O Seekers of Truth. I am the Truth; I am the giver of boons. I am He, whom thou seekest through thy sacrifice". When they saw Agni, Lord of Fire, they prostrated themselves with a joyful heart and a grateful mind and said "O Agni, O Lord of Fire, O Truth! We pray to thee, take care of the creation. Ensure that peace and unity remain always in mankind. The victorious Lord of the Wind, Mitra-Varuṇa, Heramba and Dharma are working in human society to allow us to enjoy divinity. Come and stay with us, O Immortal Guest! Maintain the Lord of the Wind's victory for ever with thy power."

Agni, the Lord of Fire replied, "So be it! I shall be a guest to mortality. The Lord of the Wind is the messenger of the Supreme Truth and the supreme commander. I shall increase his strength by bringing down power from the Supreme King. I shall bring this message for you all, when thou sacrifice thy will, thy efforts and thy desire in me."

AN ADORATION OF DIVINE INDRA

When the Aryans received Agni, the Lord of Fire, in their mortal world, they provided room for this immortal guest to always stay in this world. They told mankind to sacrifice into the holy fire their intellect, efforts and desire to obtain help from the Gods. That is why fire has officiated like a priest to all mankind and conveyed humanity's adoration to the Supreme. Through Agni, humanity's sacrificial adoration reached before Indra, the Lord of Gods. The Divine King with his thousand glorious eyes, the Emperor of all Creation, on receiving humanity's adoration, conveyed the following message to mankind through Fire, "O mortal men, I am ready to accept your sacrificial adoration and to spread the divine influence upon the earth. Purify yourself from all impurities existing within you. For this purification, sacrifice your passions, greed, anger, ego, stupidity, jealousy, pride etc, even if you have only a slight touch of it. Remove these negative feelings and offer them into the fire. Agni, the Lord of Fire, will then purify you. Sacrifice into the holy fire your individual efforts, your will, even your desire for the divine kingdom upon the earth. Then, I will manifest amongst you with my supreme power and light, with the immortal ambrosia, eternal joy and with my Truth-light."

When humanity received this divine message from Agni, the Lord of Fire, they offered their impurities into the holy fire and became purified. After their purification they heard again the message of Indra, the Lord of the Gods, "O purified men of earth, listen! Above all, I am the Lord, the Emperor, the Supreme, and I am the Ultimate. My truth, my light, and my power is for all who aspire for the divine. I am the vast, the great and the ocean. To understand me you have to be pure. To prostrate yourself before me and offer me your adoration, when you are impure, is futile. After the purification, whatever is best, great, and vast in this creation is mine. Know that there is nothing greater than me, nothing wider than me, nothing superior to me. There is no power above me. There is no victory above mine. There is no victorious conqueror that can vanquish me. Even my so-called defeats are only self-imposed strategies to experience a joy other than victory as I tire of experiencing the latter all the time. I retreat when I dislike the place or at my will. When I give the boon to be vanquished, I like to see the other as victorious as myself, or I enjoy my own defeat. Then it seems to the world that a victorious enemy arises in front of me. All is according to my wish. I am sovereign to rule my empire as I deem fit. I am the imperial Indra."

This was the message mortal humanity received from the Divine King through Agni, the Lord of Fire. When the Seekers of Truth heard this message, they offered their individual efforts to Agni. They also trained the people of the earth to sacrifice their individuality to Agni, the Divine Priest. This was an invocation of Indra, the Divine King. When hundred sacrificial flames were kindled, Indra appeared in front of the sacrifice, with his almighty power, light and wealth and received the name Śatakratu. Together with him, appeared the vast intellect and knowledge of the Supreme, the Bṛhaspati; the enormous light and consciousness, the Sūrya; and the immense ananda and joy, the Soma Devatā.

After this manifestation, and by the influence of the Divine King, humanity became transformed and obtained divine health and beauty in their bodies, as well as heavenly joy and satisfaction in their lives and minds. With divine health, satisfaction and joy they prayed to Indra, "O Indra! O King of all creation! We prostrate before Thee. Thou art the giver of light, power, love, joy, satisfaction and health. O Almighty, reign on our earth to protect it. Maintain our peace and unity and let it be everlasting." Lord Indra replied, "So be it."

In this way, and in response to the request of humanity, Lord Indra manifested the divine kingdom upon the earth. In the kingdom of Lord Indra, there were no enemies. With the help of the Seekers of Truth and other Godheads, everyone worshipped Lord Indra. They prayed, "O Almighty Indra, O Narendra, we bow down before Thee. All our health, wealth and life—all our properties are thine. Thy order is our activity and thy power is our power. O Lord Indra, remain eternally upon the earth."

Chapter 6

RETALIATION OF THE HOSTILE FORCES

Nakta, the Demon King saw that Lord Indra together with other Godheads had established the divine kingdom on the earth and that they were being worshipped by an adoring humanity. He became very angry and wanted to prove that Lord Indra was not the Almighty. He shouted, "I am the Demon King, I am more powerful than Indra. I must prove my superiority to humanity, that I am Almighty. I must conquer the divine kingdom and establish the demon kingdom upon the earth."

ASURIC INFLUENCE ON THE DIVINE KINGDOM

The devilish forces entered into the human mind and gave rise to ignorance. They made human beings doubt their own powers and convinced them that they could not achieve divine heights and become all-powerful. These forces made humanity discover many weaknesses in themselves. This occurred even though Man was like a King on the earth. Some groups of men came under the influence of this force and started to fight with the King. These misguided people fought against the King with arms under the influence of asuric forces. They vanquished the group loyal to the King. In human beings, the demonic forces subdued the divine influence. The whole humanity came under their sway. At that time, the devil kingdom manifested upon the earth. Brutality and slavery became a common occurence in the world.

MANIFESTATION OF THE DIVINE MOTHER

The Seekers of Truth observed the titanic war between the Gods and the Demons for controlling the men of the earth. In this war, the Gods suffered a defeat and were driven away from the earth. At that time, the Sages prayed to the Divine to find a force greater than the Demons. They went away from the demon-influenced human society and sought seclusion in lonely forests. They passed several years meditating to seek fulfilment of their wishes. In a trance, they had a vision of Mother Aditi, the Mother of the Gods. She appeared before them and asked, "O Seekers of Truth, I am the Divine Mother. I am Aditi, the source of all powers. Pray tell me what are your wishes."

The sages were thrilled to see the Divine Mother, with pure light spreading around her, a glorious smile on her face and her eyes full of grace. They prostrated themselves at Her Lotus Feet and said: "O Mother Divine! O Aditi! You are the giver of boons. O Mother Supreme! You are the source of peace, unity, joy and happiness. You give us all knowledge, love and rhythm. O Mother, spread your power, light, love and consciousness for divine rule and remove all demonic influences from the earth. Let the divine reign remain forever." She answered in her melodious voice, "So be it."

OPPOSITION OF THE DEMON MOTHER

On hearing the Divine Mother Aditi giving the boon of an everlasting divine kingdom upon the earth; and even before her voice had died down, the sages heard a loud terrible voice saying "No". They trembled on hearing that cry, and suddenly the Demon Mother Diti appeared in front of them. She was in her most aggressive mood, and quarrelsome attitude. She said, "No, O Men of Earth! The divine kingdom cannot be everlasting. I am the Demon Mother Diti. Humanity must also worship my sons, the demons and me. O Aditi, you are not the sole power in the whole creation. You are the Divine Creatrice and I am the Demon Creatrice. We are equal, let us divide the earth amongst both of us." The Divine Mother

Aditi replied to Diti, the Demon Mother, "Let the Seekers of Truth decide, whether or not to divide the earth. O Ṛṣis, decide whom you wish to have for the earth, Aditi with her children or Diti with her children?" The Ṛṣis replied with one voice, "We want the Divine Mother Aditi with her sons; we want the divine kingdom and not the asuric one." Aditi replied, "I bless you all, O Sages, and I give you my protection." With these words, a beam of light came out from the Divine Mother and surrounded the Ṛṣis. But Diti, the Demon Mother exclaimed, "Wait, O Aditi, You cannot do this without the sanction of the Creator." She continued to howl even louder than before, "O Creator, Break your trance; Look towards the creation and give your judgement on the activity of Aditi." With this cry, the trance of the Creator was disturbed. He got up and appeared before the two Mothers. On coming to know of the quarrel, he announced with his imposing voice, "Listen, O Aditi, O Mother Divine; O Diti, O Mother Demon; both of you have manifested from my body for the purpose of creation. Both of you created for me and the creation is mine." Both the Divine Mother Aditi and the Demon Mother Diti agreed that it was true. He added, "If this is true, then listen to me. When humanity chooses one between both of you, only one of you can stay. If the earth chooses Aditi with her children, then, O Diti, you must leave this earth together with your children."

In response, the Demon Mother Diti uttered a deafening cry, "O Creator, your judgement is biased. It proves that you prefer Aditi, with the enlightened face, and you dislike Diti with the dark face. You have no love for me. O Supreme Creator, tell me where my place is and also the position of my children." The tumultuous weeping and tears resulted in a terrible noise throughout the creation. All creations were disturbed. To stop that noise, a thunderous order came from the Creator, "O Demon Mother Diti, be quiet, listen to another proposal of mine. In front of both of you, there is Mahākāla, the Lord of Time, who at all times guides the creation with his power. Ask your children to worship the

Lord of Time. They should meditate on him, please him and then ask for a boon. On receiving this boon, your children will enjoy the earth."

On hearing the response of the Supreme Creator, the Demon Mother Diti quietened down and the Creator disappeared.

Chapter 7

DIVISION OF TIME

When the Creator announced to the Divine Mothers that they ask their sons to worship Mahākāla, the Lord of Time, there was rejoicing on the earth. The Divine Mothers instructed their own children separately to offer their adoration to the Lord of Time, Mahākāla, and thus please him. Thus the Gods and the Demons started their worship by invoking Mahākāla.

ASCERTAINMENT OF THE AGES

Pleased with the worship of the Gods, Mahākāla, the Lord of Time, appeared in front of them in the form of Piṅgala Maheśvara. He said, "O Sons of Aditi, I am pleased with your worship. Let me know your wishes." The Gods prostrated before the Lord of Time and said, "O Piṅgala Maheśvara! O Mahākāla, Lord of Time, if you are pleased with us, then help us reign upon the earth according to humanity's aspirations." He replied, "So be it. O Sons of Aditi, Satyadeva, the God of Truth, will take birth in the family of Āṅgirasas through my influence. I shall thus manifest Satyadeva on the earth. This period will be called the Golden Age or the Satya Yuga (The Age of Truth). In this Age, the Godheads will be all powerful and reign upon the earth."

When the Demons worshipped the Lord of Time, Mahākāla appeared in front of them in the form of Rudra, the Destroyer. He also asked the Asuras (the Demons), "O Sons of Diti, pray what are your wishes." The Demons prostrated in front of Rudra, "O Rudra, the Destroyer, if you are pleased with the Asuras, then help us reign upon the earth and enjoy power over humanity." He responded, "So be it, O Sons of Diti. Nakta, the Night, will take birth in the family of Kanveya under the name of Kali. You will enjoy the earth during his rule."

Thus it was decided that the two opposing powers would rule over the earth. With the help of Mahākāla, the Lord of Time, Satya (Truth) and Nakta (Night) would take birth in the family of Rṣis. These would at their appointed times act as Guide of the Age and influence the earth for a predetermined time. At first, Satyadeva took charge of the Time Wheel and influenced the earthly creation. During his time, the Gods were active and a divine kingdom manifested on the earth. But this did not last forever. Then came the time of change and Kali took charge of the Time Wheel. At that time the hostile and negative forces became active on the earth. The activities of the Gods came to a standstill and Satyadeva disappeared from the Time Wheel. Then the Gods and Ṛṣis understood that their time had come to an end. Henceforth, Kali would hold the Time Wheel and guide the creation. During this time period, devilish forces would have absolute power in the world.

In order to lessen the impact of Kali, and to ensure that his ruling did not last long, the Gods and Ṛṣis worshipped Mahākālī, the power of Rudra. They invoked her thus, "O Mahākālī ! You gave a boon to the Demons. O Mahāsurī! Through your boon the Gods are suffering. They have lost their kingdom on the earth. O Rudrāṇī, we pray for your grace." They continued thus their long prayers in the silence of the Himalayas. Mahākālī was pleased with the homage offered by the Gods and the Ṛṣis. She appeared before them in the form of a young girl and enquired, "O Gods! O Ṛṣis! Whom are you all worshipping?" They replied, "We are praying to Rudrāṇī, the Mahākālī." Receiving this reply, she enquired again with a smile, "Why are you invoking Mahākālī? She was kind to the Demons and has appeared in front of them." The Gods and Ṛṣis answered, "We are praying to Mahākāli for this reason only as we want to shorten the period of the Demons." She added smilingly, "Why are you worshipping Mahākālī for this. You can shorten the period of Kaliyuga by asking the sons of Aptya Ṛṣi, Trita and Dvita, to influence three fourths of the time of Kali and leave only one-fourth to Kali. This would diminish the influence of Kali. If during this period, the demonic activity increases then, O Ṛṣis, O Gods, call upon Lord Viṣṇu, the greatest Fighter of all creations, and the Protector, to come down to the earth and vanquish the hostile forces."

On hearing such an easy solution to their problems from such a little girl, the Gods and Ṛṣis were absolutely astonished and they asked her, "O little girl! Tell us who you are? You have solved the complex problem that we found impossible? Are you the power of Mahākālī playing with us in this way." The little girl smiled again and changed her shape. She appeared before them in the form of Durgā Maheśvarī. They saw a Goddess of eternal divine beauty, full of divine harmony, having the magic of an irresistible universal charm. She said, "I am Durgā, conqueror of all difficulties and problems, O Ṛṣis ! O Gods! I am the Mahākālī come to favour and to save you all." All the Gods and Ṛṣis bowed down in front of her and said, "O Mother Durgā! O Maheśvarī ! You are Mahākālī; You have taken a graceful shape for the Gods. We offer our adoration to You with all our powers, weapons and riches." She smiled, looking very radiant and asked in a melodious divine voice, "Pray ask for a boon, O Gods! O Ṛṣis! I am pleased with your prayers and worship." They replied, "O Mother Durga! Help us always in our difficulties and in our sufferings."

She answered, "Whenever you will call me in your difficulties and your sufferings, I shall appear and solve your problems." Then the Goddess Durgā disappeared.

THE ARRANGEMENT

Then the Gods went to the Creator and told him, "O Father, we worshipped Mahākāla and he became pleased with us.

He appeared before us in the form of Piṅgala Maheśvara and gave us a boon that we would influence the world for a certain period of time. Mahākāla also manifested in front of the Demons in the form of Rudra Maheśvara and gave them a similar boon. With this boon, time on the earth was divided between Satyadeva, for the Gods and Kali, for the Demons. To obtain relief for humanity under Kali, we prayed to the power of Rudra, Rudrāṇī Mahākāli. We received a boon to shorten the period under Kali to only one-fourth of the allocated time with the help of Trita and Dvita, the sons of Ṛṣi Aptya. Still, if the demonic forces became unbearable for suffering humanity, to invoke Lord Viṣṇu to come down to the help of the earth. But, O Father, for one-eighth of the time cycle, Kali will be all-powerful together with his Demon friends. Tell us how do we pass that period." On hearing their explanations, the Creator answered, "O My Divine Children! For one-eighth portion of time, let the sons of Diti play on the earth and you rest." Then the Gods asked their father again, "When the rule of the Asuras ends, and the period of Kali finishes on the earth, how will we come again to influence the earth" The Creator replied, "I myself shall go to the earth with your mother Aditi to prepare the way for you to enter into the world."

On hearing this, they asked Marīca-Kaśyapa, "O Father, how will you make an opening for the divine kingdom upon the earth." He replied, "Listen, O Ādityas, at the end of Satya Yuga, Kali will not be able to manifest fully upon the earth due to the valiant fighters, Trita and Dvita. However, at times, the hostile forces will gain more power. Then as the Mahākālī says, Lord Viṣṇu will descend on the earth to save it. Three-fourths of the time under the influence of Kali will pass like this. At the end of the Dvita Yuga, Kali will fully manifest upon the earth. Under Kali's influence, all dark and sombre forces will gain in influence and all unity and peace will vanish from the earth. As a result, there will be many states, innumerable languages and several religions to add to the confusion in the world. Fear will be predominant. In spite of religions, there will be neither dharma, nor right conduct, nor spirituality. Mankind will not believe in the existence of Gods. At the end of Kali, kingdoms and royalty will vanish from the earth. When people observe the deficiencies in kings and kingdoms, they will try to achieve peace and unity without Gods and kingdoms."

"O my children, it is impossible to have world peace and unity without Gods and kingdom. At that moment, I, myself, with Your Mother Aditi will come to the world in a human body and announce the reality of the existence of Gods and the necessity of kingdoms. At that moment, the giver of boon of the Golden Age, Piṅgala Maheśvara, will bring down the divine epic on the earth and relate the history of creation to mankind. Then only humanity will become aware of Gods and invoke you upon the earth. Thus your path will open for manifesting the divine kingdom."

The Gods enquired again, "O Father, when you take birth as a human being on the earth, tell us about our work." The Creator replied, "You have nothing to do at that time, your Mother will open the way. You should adore and worship your Mother only. She will do the needful." Then all the Gods went before Aditi, and they paid homage to the Divine Mother, "O Mother, you alone can solve our problems. You alone can open the path for us in the future. You are the giver of life and consciousness, power and bliss. We sleep under your protection during the period of Kali. We will awaken with your power by the advent of Truth. O Mother, we kiss your feet before our sleep and at the beginning of our work."

BIRTH OF THE AGES

The Lord of Time, Piṅgala Maheśvara, decided to divide time between the Gods and the Demons, the period of Deva for the Gods and that of Kali for the Devils. To reduce the period of Kali, Durgā Maheśvarī gave the boon to humanity that

Trita and Dvita, the sons of Ṛṣis Aptya, would be all powerful during a major part of the time given to Kali.

The Gods waited around the Supreme Creator, Kaśyapa, after receiving blessings from the Divine Creatrice, Aditi, to find out how they could commence their work. The Supreme Creator was in a very deep trance and the Gods observed the pure, calm and silent atmosphere without any movement. In that profound silence, the Creator felt the presence of Gods and broke his trance. He opened his eyes, pure and full of grace and looked at the Gods. He asked them, "O Gods, what is your problem now?" All the Gods prostrated before him and appealed, "O Father, Mahākāla Piṅgala said that the Lord of Truth, Satyadeva, will take birth as a manifested being so that we could increase our influence in the creation. Please tell us when and how the Lord of Truth will manifest." The Supreme Creator told them to go and seek the Seekers of Truth and help them to realise the Truth.

Subsequently, the Gods obtained Kaśyapa's blessings and left that plane. When they descended down to seek the Seekers of Truth, they saw massive preparations made for a sacrifice where all the Ṛṣis had gathered. On seeing the Yajña, the Gods were filled with astonishment. They enquired from the Ṛṣis, "O Seers! Tell us about your deeds here? For which ceremony have you made these elaborate arrangements?" The Ṛṣis were pleased to hear this question from the Gods and they said, "O Sons of Aditi, you all have come to help us. We knew that you would join us us for this sacrifice as this had been decided by the Supreme Creator. We shall now invoke the Supreme Truth and call for its manifestation. Help us in invoking the Lord of Truth, Satyadeva."

The Gods joined in the sacrificial ceremony as arranged by the Ṛṣis and they took part in burning the sacrificial flame in the Yajña. Śauciki, son of Agni, was the priest performing the ceremony and the son of Aṅgirā, Abhivarta, was the holder of the Yajña. There they chanted the Hymns to the Deva, as given in the Ṛgveda (tenth maṇḍala, 51 sukta, 1-5 ṛks).

महत्तदुल्बं स्थविरं तदासीद्येनाविष्टितः प्रविवेशिथापः ।
विश्वा अपश्यद्बहुधा ते अग्ने जातवेदस्तन्वो देव एकः ॥१॥

1. A being above the supermind has manifested in this creation, who is maintaining eternal ānanda and consciousness. O Agni! Enter there and look at the manifold creations. For their happiness, manifest a Deva with delight, power and truth.

को मा ददर्श कतमः स देवो यो मे तन्वो बहुधा पर्यपश्यत् ।
क्वाह मित्रावरुणा क्षियन्त्यग्नेर्विश्वाः समिधो देवयानीः ॥२॥

2. We have not seen the Deva. His appearance also we do not know. We have heard that He will manifest in these manifold creations. O Mitrā-Varuṇa! Kindly light the sacrificial flame and manifest the Devāyaṇa with the help of Agni, the Lord of Fire.

ऐच्छाम त्वा बहुधा जातवेदः प्रविष्टमग्ने अप्स्वोषधीषु ।
तं त्वा यमो अचिकेच्चित्रभानो दशान्तरुष्यादतिरोचमानम् ॥३॥

3. By kindling the Devāyaṇa, O Agni! O Jātaveda! Enter into the manifold creations in the water, plants and trees. O Yama! Wake up that Puruṣa who is unconscious in the creation. Let him become conscious and manifest in all with his own light.

होत्रादहं वरुण बिभ्यदायं नेदेव मा युनजन्नत्र देवाः ।
तस्य मे तन्वो बहुधा निविष्टा एतमर्थं न चिकेताहमग्निः ॥४॥

4. O Varuṇa! Give your sacrificial offering; through that we shall attain the young born Deva. We will direct him to the manifold creations. In this way you will increase the power of Agni.

एहि मनुर्देवयुर्यज्ञकामोऽरंकृत्या तमसि क्षेष्यग्ने ।
सुगान्पथः कृणुहि देवयानान्वह हव्यानि सुमनस्यमानः ॥५॥

5. We have burnt here the sacrificial flame for men, O Agni! Let the divine food be ready for Deva, let the path of advent of Deva be facile, let our sacrificial offering be accomplished successfully and let the Devāyaṇa be opened.

When they were fully absorbed in chanting these hymns to invoke the Deva with Ṛṣi Śauciki, at that time Mahākāla Piṅgala Maheśvara appeared before them and said, "Behold! O Sons of Aditi! O Ṛṣis! In the sacrificial flame, a golden young boy with four hands is appearing. He is holding the Vedas in his hands as well as a pot of Amṛta, the divine nectar. He is Deva for whom you have burnt this sacrificial flame and whom you have been seeking through this sacrifice." Among the Ṛṣis, the eldest was Abhivarta and thus the King of the Ṛṣis. He made the following appeal to Deva to have him as his son.

He said, "O unknowable Truth! O unrealised Deva! Today thou hast manifested thyself as a young boy. O Lord of Truth! Enter our house as our son. Let us nourish you. Grow up in our house and play in our sacrificial garden. Play also throughout the creation to enlighten it with your immortal light and joy, and manifest the Gods with their accomplishments upon the earth."

The Deva, pleased with this appeal of Abhivarta, replied, "O King of the Ṛṣis! I accept your wish. I shall enter your house for guiding this creation together with Gods to transform the earth into heaven. O Father! Embrace me as your son."

Thus was the manifestation and birth of Deva or Satyadeva as the Ṛṣis called him. He held the Time Wheel, the Kālacakra, to guide this creation. When he entered into this creation, he removed all malformations as desired by the Gods merely through his touch. A transformation took place in human beings and their bodies became beautiful like Gods. Through his immortal influence, men became conscious of their divine nature, attained the supreme knowledge and drank the heavenly nectar. At that point of time, all Godheads entered into the human body as mentioned in the Aitareya Upaniṣad. Each took control of its own area and started their divine work on the earth. Earth became like heaven. The people of the earth were like Gods. They became immune to all negative forces through the influence of Satyadeva. This Age was known as the Golden Age or the Satya Yuga, where Truth was all prevalent.

On observing that life on earth had become immortal and seeing the play of the Gods upon the earth, the Asuras the Demons became jealous. They wished to also have an Age when they would reign supreme. They had received the boon from Mahākāla Rudra that they would have a period when they would be all—powerful. They became friendly with Śani, the son of Sun God, Sūrya. They asked Śani, who was irreligious, to enter and facilitate a demonic birth in a family of Ṛṣis. His aim was to look divine but to work for them. To increase the demonic work on the earth and to allow the negative forces to become all powerful on the earth, Śani moved amongst the family of Ṛṣis to have a chance for the birth of Nakta, the Darkness.

During the marriage of Pragatha Kanveya, Śani, with the help of Śukra, influenced Pragatha on the night of the marriage. Thus Nakta, the dark force, entered the womb of Gathini, who had just married Pragatha, during the most inauspicious time of the Kāla-Rātri, i.e. the night of the wedding or the next night. In India, these two nights are considered very inauspicious for marital relations. This custom is still followed and wedded couples are not supposed to have any intimate relations during the first two nights. As a result of this mishap, Kali was born as the son of Pragatha. He grew up in the family of Ṛṣi Kaṇva and was inherently evil from birth. He became more and more destructive as he grew up. All the members of the Kaṇva family were disturbed through his actions. Particularly, Nārada, his uncle, was so alarmed and upset about him that he was unable to remain in the same place as Kali. He left the house. Kali became even more anti-Deva and anti-Ṛṣi through his education with Śukra.

Śani (Saturn) was his constant friend. Through him, Kali became very intimate with the Demons, the anti-divine beings,

Rākṣasas and snakes. He married Mṛtyu (death), the sister of Śani. With the help of these hostile forces, he became extremely powerful. He started to negatively affect the human society. For example, he brought about a catastrophe at the sacrificial Yajña of Dakṣa.

Śatī, daughter of Dakṣa, and the consort of Lord Śiva, willingly left her body in the sacrificial flame of the Dakṣa Yajña as she sensed an insult from her father to her husband, Lord Śiva. On hearing about her sacrifice, Śiva became Rudra out of an all-consuming anger. Wishing to destroy the whole creation, Rudra started his destructive dance as he realised that Satī had sacrificed her life for him. At that time, Deva disappeared from the creation. All the Godheads were terrified, as they feared that the whole creation was going to be destroyed by the destructive dance of Rudra. They went to pray before Lord Viṣṇu, "O Lord Viṣṇu! Willt Thou save us from destruction? Will Thou stop the dance of Naṭarāja?" Lord Viṣṇu affirmed that he would do so and asked them to wait.

He snatched the body of Satī from the shoulder of Rudra, who held her inanimate body on his shoulder while dancing. Lord Viṣṇu dissected Satī's body into fifty-two pieces with his weapon, the Sudarśana Cakra, and threw them onto the earth. The places, where these pieces fell, were called Pīṭhasthāna and they still exist in India. These holy places are still worshipped by the Hindus and they call them Tīrthasthāna (a place of high merit). After Satī's body was snatched away from Rudra, he quietened down and all the Godheads were relieved that the immediate danger and fear confronting them was no longer there. When everything quietened down, they saw that Dakṣa had been killed and his head destroyed during Rudra's terrible dance, but his body remained. The Creators gave life to Dakṣa by attaching the head of a horse to his body. With this change, he was known as Hayagrīva.

The Gods wanted to know the reason for this catastrophe and discovered that Kali was holding the Time Wheel, the

Kālacakra. Deva had vanished and was no longer there. They realised that the time of Deva was over and now Kali would gain in influence. Then they remembered the advice of Mahākāli on how to lessen this evil time. To stem the advance of Kali, they called upon the sons of Aptya Ṛṣi, Trita and Dvita, to control the Time Wheel. Dvita was the eldest son of Ṛṣi Aptya. His mother, the Ṛṣikā Ambhrinī, was cursed by Ṛṣi Bharadvāja when she was still carrying Dvita in her womb. Through that curse, the infant was half burnt in the womb and was born as Dvita, having only half of his strength. The other son, Trita, was also affected by the same curse and was lame in one leg. But he had his full strength. The Ṛṣis and Godheads observed that Trita was more powerful and would be in a better position to limit the baleful influence of Kali. They chose him to hold the Time Wheel and to guide this creation, maintaining the ideals of Deva.

TRITA YUGA

In the meantime, Kali was in the process of occupying and influencing this creation with his demonic friends. Trita was married to Yamī, sister of Yama. When Trita tried to take up his duties, he discovered that Kali had already occupied half of the creation. Trita started to fight with Kali to restrain the demonic forces. He conquered Kali and removed his dark forces from the creation. Kali then encouraged Rākṣasas and Demons, terrifying beings of the lower vital, to proliferate and occupy the creation. At this time, Rāvaṇa became all-powerful and the Lord of All through his intense sacrifice and efforts. He became victorious over all. He conquered the three worlds from the Gods and rejoiced in obtaining the wealth of the Gods and enjoying it.

The earth was undergoing unbearable pressure and pain through this demonic influence. To remove the pain of the earth, the Ṛṣis with the help of Trita, the upholder of the Time Wheel, invoked Lord Viṣṇu to descend in a human body. Thus, Śrī Rāmacandra, an incarnation of Viṣṇu, took birth as the eldest son of Daśaratha. He fought Rāvaṇa and defeated him, liberated the Gods who were held captive by Rāvaṇa and removed the demonic influence from the earth with the help of the monkey regiment. Still, Kali did not lose heart. He tried to influence the ignorant people by planting doubts about the chastity of Queen Sītā, King Rāmacandra's consort, who had already proven her purity through fire. As a result, people started wondering and doubting whether she could still be pure after remaining captive for a year in Rāvaṇa's garden house Aśoka Vana. On seeing the mood of the people, Śrī Rāmacandra banished her into the forest. She came in front of her husband again many years later when she was invited to the Aśvamedha Yajña. Under Kali's doubting influence, the Ṛṣis demanded that she prove her purity through fire again. That proposal caused her deep pain. She asked Mother Earth to accept her back. Then the earth split and she entered and vanished into the earth. Trita was not able to tolerate this sad event; he disappeared from the Time Wheel.

The Ṛṣis became conscious themselves that it was all due to Kali's malefic influence that the people had started doubting their King and Queen. The Ṛṣis had also came under the same negative influence when they started to doubt the purity of Sita. Furthermore, Kali also ensured the exile of Lakṣmaṇa, the beloved brother. Kali went to meet Śrī Rāmacandra and extracted a promise from him that anyone disturbing their talks be banished. Then he ensured that Ṛṣi Durvāsā, known for his uncontrolled anger, came to demand an audience with Śrī Rāmacandra at the same time. When Lakṣmaṇa went to ask his brother to see the Ṛṣi urgently, he apparently violated this condition and thus had to be banished in exile.

DVITA YUGA

On seeing the increasing power of Kali, the Ṛṣis again remembered the words of Durgā how to shorten the influence of the dark forces. They called upon Dvita to control the Time Wheel. Dvita, however, was weak and could not stem the advance of Kali. At that time, Ṛṣi Mārkaṇḍeya, the Guru of Dvita, taught his disciple to worship his own mother, Ambhriṇī, as the Universal Divine Mother and to seek her strength to protect the creation from Kali's influence. He gave instructions and the relevant mantras to Dvita. In response to Dvita's prayer, his mother Ambhriṇī appeared before him and gave her unique Divine Gospel to Dvita. This was the Devīsūkta of Ṛgveda as uttered by her daughter Vāk. Dvita attained the power of the universal mother. With that power, he was able to hold and control the Time Wheel and drive Kali away. Still, half of the creation came under Kali's influence; during the Trita Yuga, only one fourth of humanity was affected. At that time, Ṛṣi Mārkaṇḍeya went around singing mantras of the Universal Mother's glory and her achievements amongst people. This was Caṇḍī.

Kali, however, did not remain quiet during this period. With his encouragement, some Devils managed to increase their power in human society. As a result, some Kings became powerful and spread their influence over the whole world. Suffering under their demonic activities, the earth became very oppressed. Seeing her tears, the Ṛṣis prayed again to Lord Viṣṇu. He descended once more on the earth in a human form and took birth from Devakī's womb as Kṛṣṇa. She was the sister of the powerful Devil Kaṁsa. At that time Kaṁsa, Jarāsandha, Śiśupāla, Dantavakra, Śakuni and Duryodhana with his hundred brothers and others were going from strength to strength with the active help of hostile forces on the earth. To fight these forces, Lord Kṛṣṇa descended on the earth together with other Godheads, the Pāṇḍavas. Lord Kṛṣṇa killed Kaṁsa and became the King of Mathurā. Due to this, Jarāsandha, King of Magadha, friend and relative of Kaṁsa, became his most bitter enemy. To protect himself from repeated attacks by Jarāsandha, Kṛṣṇa quit Mathurā and made his kingdom in Dvārakā, an island. Kṛṣṇa's friends, the Pāṇḍavas, helped him in defeating Jarāsandha.

The other Godheads were the Pāṇḍavas. They had to struggle always against their cousins the Kauravas, Duryodhana and his hundred brothers. Even as a child, Duryodhana was bitterly jealous of the Pāṇḍavas. Soon the jealousy reached such a stage that the Kauravas wanted to kill the Pāṇḍavas at Varaṇāvata. Luckily, the Pāṇḍavas escaped and proceeded to Pañcāla through the forests. There, Arjuna won the hand of Draupadī, the daughter of Drupada, King of Pañcāla. Through a twist of fate, Draupadī became the wife of all the Pāṇḍavas. The Pāṇḍavas made a new city named Indraprastha, which was the capital of their part of the kingdom. The Kauravas had the other half with Hastināpura as the capital. Duryodhana was bitten by jealousy on seeing the wealth of the Pāṇḍavas during the Rājasūya Yajña, where they had been invited as guests. He was also angry at seeing the respect and love that the Pāṇḍavas received from other Kings and the people. After the royal sacrifice ceremony, which made the Pāṇḍavas very famous, Duryodhana invited Yudhiṣṭhira to play dice with him. The prize would be the promise of wealth, property and kingdom. The Pāṇḍavas agreed. It was decided that Śakuni, the maternal uncle of the Kauravas, play on behalf of his nephews. In this game, the Pāṇḍavas were defeated. They lost their property and their kingdom. Additionally, they had to go and live in the forest for twelve years. The thirteenth year they had to live incognito.

After completing their exile, when the Pāṇḍavas approached the Kauravas to regain their kingdom, they were informed that without a fight, they would not receive even land as big as a pinpoint. The war of Mahābhārata started at Kurukṣetra, where the warriors and military forces of India were divided into two sides.

The fight was between Duryodhana and his friends, on one side, influenced by the negative forces, and on the other, Yudhisṭhira and his friends by the divine forces. There were some great souls among the Kauravas like Bhīṣma, Droṇa, Karṇa, Aśvatthāmā etc. but they were under the influence of the devilish forces. Lord Kṛṣṇa himself, who was divine, was the leader in the battlefield to defeat the forces of evil.

After the battle of Kurukṣetra, which ended in the divine victory, Aśvatthāmā, under the influence of Kali, wrought a havoc of destruction in the fort of the Pāṇḍavas. He killed the sons of Pāṇḍavas thinking that he was destroying the Pāṇḍavas themselves. Nevertheless, the Pāṇḍavas recovered from this terrible onslaught with the help of Kṛṣṇa and they established their kingdom. Subsequently, they organized the Aśvamedha Yajña, the world peace ceremony, and brought relief once again to the troubled earth.

After a few years, another catastrophe occurred in the family of Lord Kṛṣṇa. Under the influence of Kali, there occurred an internal quarrel amongst the family, which led them to their destruction. Through this fight, the whole family of Lord Kṛṣṇa was eradicated and Kṛṣṇa and his elder brother Balarāma left this earth. The only members remaining in the family were the Yadav Queens and some other female members. At that moment, the third Pāṇḍava Arjuna visited Dvārakā and saw the plight of the Yādava family. He took them to Indraprastha. When Yudhisthira came to know about this havoc in Lord Kṛṣṇa's family, he lost interest in life and decided to leave this world. He asked the wise seers in his royal chamber the reason for this catastrophe. They told him that the reason was the expansion of Kali's power. Soon his influence would cover the whole earth. On hearing this explanation, Yudhisthira became disheartened and decided to leave this earth together with his four brothers and Queen Draupadī. He gave his kingdom to Parīkṣit, Arjuna's grandson and ascended to heaven from the Himalayas.

At that moment, Dvita disappeared, as he was unable to control the Time Wheel any longer. When the Ṛṣis saw the disappearance of Dvita and that the spread of Kali could not be controlled, they also decided to leave this earth. One by one, they started to depart. Amongst them, were some who wished to help mankind maintain the memory of Truth and the divine ideal in the world, particularly in the time of Kali. However, they failed in this attempt, as King Parīkṣit could not complete his sacrificial oblations. A Brahmaṇa cursed the King that he would die of snakebite within seven days. In this short period, King Parīkṣit decided to hear the recitation of Bhāgavata, the life story of Lord Kṛṣṇa. With full determination, he established the memory of Lord Kṛṣṇa for the period of Kali. He died within seven days by the bite of Takṣaka, a snake.

His son Janamejaya became depressed, and then very angry. He wished to take revenge and eradicate the snakes from the earth. He was encouraged by some Brāhmaṇas to burn a sacrificial fire and thus attract the presence of all snakes so that they could be destroyed. The sacrifice proceeded successfully but at the moment of completion, a powerful holy man belonging to the snake family named Āstīka, son of Jaratkāru, came there and stopped the snake sacrifice. In this way, Janamejaya was unable to complete the ceremony. Then he tried to perform the Aśvamedha Yajña to re-establish world peace, but could not complete this ceremony as well. At the place of sacrifice, Kali influenced the sacrificial horse, which had been divided into two pieces. From the head of the horse, one heard the horse neighing. Janamejaya was very shocked to see this. At that moment, a Brāhmaṇa laughed on seeing and hearing the horse's head moving and neighing. The King thought that the Brahmin was mocking him, so he became enraged and killed the Brahmin. As the King had committed a great sin by killing a Brāhmaṇa, a very severe earthquake shook and destroyed his capital city. This was the moment when Kali fully manifested himself on the earth.

Chapter 8

THE IRON AGE APPEARS

Ṛṣi Vyāsa came to King Janamejaya and told him that Kali, the Lord of the Iron Age, had completely manifested on the earth. He said, "Listen, O Janamejaya! This is not the moment for holding an Aśvamedha ceremony for world peace. Kali has fully manifested before us and from now on he will have complete power over the whole creation. His will be the only influence on human activity. There is no power that can control his power, because it was so decided by Mahākāla Rudra. This is the time when the devilish forces will be let loose on the world. At this period, world peace and unity will be impossible. Kali's influence will divide the world into many states. There will also be many castes instead of the four varṇas. They will not be based on the Guṇas. There will be many religions in place of the one united spirituality of the Vedas. The Vedas will cease to exist, the Ṛṣis will disappear, and Gods will remain inactive and asleep."

BALEFUL INFLUENCE OF KALI

"O Janmejaya! This will be a terrible situation on the earth and amongst humanity. There will be many languages, castes, religions and states in the world. Therefore, the people will be divided. Amidst this plethora of diversity, human beings will fight amongst themselves for their state, religion, caste and language. The Vedas will not exist and mankind will have no real knowledge. Human beings will study nature by neglecting the soul. That will be the foundation of their knowledge. From nature, they will earn their vital food. They will give much more importance to the wealth given to them by nature. Their religion, social affairs and knowledge will all depend upon the extent of their discoveries in nature. Love will be converted into sexuality and human birth will be similar to animals."

"At that moment, money will count for more than spirituality. Military power will be controlled by money. Without money, there will be no meaning in life, and life will become a burden. People will consider life full of misery. With the power of money, human beings will attain power. If a fool has money, he will be considered wise; whatever his character, he will be worshipped by others. A coward will become victorious with money power. Through the influence of Kali, even books of knowledge will worship money. The sword of a victor will bow down before it. Money will have a vital importance for men. Knowledge of the soul will be hidden by the power of Kali. Birth will take place due to sexual enjoyment. There will be one great fear for human beings, and that is death. People will conclude that the aim of life is enjoyment and the level of enjoyment will be controlled by the power of money."

"The enjoyment of life will give rise to an increase in passion, greed, anger, ego, jealousy and stupidity. Diseases will be rampant throughout mankind and life will become a mockery. The soul is immortal and rejoices in the joy of immortality. However, being detached from the soul, people will suffer from troubles, disharmony, and diseases around them and will die helplessly. They will consider that they take birth to suffer and die. Thus, the influence of Kali will remove the knowledge of the soul and intensify the sense of suffering in birth and death."

"For life to continue as it has manifested, it would be essential to satisfy the gnawing hunger. One must eat to increase life energy. To counter inactivity and tiredness, and in order to work more, one must sleep. Without knowledge, people on the earth will fight each other to earn their necessities, to fulfil their needs of hunger, thirst and sleep.

They will live for a very short period; pain, sorrows and repentance will be ever-present and reduce their longevity."

When King Janamejaya heard the words of Vyāsa and saw the frightening picture of mankind and the earth during the Iron Age, he fell down at the feet of Ṛṣi Dvaipāyana and asked him, "O Seer! What shall I do for the people of the earth? How shall I rule this world?"

Rṣi Vyāsa replied, "Listen, O King! Call a conference of all your friend Kings and hear the Mahābhārata from my disciple and son Vaiśampāyana. In this epic, I have written about the life of Dharma to remove the influence of the negative forces. On hearing the Mahābhārata you would be freed from sin. The sin that you have committed by killing a Brāhmaṇa, which has caused pain to the mother earth, will be wiped off. During the period of Kali, people influenced by the Lord of the Iron Age will commit many sins. There will be sins such as killing the mother, father, brother, sister, son, wife etc. There will be other crimes such as robbing, stealing, betraying friends and relatives to attain the wealth of others or wife or prostitute. Drinking of wine would be another sin. These are the great sins. Announce through your royal edicts that people should read and hear the Mahabharata to escape from the influence of Kali."

King Janamejaya asked Ṛṣi Vyāsa, ""O Seer! How shall I know that after hearing the Mahābhārata I shall be freed from the great sin that I have committed?"

Ṛṣi Vyāsa replied, "Listen O King! Fix a black canopy above your head in the place where you will listen to the Mahābhārata with your friends. That canopy I shall influence through my mantra. You will see that the black canopy will slowly change into white. It will prove to you that your inner being has been liberated from sin. Be happy and accept my blessings."

Subsequently, a place was constructed with a black canopy over it and Ṛṣi Vyāsa put his mantric power on it. When Ṛṣi Vyāsa was leaving that place, King Janamejaya exclaimed, "O great-grandfather, there is one question which I need to ask."

IRON AGE AND ITS FUNCTIONS

Ṛṣi Vyāsa turned back and asked King Janamejaya about his question. King Janamejaya enquired eagerly, "O Seer! Explain to me what will be the middle of the Kaliyuga and how will it end?" On hearing this question from the King, Ṛṣi Vyāsa's face became very serious and his forehead wrinkled with great concentration. He gazed at the blue sky and for a short period, remained silent. Everyone was observing the Sage intently. They were concerned on seeing the serious face of the Ṛṣi.

Then the Ṛṣi smiled and said, "Listen, O Pāṇḍaveya! Mankind will doubt the presence of Gods. Fear will be ever-present. During the Kali Yuga, the Gods will rest, they will not be active and thus people will have doubts about their existence. Under the influence of Kali, men will be doing many evil deeds. People will be obliged to worship the power of the snake, Arbuda, the giver of wealth and the creative power of Kāmadeva, who will maintain the earthly creation. Under the rule of Kali, Kāmadeva will be the Creator and Arbuda, the giver of wealth, will also be responsible for the physical birth. Mṛtyu (power of death), the undivine power, will be responsible for death in place of Yama, the divine. Śani (Saturn) will replace Dharma and rule over the physical creation. He will use his power to deflect mankind from immortality to mortality, whereas Dharma steers mankind in the opposite direction. You can imagine what the condition of the earth would be in such circumstances. If Śani stands on the way to spirituality (who directs the stars and planets in the firmament to affect human fate), then there will definitely be no spiritual development in human society. Instead of spirituality, people will have faith on fate. There will be several religions. Not everyone will be satisfied with religion as the observance will be on rituals and external activities only. Men will seek to have some satisfaction in religion. To this end, some immortal beings, who had reached an advanced stage through their tapasyā, their sacrifice in the previous Ages, will incarnate. They will take human births in different parts of the world. Through their particular gospel to humanity and their activities, several religions will be formed."

"When the snake king Arbuda is responsible for birth and for providing wealth, the higher souls, those who are spiritually inclined, do not seek to take birth. Instead, many will be born who are willing to do the bidding of the Devil. However there will be some advanced souls who will take birth to do good deeds and confound the rules set by Arbuda. Consequently, they will have to undergo great suffering. Such souls will face determined opposition to their work, face poverty, as Arbuda will be in control of money. They will be opposed if they try to guide humanity to higher goals. Their wishes, once expressed, will soon be distorted due to Śani's influence. Any mention of immortality will result in detractors demonstrating the mortality of the human body. Death will be the one constant factor for all humanity."

"When Mṛtyu (death) will be responsible for changing the mortal body, there will be an early death and the soul will return back to the earth for re-birth. Death will come through all kinds of diseases. Accidents will also help in snuffing out life from the human body. All will fear death and this fear will be inborn due to Kali's touch. Death will also occur through famines, epidemics, floods, earthquakes etc. This fear will counteract all positive developments made through human effort and will be supreme over all humanity. Death's devil brother, Śani, will continuously provide floods, earthquakes, epidemics, famines, heavy rains or drought. Death will dance in all misfortunes of men, which will bring great destruction to mankind. With the assistance of diseases and natural calamities, death will banish immortality, established by Satyadeva and maintained by Trita and Dvita in their Ages."

"With Śukrācārya (the Demon Teacher) in control of the future of life, mankind will be faced with a hopeless dilemma. Men will find mortal birth a misfortune and death a jump in the unknown. Life will consist of facing big problems. The reason of birth and death will be hidden. Some will consider that birth takes place due to their parents' sexual attraction. Thus, men will decide that the aim of life is enjoyment. Others will find this a ludicrous idea. They will claim that liberated souls take birth to gain more experience. Through renunciation, they will find out about their immortality and will rise above birth and death. They will say that to enjoy life is evil, and will advocate that renouncing material pleasures is the aim of life. Some others will question that when all souls are liberated, why do they take birth to have an experience. Why is it necessary to completely renounce life to go beyond birth and death?"

"Others will say look at the beautiful earth, with a wonderful blue sky. Observe the play of clouds, colourful sunrises and sunsets. See the peaceful high mountains, covered with shining white snow, dazzling under the sun. How beautiful it is when the rivers and rivulets rush down the mountain, flowing through the forest glades and the wide green land with a soothing murmur in their way to the sea. Look at the seas and the oceans! Look at the waves how they rush towards the shore. From the shore, the horizon looks as if the sky is touching it. Observe the beautiful sunrise, when the sun rises from the ocean and the sky becomes a glorious canvas. How beautiful are the forests with their animals and birds. Look at the soothing sight of dawn with the manifold canticles of birds. Others will contradict these views and say that these sights are beautiful only for poets, artists, and philosophers and those who have an imagination. Think of those people who have no houses to live in, no clothes to cover themselves and no food to fill their belly. For them such a dawn is mockery. Life with all its demands paints a sorrowful picture for them. Thus, there will be many ways of looking at the same facts. These will give rise to conflicting opinions and result in unending arguments and discussions. Each side will try to prove the Truth of its opinion, which will result in continuous quarrels amongst differing groups. Through these fights, people will face constant fear and havoc. They will become very tired of these disputes. Each party will be completely divided from the other. They will each try to build up on their conflicting views. At that moment, some immortal beings will take birth."

"This will occur during the middle of Kali, when mankind will be divided into many groups. Spiritual knowledge, the knowledge of the soul and experiences of Vedic Truth, will be completely lost. Their experiences will be based solely on material Truth. They will all try to spread their own views amongst others, which will give rise to widespread discord. At that moment, to achieve a united consciousness and to realise peace on the earth, there will be six incarnations of immortal beings one after the other. However, through the influence of Kali and his sombre forces, the teachings of these immortal beings will become so warped and distorted that this would lead to formation of different groups. These groups will then consider their incarnated being as a direct representative of the Divine, and with his gospel, they will make a particular creed. Religion in Kaliyuga will take the place of spirituality. With the other incarnated beings, a similar process will occur. As a result, there will be many different religions with their own gospels and creeds on the earth. These varied religions will further separate into groups, inimical to each other, in which, additionally, the previous divisions of humanity in four castes will remain. Further division will be caused due to the multitude of languages existing in the world. These groups will be under the control of various religious creeds."

After giving these details to King Janamejaya, Ṛṣi Vyāsa wished to leave and said, "O Pāṇḍaveya! I have given you an account of the future activities of Kali. If you have any further questions, you can ask your Guru, Śukadeva, who is my son. He was also your father's Guru. He is in your royal chamber as a Prime Minister. He provides you with important political guidance on how to govern your vast kingdom. He is spiritually as wise as I am. Now I must depart with this knowledge, as Kali's influence on the creation will spread soon. I have to leave without the Mahābhārata but with the knowledge of the Vedas which is above all creation, and place it in the chamber of Brahma." Saying these words, he disappeared.

THE MATERIAL CONSCIOUSNESS

After the great Seer Vyāsa disappeared from the Royal Conference of King Janamejaya, where the Mahābhārata, the epic, was being recited for the King, Vaiśampāyana, son of Vyāsa, took his place and the recitation continued.

Vaiśampāyana told the detailed story of Mahābhārata to King Janamejaya during a month. The King was then liberated from sin. Everyone saw that the black canopy had changed into white. Although the King was glad of his own purification, he remained concerned about the people of his state. He decided to circulate the Mahābhārata throughout his kingdom and took this up as a state duty. He himself moved through the country with some orators to spread and circulate the story of the Pāṇḍavas. While he was touring the land, he saw that a cowherd boy, having a strange shape, was beating a one-legged cow mercilessly with a stick. On seeing this, the King approached the boy and asked him why he was thrashing the cow so mercilessly. The boy continued his brutality without paying any attention. Then, the King became angry and said, "O foolish boy! Do you not hear what I am telling you?" The boy looked at the king for a minute but then continued to beat the cow. King Janamejaya became very angry. He took his sword and shouted, "O disobedient boy! Stop this cruel beating immediately."

As the boy did not pay any heed to him, the King struck the boy with his sword to stop him. All of a sudden, the scene changed completely. The King saw that there was neither a boy nor a cow. Instead of the boy, Kali, the Lord of the Iron Age manifested, having three eyes and four hands. He shouted, "I am Kali, O Janamejaya. This is my Age. Here only my Will is supreme. You saw an example through the cowherd boy and the cow. You cannot rebel against me. Obey my rule, prostrate before me and take my blessings. If you worship me only, then I will establish you on this earth."

On hearing the voice of Kali, King Janamejaya became furious. He said, "I have been born in the divine family of the Pāṇḍavas. O Kali! O Antidivine! I cannot accept you. Until now, I have only heard about your evil deeds from the Seers. I was eager to meet you." Kali asked the King why he wanted to see him. The King replied, "I wanted to fight with you, O wicked guide of the Kālacakra, the Time Wheel. I will not accept your evil rule. O Kali, I must fight you. Either you conquer me to establish your rule or I must conquer you to establish the divine rule upon this earth." With these words, the King attacked Kali with his sword. Kali disappeared. The King heard only this voice from the clouds, "It is impossible, O Janamejaya, to conquer me. You are vainglorious that you wish to fight with me. You will be punished in time."

The King heard this sentence of Kali and stood still pondering on the problem. He thought of ways on how to start a fight with Kali, how to control antidivine work and how to counter the devilish influence on the people of the earth. With these sombre thoughts, he finished his tour and returned to the royal palace. After a short rest, he entered his royal chamber. He informed himself about the political activities of his ministers in his absence. Then, he told his Guru Śukadeva about the success he had in spreading Mahābhārata in the country as well as his encounter with Kali. When Śukadeva heard about that incident, he said, "O Janamejaya, I will explain to you the vision you had relating to the work of Kali. O King! The cow is the symbol of this earth. The four feet are the symbols of her spiritual base. The boy himself was Kali as you yourself recognised later. Now you can observe the work of Kali. He has reached the material consciousness and taken it under his control. As you have seen yourself, the three feet of the cow are already broken. She is standing on her last leg and Kali is beating her mercilessly." King Janamejaya was full of fear as he asked, "O Guru, please explain to me the significance of her different legs? Which three have been broken by Kali? How has he broken them? On which leg is she standing now?"

Śukadeva replied, "Listen O Janamejaya! Observe the present condition of the material consciousness. The earth has lost already tapasya (meditation) on Brahman, knowledge of the Vedas, Yajña (sacrifice) for the Gods. Now, she is standing on Dharma (right conduct) of human activity. These are the four feet of the earth—tapasyā, knowledge, yajña and dharma. This is Kali's victory as he has really hurt the cow, the symbol of the mother earth. O King, you do not know with what love Brahmā, the Creator, has shaped this earth. All the beings he created, he placed in her, with his blessings to the earth. "O Mahī! Thou wilt be perfect within thyself. Thou wilt be able to take any shape you like."

"To conquer material consciousness means to have complete vicrory. Kali has now attained this victory. Now, Kali will manifest on this earth under the following arrangement. Śukra, the Demon Teacher will be controlling the intellect of the being to guide the mind in the false direction. Śani, the Devil, will govern the whole creation in the place of the Divine Governor, Dharma. Mṛtyu, Death, will be the effective power in place of Yama to detach the soul from the body and Kama, Passion will be the Creator for the physical birth. Arbuda, the Snake King will be the master of wealth. Hunger and thirst are important for the vitality of the being, for which one has to do divine sacrifice for the health and growth. Instead of divine sacrifice, there will be greed. People will become greedy for food as well as for desire and passion. They will want more and more. Desire and passion will become more powerful and they will fully influence the people of the earth. Thirst of the soul will be corrupted and influenced by anger. Anger will consume the life juices to nourish the ego in place of the soul. Ego will become all-powerful throughout mankind. People will be egoistic without any knowledge of the soul. The whole humanity will be fully covered by the shadow of ego and desire. They will be deflected from their own divinity. Humanity will consider the ego as the soul or as the self itself."

"What you saw in your vision was Kali hitting the base of religion of the material consciousness. Now we have to discuss what is the right conduct of the earth. It is religion or right conduct to believe in the existence of Gods, their works for the growth of the earth, to manifest purity, peace and joy for the immortality of the earth and to worship the Gods for the earth's perfection and development. As Kali has touched the earth now, she is bound to worship Him, lose faith in Gods, and neglect them. Earth will be forced towards ruin by impurities, diversities, sorrows and repentance. The dark forces will influence her during the period of Kali. The material consciousness is the base of life, which acts mechanically through life energy. The whole day's active efforts' fail to act in sleep with the result that gains are lost. At such a moment, men are helpless to control the action of material consciousness. O Janamejaya, as Kali has touched this consciousness, mankind will evolve without any succour in the frame provided by Kali. They will commit evil deeds themselves and be miserable. Finally, they will ruin themselves and have a peaceless, sorrowful life without any relief in future."

THE LIFE ENERGY

When the king heard the condition of the material consciousness, as guided and moulded by Kali, he became afraid and asked Śukadeva, "O Guru! You say that Kali will act through the material consciousness and colour the mental being according to his own nature, which is evil. Would there be no help from other forces to direct the life energy on the right path?"

Śukadeva replied, "Yes, there is a way to direct life towards the Life Divine. Listen, O Janamejaya! Look inside your body through the assistance of my power of tapasyā. Close your eyes, try to see inside your body and concentrate on your breath. Try to penetrate deeper still." Śukadeva touched the forehead of the King with the index finger of his right hand and asked, "Tell me, O Son of Parīkṣit, what do you see now?" The King replied, "I see, O Guru, a vast void before me and a wind blowing with a great noise." Śukadeva said, "Concentrate still more and tell me what you are seeing." After a while, the king replied, "Now, I see a fire burning which is touching the sky." Again Śukadeva repeated, "Concentrate, O King, on the fire and tell me what do you see?" After some time had passed, the King murmured, "O Guru! I see in the fire a space where a very beautiful girl, eight years old, is sitting with her loose curly hair falling around her to the ground. She is looking towards the sky with her eyes like a lotus, her motionless pupils seeming like black drones seated on the lotus petals with dewdrops around her. Adjusting her two hands just in front of her mouth, she is praying to something, as she is gazing at the sky." Again, Śukadeva asked the king to tell him what he saw. The King replied, "I see a snake behind her in a semi-erect position having several heads, and holding the creation on its head. I see another snake approaching, who also has several heads and is ferocious looking. He has started to attack the former snake, that is holding the creation, with his head. But the former snake is strong enough to resist this attack and remains still without any movement. He is standing like a pillar. Then the second one arose and, becoming very vicious, started to poison the creation." Śukadeva asked the king to come back to the present to hear the significance of the vision. Then the king came out of his vision, became normal and was curious to know the meaning of the vision.

Śukadeva replied, "Listen carefully, O Janamejaya, this vision has a special meaning. The space or the void you saw is the gap between the material and the subtle consciousness.

Then you saw a fire burning in the space and that is the Vītihotra, (the aspirant fire). In that fire, the little girl symbolises the psychic being. As she is seated, she symbolises the psychic prayer for the supreme. This is the prayer for the Truth that has disappeared from the earth consciousness. The snake holding the creation on his head is the life energy based on material consciousnesss that is holding the mental creation. The Purāṇa gives him the name of Vāsuki. Vāsuki serves the Divine and gets energy from Marut, the Lord of the Wind. By his efforts to attain the Divine, he has attained immense strength, which cannot be measured. He is immortal and will always stand holding this creation."

"The other snake, which appeared afterwards and attacked Vāsuki on the face, is Arbuda, under the influence of the dark forces. He is the brother of Vāsuki. He did a great tapasyā for attaining immortality, but he did not succeed. For this reason, he became full of vengeance and wanted to harm the divine creation and activities. Then Kali made him an instrument for his devilish work. The significance of his coming afterwards, means that he will come one day to poison this creation. That will occur during the period of Kali." Then the king demanded why Arbuda, who was incorporating vital energy through the influence of Kali, was not trying to poison the little girl, as she was the psychic being.

Śukadeva replied, "See, O King, a fire is burning around her. This is Vītihotra, an aspirant fire, and the psychic flame. By the power of that flame, she is protected. The snake, influenced by the Devil, cannot enter there. That flame came out from her own penance. This was so established by the Ṛṣis when Satyadeva (Leader of the Golden Age) disappeared from the Time Wheel."

THE MENTAL CREATION

Then King Janamejaya questioned his Guru about the nature of vital energy. Śukadeva replied, "Listen, O Janamejaya! Vital energy has no other function but to poison the being; it is according to the power of time. Let us go to the mental creation and see the activities of vital energy."

Śukadeva again touched the forehead of the King and asked him to go deep within himself. There the King saw that his Guru was ablaze with light like the sun at noon. Then he looked at his own body. He saw he did not have the golden red colour (the actual colour of his body as he was born in a family with a divine descent). In place of that luminous colour, his body was dark brown without any light. He requested his Guru the reason for the change in his skin colour. The Guru replied, "Janamejaya, do not be afraid. This is not your physical body, which has a golden red colour due to the blood of your forefathers. This is the subtle body, which you have acquired with your own efforts. My subtle body is full of light like the sun as I did a long penance (tapasyā) even before my birth. When the time came for me to take birth I remained in my mother's womb reciting the Vedas and ten months passed. I did not wish to leave my mother's womb as I saw that the world was full of attachment. Consequently, I passed twelve years in my mother's womb in the shape of a small baby. My father requested me to come out into the world to relieve my mother. I did not agree. I told my father to request the Creator to withdraw attachment from the world, and then I would take birth. In response to my father's request to the Creator, He agreed even though it was impossible, to withdraw māyā for one moment from the world so that I could take birth. That occurred and I was born. After the delivery, my small body expanded and I became like a young man. I went immediately to the forest for my tapasyā. Not even for a day did I enjoy my body. For this reason, you saw that my body is ablaze like the sun. The dark brown colour of your body is the effect of enjoyment. Through enjoyment, the light of the body goes away and then enter disease, old age and death. Now, let us go to your goal."

King Janamejaya and his Guru Śukadeva started their adventure. They went through a vast green land and then through certain areas, which looked like a desert without any trees or green grass. At last, they reached the shore of an ocean. This ocean was so vast that they could not see the other shore from where they were standing. They saw a bridge with people coming and going in a queue. Śukadeva asked the King to follow him and he started walking on the water. King Janamejaya was astonished to see that Śukadeva did not sink into the water. His Guru was walking so fast that he had to follow him. He was not able to ask him the reason. However, the Guru understood his unspoken wish and told the king to follow him as a silent spectator until the adventure ended. This the King did. After some time, he saw that the bridge collapsed into the ocean taking down all the pedestrians on it. The King was shocked to see the catastrophe. Then he saw that the bridge arose from the ocean with only a few pedestrians.

When they reached the other shore, they saw a land with a wonderful creation. The gate was a bit further from the bridge, which was the only entrance to that enchanting place. A very good looking man, fully armed, was guarding the gate and controlling the people who were entering and leaving there. When both of them reached there, the gate keeper gave a long salutation to Śukadeva and told him, "Enter, O Ṛṣi, this door is always open for you." On Śukadeva's request, the king was also allowed to enter inside. When they entered, they observed that they were in a wonderfully created world, which, in comparison to the earth, was gigantic. All that exists on the earth mountains, trees, animals, birds, human beings even houses, boats etc. were all in this world, but they had an immense size and the quantity was much greater. They moved through these multitudes and finally came in front of the Creator. The Creator was creating all that he liked but the only difference was that everything was conscious. Also all creations were in motion, even the things that are immobile on the earth, like mountains, houses, trees etc. They all moved according to their own will. There were many mental creators and they were making innumerable creations. They were not looking at their own creations, not even at the strangers Śukadeva and Janamejaya. They were gazing at the sky. Śukadeva and the King Janamejaya, on his part, looked at the scene with mounting astonishment.

After observing for a long time they saw a many-headed snake rising slowly from below, which touched the creators with his forked tongue. Through that touch, one by one, they all became conscious. Then they started to shout at the same time, "This creation belongs to me. Look, how beautiful it is. I am the creator of this world." When the creators were all busy shouting, at that time they heard another voice, "You all are the creators but I am the Lord of All. Remember, O Creators! I am the King of this world, who protects you and your creations. Thus, I am the owner of this creation. This belongs to me, and how beautiful it is. I am the King and I own it all." On hearing this, all the mental creators became quiet and disappointed. They started to brood on this issue.

After some time, there arose another big commotion. "The King may be the owner, but we are the protectors, so these creations belong to us." When the King heard this, he came out with a sword to subdue them. He told them, "Be quiet, and do not make any noise. You are all my slaves. You are here to serve. You have nothing to do with these creations." They replied, "But you are not the Creator. We have created these worlds for ourselves. We wish to rejoice in them."

The King replied, "This is not true. You all have created for me so that I can rejoice and rule over them." They agreed that that was the case. Then the King became very annoyed with them and started to strike them down with his sword. They fought against the sword to save themselves. At the end of the fight, the King vanished. Without the King, they became powerful and occupied the creations. They ruled over the creations. Then a fight started amongst them on how to divide their creations. The fight went on intensifying and went from bad to worse. The mental creators became afraid that they would not be able to save themselves and their creations. They worried that their creations were going to be ruined by the fight. They were repentant. They said, "We have had very bad luck. Now where do we stand? Our own creation refuses to accept us." The creations shouted back at them, "O creators, take our side, remain untouched and out of danger under our protection." The mental creators considered it very disappointing that they were becoming controlled by their own creations. Then the mental creators, together with their creations, became divided into many parts. To fulfil their necessities and to bring satisfaction, they started to create. But this creation was completely different from before. These could in no way be compared to the previous ones. Moreover, there arose a need amongst the groups to gain supremacy amongst the others. To fulfil this demand there were further creations. However, these creations became awe-inspiring and fearful and the mental creators became afraid that their creations would annihilate them. They asked themselves who could save them in this hour of dire need.

After some time, the mental creators saw that their creations were heading towards extinction by their own fight. There was nobody to save them. The desperate creators looked above them and saw a golden sun. This was not the sun as they remembered. They saw a being with a halo around his body and from him they heard the assurance that he would save them all from catastrophe.

After that both Śukadeva and Janamejaya returned to their body consciousness, by descending into the physical plane. The king asked, "O Guru, will you please explain to me the meaning of the vision of the mental creation that we saw just now."

Śukadeva replied, "Yes, my disciple, listen to the significance of the present vision. As we came out of this physical body, you saw that we had a subtle body. With these bodies, we started our adventure in the mental creation. We went through the "Antarikṣa"—that is the inner space between the mind and the physical. This was the vast land, where we saw green earth as well as deserts. Subsequently, we arrived at the shore of the life ocean, which we call the ocean of longevity. Over this ocean, there was the bridge constructed of life power, which is connecting the mental and the subtle plane. As you remember, the bridge collapsed suddenly into the ocean and you cried out when you saw the catastrophe. After a while, you saw that it rose once again from the ocean and became fixed at the same place. When it had collapsed it was full with pedestrians, when it arose again it had only a few. O Pāṇḍaveya, this happens all the time. Innumerable mental creations pass over the bridge. When it becomes overloaded, then it collapses; most of the mental creations go down and lose their life strength. A few of them survive as they are blessed with longevity from the ocean of longevity. They are then able to go to the subtle plane to have a subtle body." Then the king asked, "Why do so many gather at the same time on the bridge of longevity." Śukadeva replied, "They have to receive the boon of longevity for crossing the bridge, otherwise they have to wait there. That is the reason why all mental formations do not take a shape. Whatever is formed at the mental plane is usually destroyed in the ocean of longevity. Most of the mental formations remain only in the imagination. Only a few come to the physical plane and take a physical form. Do you understand now, O my disciple, why all the mental thoughts do not become reality?"

"Now we come to the crossing of the ocean. When we reached the shore, we saw a little gate aside from the bridge. This gate is the entrance and exit of the mental creation. There you saw a male being with an impressive personality. He is Bhavyavaya, who directs all thoughts created on the mental plane to the subtle plane. Then, we entered into the mental plane and saw many formations or creations, all of them conscious, which can move, having the shape of *bhāva* (*bhāva* is the source of thoughts. It is formed in the superior part of the mental plane. An idea is the effect of the thought and it is made in the inferior part of the mental plane). In addition, Bhavyavaya guides these bhāvas to the vital plane. For that reason, the Ṛṣis called them bhāvanā. Those bhāvas who manage to pass over the bridge are bhāvanās or thoughts. Only when they take shape on the physical plane, they become alive. Then these very thoughts manifest physically to have an impact on circumstances in our lives."

"You recall that on the mental plane, the mental creators are busy creating new thoughts according to their wishes. There is no plan behind them. In the human mind, the presence of thoughts comes after their creation. When the individual mind comes into contact with these ideas, they consider it as their own concept, plan or idea." King Janamejaya asked his Guru, who was the individual being who finally came into contact with the ideas as men give them various names such as I, you, he.

Śukadeva replied, "No, my disciple, this is the name given to all who are alive. When these mental formations come into contact with life, in other words, with someone who is alive, then they become real and take shape."

"Subsequently, you may recall, we saw a many-headed snake rising up there. This is life energy influenced by Kali. You saw that this snake touched the heads of the mental creators with his forked-tongue and gave rise to ego in them. As a result, the silent creators started claiming that they were the ones who had created these thought-formations. You remember, before Kali touched them, they were not conscious about their own creations. But Kali's touch poisoned them and they became infected with the idea of mine and thine. With these claims, the ruler of the mental plane shouted that he was the one who owned the whole creation. This clearly shows that the effect of Kali's poisonous touch is that all will feel that the thoughts belong to them. The ruler will think the thoughts are his and the worker will consider them as his. The situation will deteriorate to such an extent that the people will remove their ruler and form many parties. Then the competition will start amongst these parties and in the end, they will ruin the creation. At such a moment, the people will be invited to join these parties for their own safety. Everyone will come under their influence, people will be helpless and they will be forced to serve them. The creators will realize that the creations are at the point of extinction. They will feel helpless and afraid to stand there. Then they will look upwards and see a new Creator with a glowing light who will support them to achieve victory. The aim would be to have a total change so as to achieve a complete transformation.

KNOWLEDGE AND IGNORANCE

The King asked Śukadeva, "Tell me, O Guru! When will these creations be destroyed? Tell me about human activity at the period of Kali?"

Śukadeva responded, "Listen, O King! During this time, mankind will remain distant from knowledge of self and will work only through ignorance. Here, I will try to explain to you in more detail the idea of knowledge and ignorance. First, let me tell you about knowledge. All creative thoughts and inspirations come from Brahmā, protective and constructive ideas from Viṣṇu, and destructive and reconstructive insights, from Rudra. Those who are conscious about the origin of thoughts through meditation can themselves become instruments of creation. They can realize all their wishes and be an instrument of the Divine. In fact, they can even rule over the earth. They can become an instrument of the power of destruction, destroy their opponent, and even reconstruct that which was chosen from the original source. A man, who knows this secret, can become a poet, a discoverer, an inventor, or a powerful ruler, a great hero or a determined warrior. To know about the origin of the manifestation of thoughts that is real knowledge. With this knowledge, an ordinary man can become a superman. The most important factor is to become conscious of the self or "Ātman" which is always connected with the supreme self or "Paramātman" and then to establish the connection between the two."

"In this Age, there will always be an inspiration to work for self interest, for one's own purpose, for one's own vital satisfaction. No one remains satisfied without work, no mind without thoughts. Human beings have to work and think always because there is a constant pressure on a person through the demands made by hunger and thirst. Most of the human efforts are made to safeguard themselves against these demands. In addition to these, other compulsive needs influencing human beings are ego, passion, greed, etc. Men are ignorant and self-conscious, which leads them to behave like beasts. Their main interests are to eat, to sleep and to have children so as to continue the family. They can even become violent and brutal to satisfy their own interests, needs and desires. This creates disharmony. They become merciless, have no sympathy, and could even kill others for their needs and necessities. To control these violent emotions, rational behaviour could be of help. With a rational mind, people become considerate in the satisfaction of their needs and necessities. They can control their baser instincts, which lead them to brutality and violence. Reason can control the intensity of vital cravings and demands for the necessities of life. A rational mind is like the twilight before dawn. We cannot have a clear vision to observe the complete Truth. For example, what reason decides is good for humanity, for the country, or for the individual self, could be only partially good for the party, for the divided country or for the divided self-fulfilment. At this moment, the whole of mankind, the earth, spirituality, religion, social affairs or other activities are guided by reason, which can benefit only some parts of the world, not the whole. To acquire knowledge, for various reasons, such as for the development of the country, or to secure freedom, will, when guided by the rational mind, be only partially helpful. Reason shows everything bathed in the mental light, which is like twilight based on ignorance."

"O Janamejaya! You saw that, when all was on the point of being destroyed, a luminous being over this mental creation told the creators there that he would save them. They should always remember that the sun like manifestation is the real knowledge. This is not to be guided by reason, but is beyond it. Action should be without any efforts. All labours are to be smooth. Understanding is not to be vague, to be scrutinised by reason, to be judged either good or bad, or right or wrong, divine or undivine. Everything is evident, self-manifested like the sunshine. No dissection or deviation, neither partial good nor partial activity is integral knowledge. This allows us to see the united whole that is good for all. It is beneficial for the whole humanity, for the whole country, as well as that, what is healthy for the whole society. This would be auspicious for all parties, bringing gain to all. There the whole earth will appear as one country; all men of earth belonging to one caste; one group of descendants of Kardama; a united race of Manu, with one language for all, where one feels and lives with a divine rhythm. There is no separation between beings; no activity by which one profits and the other suffers. There is no occasion where one laughs, dances and sings and the other cries with sorrow, shouts for revenge or repents for certain deeds. That will be the united consciousness, which only shows itself in the light of this realisation, discovered by the Ṛṣi Mahachamasya. This is called Mahas or the supramental."

"O Son of Parīkṣit! Are you clear about knowledge and ignorance? Then follow me. During the period of Kali, the whole earth will be fully covered by ignorance. There will arise ego and desire in human activity. They will lose faith in the existence of Gods and their work in the human being or on the earth. Fear will be all-prevalent. Death will face mankind at all times. Although humaṇity will not believe in Gods, they will accept the reality of death. To them, the books of knowledge like the Vedas, Upaniṣads, Purāṇas, Rāmāyana, and Mahābhārata will be of no use. They will not be able to understand the reality of these scriptures through the influence of ignorance. When they will follow them without understanding, they will use them without meaning. When they accept past sayings on faith, and then not see any results; they will lose faith day by day. Then they will treat these books of knowledge as ordinary books. They will be irrelevant for their daily life. They will even try to misuse this secret knowledge for their own purposes and will be disheartened on seeing no results.

DISCOVERY OF SUPERMIND

The King exclaimed, "O Guru! You have described a very agonizing picture for the future of mankind on the earth. Will you please enlighten me how we will be able to become liberated from it in the future? Is it not possible to do something now for the future with your wise help?"

Śukadeva replied, "No, my disciple, it is not possible to do anything for the future. But listen, O Janamejaya, a few steps could be taken to change and be liberated from the influence of Kali."

"First of all, this earth and the whole creation will be fully covered with the darkness and ignorance spread through the influence of Kali. There will be many divisions in mankind; these divisions will also be prevalent even in the country itself, even amongst people speaking the same language. Vital forces like ego and desire will be very prominent. A quarrelsome attitude and selfishness will be widely prevalent in everyone's life at this time. People will be completely devoid of the knowledge of the Vedas. They will be totally unaware of spiritual knowledge and works, as I had told you before. The books of knowledge will be misused to fulfil, satisfy and serve their own self-interest. The knowledge people obtain from the Vedas will be used wrongly. Thus the results will be harmful. Day by day, they will lose faith in this ancient wisdom."

"In their social life, they will always be troubled by selfishness and jealousy. These two powers will result in quarrels and unpleasantness, which will disturb their harmonious life and work. They will feel increasingly miserable. Accompanying these negative feelings, Kali will also bring about natural catastrophes. Through his influence, fear will be prevalent in a vicious form throughout mankind. There will be great destruction at times from flood, famine, earthquake and epidemics."

"To develop trade and business, and to promote the export and import of goods, human beings will improve the means of conveyance by air, by land and over the oceans. To fight famines, they will discover ways of quicker and increased production of food. To this end, they will manufacture fertilizers and invent machines to assist in preparing the soil, providing water for agriculture and harvesting. They will study the soil, water, movement of stars and planets for the prediction of earthquakes and floods. They will make efforts to predict accurately the lack of rain or an excess of rainfall. They will try to solve their problems by trying to travel to the stars and planets, to survey the ocean beds and to penetrate into the earth. They will depend on their eyes, their machineries, their instruments and incredible weapons to find an explanation of the problems facing them. Developing their knowledge in these fields, they will call it science.

"They will try to ascertain spiritual knowledge or events occurring in their past history on the basis of concrete evidence. These will be the facts in which they believe. Their knowledge in various fields will be based on proof. In their eyes, only science will provide them with Truth, which can be believed. Only when objects are visible will they consider it the cause or the Truth of events or happenings. This will be known as the scientific method."

"Science and history will prove to mankind that they are greater than all beings in the world. Through their astonishing discoveries, they will have more confidence in their mental intelligence, reason and judgement. However, their satisfaction will be based on ignorance. After a little while, they will again become restless. Developments in science will help to a certain extent. With these, they will be able to attain supremacy in the material sphere."

"Their mental ego will become monumental through their amazing discoveries. On this basis, they will try to prove that they are more advanced than in the past, that they have discovered more than their forefathers and that they have made much deeper progress. However, the results will be evil, as they will consider themselves wiser than the sages of ancient time. This egoistic knowledge will create increasing problems for them. They will try to solve one problem after another but the problems would be never-ending. Countries or states will be without a king. Instead, they will try to establish peace and harmony by inventing many new theories or "isms". In the meantime, through scientific and material developments, other stubborn problems will arise which will cause even more difficulties than before."

"However, their efforts will be in vain. Problems will remain in achieving and maintaining peace, the reason being that they will not be able to achieve perfect peace and harmony and resolve their differences, quarrels and difficulties. Their method of discovery of Truth and their efforts will not lead them anywhere. When they see no solution to their problems, they will declare that life is meant to be a struggle and that there is no life without difficulties. One who battles life is a hero. They will stop expecting perfect peace in life on account of the diversity of nature."

"At that moment, there will be a divine descent on the earth from the supramental plane. A Supramental Creator will take birth on the earth as a human being. He will suffer all the pain that mortal men have to undergo. He will live like an ordinary man and will try to uplift humanity from its chaotic, peaceless condition and lead it to harmony and peace by announcing the supramental descent. This could be achieved in two ways, either ascension of the whole humanity to the Supermind or a descent of the Supramental consciousness into humanity to help it evolve into a higher plane, transforming mortal life into the life divine."

REALITY OF THE SUPRAMENTAL PLANE

"However, the scientists, the wise historians as well as the followers of the ancient scriptures, (the orthodox learned persons who implicity believe and follow the ancient scriptures, without understanding the meaning) will refuse to accept the reality of the Supermind. They will feel, see and decide that this state is impossible. The scientific brain will refuse to accept that man can be transformed, be divinised, become immortal when he has so many defects, failings, and mental problems. The wise historian will say that this thought is absurd, as it has never happened before in the history of the world. If it has not happened in the past, how can it happen now? The followers of the ancient scriptures will say that there was a Golden Age on the earth. At that time, the human beings were good and they had a high and elevated character. They followed all the moral rules. However, to expect such a monumental event at present is irrational. It is true that the scriptures have mentioned, that there would be a Golden Age once again. But for that, we will have to wait a much longer time, perhaps thousands and thousands of years."

"O Janamejaya! How can they know about this secret? This is neither a dream nor an imagination. When Satyadeva withdrew from the Time Wheel, He took this secret with him. The golden moment had disappeared from human sight and memory. After the Golden Age, the Silver Age began and since then the world has passed through two different Ages. Now the third one, the Iron Age will start which will be completely different from the other two. Naturally, there are no traces of the Supramental or Mahas in the human mind. From the Silver to the Iron Age, the Brahmins will know and recognise three planes. These are Bhūr—the physical plane, Bhuvar—the vital plane and Svar—svarga, heaven, which is the mental plane. In these three planes, the influence of Kali will be evident. During this period the Gods will be resting, they will not be active in any way."

"The Ṛṣis of the Silver and the Bronze Ages remembered the supramental plane when they decided to leave this earth. They knew that the only way to get rid of the influence of Kali is through renunciation. That is the reason why they showed us the path of detachment and of sacrifice, tapasyā etc."

"Today, I will tell you, O King Janamejaya! The secret of the Golden Age, which had occurred a long time ago, was kept well hidden. This was the knowledge of Mahas (the supermind). After the disappearance of Satyadeva from the creation, this secret was kept by a society of Ṛṣis who gave their knowledge to chosen disciples only. This concerned immortality, the experience of unalloyed joy, the complete immunity of the body, ways to increase and decrease the body (consisting of fire, water, ether), and how to obtain a body directly from nature without going through the mother's womb. These were the secrets that the Ṛṣis taught their disciples, which would seem impossible to modern man. Kali came to know about the activities of these Ṛṣis and became very annoyed. He felt that if this knowledge remained on the earth, then people would not believe in the tenets of his Age. He gave instructions to the hostile powers under his control to destroy the forest together with the Ṛṣis and their disciples. There was a flood in the middle of the night when the forest together with the Ṛṣis and their disciples disappeared, leaving no signs of their existence.

At the time of the flood, a bird named "Tittiri", living on a tree there, escaped and came flying to Mithilā where Rājarṣi Janaka was holding a spiritual conference. The Ṛṣis, fully knowledgeable in different parts of the Vedas, completed their contribution, and King Janaka received the secret knowledge from different parts of the Vedas. However, he did not receive an important part of the Yajur Veda. He was looking for that information, which none of the Ṛṣis could provide. At that moment, the bird Tittiri spoke from the tree to King Janaka. All present were surprised to hear an unexpected voice coming from a tree. The bird said, "O King! I am coming from the ashram of Ṛṣi Mahacamasya, where they were developing that part of the Yajur Veda, which you are seeking. Those Ṛṣis in that forest are no more and have now drowned in the floodwaters. That knowledge is now lost."

When King Janaka heard of the disappearance of an important part of the Yajur Veda, he was very sad and disheartened. After a while, he asked the bird Tittiri to tell the Conference what it had heard from the Ṛṣis. Now the bird, Tittiri, had heard the daily chanting of the Vedic hymns by the Ṛṣis. It told all what it had heard and understood from the Rṣis and that is the basis of the Taittirīya Upaniṣad. Here I will give you a portion, which will prove to you the reality of the supramental world. "Bhūr, Bhuvar and Svar" are the physical, vital and mental planes. Above these three planes, there is one more plane announced by the Ṛṣi Mahacamasya and that is the Mahas (the supramental plane). This is the plane for Brahman; he is the Ātman (soul) with all the Godheads. In short, Bhūr is the earth, Bhuvar is the antarikṣa (the plane existing between earth and heaven), Swar is the heaven and Mahas is the plane above heaven, the plane of the Sun (Ādityaloka—the Supramental plane). Now you can understand that the Supramental plane is a Truth, and the plane Maharloka exists forever. It is neither a dream nor is it a new concept that needs to be introduced into human society. So its manifestation is inevitable in the course of time. The time, when it will become evident to all, depends on the movement of the Kālacakra."

THE DESTINY

"As you say, O Guru! You know the secret knowledge of the Golden Age as well as the immortality and immunity of the human race. Will it not be possible for you to disclose it to me now? Can we not have this Age here now with the help of all the royal power under my command supported with military power? Is it not possible to teach and train some selected persons on the earth to keep the information of the Golden Age for the future. If it is possible, O Guru, then I pray to you to please do so. I have failed miserably in this attempt. In your absence, I tried to perform an Aśvamedha Yajña, the horse sacrifice ceremony, in which I did not succeed. The snake sacrifice ceremony that I started could not be completed as well."

"It was one of the largest ceremonies of its kind. All the powerful Brahmins were gathered there. A huge number of snakes were destroyed during this ceremony. They were drawn to the sacrificial flame in great numbers. They jumped into the pyre through the power of the mantra, a specific incantation. Not only the snakes near the capital or those living in India were so affected. Even those who were living in far-flung areas of the world and those living hidden from all beings were similarly affected. Almost all the snakes had jumped into the flaming pyre and sacrificed themselves. Only Takṣaka the snake, who killed my father Parīkṣit, survived. My aim had been to kill him together with his family when he was drawn to the fire. He had also reached the sky above our sacrificial place. At that moment, a powerful Ṛṣi came. He was Āstika, son of Jaratkāru. (Jaratkāru married the sister of snake king Vāsuki, whose name was Mānasī. Āstika was born from her womb.) He wished to save his maternal race. By his power, he controlled Takṣaka's advance and stopped all Brahmins from pouring the sacrificial offering. He requested me not to proceed further and gave me a long, learned and interesting lecture on the necessity of having snakes in the creation. I was forced to stop the ceremony." After this the King paused. Being very emotional, his voice became heavy and his eyes filled with tears of frustration. Śukadeva said in a loud voice, "O Janamejaya! I know the details. You do not have to tell them to me."

After a little while, Janamejaya said, "O Guru! I wished to establish peace in the world as my great grandfather did. I organised an Aśvamedha Yajña, which could not be completed. After my forefathers departed from the earth for heaven, my father Parīkṣit tried also but it could not be completed due to his early death. After his departure from this mortal world, global unity became disturbed. Many states were formed having their independent rulers. I wanted to unite them again. Although, I conquered all those States, which were opposing me, still I could not re-establish the inner unity. I failed miserably; I could not complete the sacrificial horse ceremony. Instead, I committed a terrible sin, which caused the devastating earthquake in which my capital city disappeared. Due to the noble deeds of my forefathers, I was saved from this cataclysm by the sudden arrival of your father, the great Ṛṣi Vyāsa. He told me how to do penance for the unpardonable sin that I had committed. He told me to listen to the epic Mahābhārata from his disciple and son, Vaiśampāyana. After hearing the Mahābhārata, when I saw that I had become liberated from my sin, I realized that listening to this epic was a great virtue. I felt encouraged to spread the glory of this epic amongst my people. But I could not complete my mission due to the opposition of Kali. You told me then the reasons why the influence of Kali is bound to spread. O Guru! I have completely failed in bringing back the divine rule back to the earth as my great grandfather did before. If there is any possibility that I could succeed in this mission, then please tell me."

On hearing King Janamejaya's impassioned appeal, Śukadeva replied, "O King, I have told you the details about the present situation. Let me see if as a last attempt you could do something in this direction."

Then both of them stopped their discussion and became engaged in their normal work. After a few years, Śukadeva called Janamejaya and asked him to meet him one night. When the king went to him Śukadeva told him, "Every night,

I have seen Kali moving here and there in Indraprastha. I can show him to you. If you can call him and defeat him in an open fight then there could be a possibility to bring down again the secret knowledge of the past." On hearing this, the King was overjoyed and he was ready to do battle. He said gladly, "O Guru! Show me the place where he is and I will fight Kali and conquer him with my divine weapons. With these arms, I will definitely conquer Kali. Tell me, O Guru! Has there been anyone who has conquered Kali in the past?"

Śukadeva replied, "In the beginning of the Dvāpara Yuga, there was King Nala who fought with Kali in the forest. He fought because he found out that Kali had engineered his entire misfortune. He became determined to conquer him."

"King Nala lost in the game of dice with his own brother, Puṣkara and was driven out of his kingdom. During the deep dark night, he walked through the forest with his wife Damayantī carrying a small packet of clothes and some ornaments. He reached the bank of a river, wished to cross the river and reach the other bank. At that moment, a boatman came and promised to ferry them to the other bank. He proposed that as his boat was small he could take them one after the other, but not both at the same time. The boat could not bear the weight of two persons. Nala thought about this proposal for a long time, but he could not leave his wife alone in the forest and go himself to the other bank. Also, he could not send her alone to a place, which he had never seen himself. He said that only if the boatman could take both of them, then they could cross the river otherwise they would still wait. The boatman replied, "I can take both of you carefully to the other bank of the river. Although the boat will be overloaded still I can try. However, I cannot take the packet you have with you. The weight of your packet will really sink the boat. Give me your packet, first I will take it to the other bank and then return to pick you both. As arranged, Nala gave his packet to the boatman, he took it away but did not return."

"Nala understood then that it was the work of Kali. Then he started looking for some food, because both of them were feeling hungry. After some time, Nala saw a bird near him. He wanted to catch it but did not have anything with which to catch it. He thought he would use his clothes to capture the bird, as no one was there who would see him. When he tried to catch the bird, it flew away with his cloth. Thus, he was standing there completely naked, perplexed as to what he should do. Then his wife gave him half of her sari to wear. He wore half the sari but it was difficult, as they had to do everything at the same time. They walked for sometime together, and then as they were tired, they lay down under a tree. In a short time, his wife was asleep. He was worried that his wife was suffering because of him. She could easily return to her father and live safely and in comfort there. He had told her often to return, but she would not listen to him. He thought that if he could cut the sari in half, he could leave her there and hide in the deep forest."

"When she woke up, she would find herself alone in the forest, and then, out of fear, she would return to her father. At that moment, he saw a sword lying just near by. He took the sword and cut off the cloth between him and his wife in the middle. He then left his wife Damayantī, fast asleep, alone in the middle of the deep forest. When Damayantī woke up, she did not find her husband Nala and felt very afraid. She started weeping. At that moment, a hunter appeared in front of her. He sympathised with her and was attracted by her beauty. Sensing herself in danger, she played a trick. She showed the hunter that she was interested in him, asked him to take her to his father's hut and save her from the ferocious beasts in the forest. When the hunter took her to his hut, the hunter's father asked her about her family. On coming to know that she was Rājā Bhīma's famous daughter, his father took her back and the King rewarded the old man."

"In the forest, Nala walked very far in the deep forest. On becoming tired, and feeling hungry and thirsty, he sat down for some time on a log of wood. However, what he thought a log of wood turned out to be a big snake and Nala was bitten. With that bite, Nala, whose good looks were envied by the Gods, became ugly and disfigured. He looked like a completely wild man."

"Nala started to consider his next step. At that moment he heard a voice near him. It scoffed, "O beautiful Nala! Where are your good looks now? Where is your wife, your wealth and your kingdom? I have taken everything away from you, O follower of Dharma. If you agree to follow me, to forsake right conduct and to give up your principles, then I will return everything to you. Otherwise, you will have nothing and suffer like a beggar. This is my punishment to those who disobey and neglect me. I am Kali, the Lord of the Iron Age, the guiding power of the creation. You must obey me, otherwise you will be ruined and remain in this wretched condition."

"When Nala realised that Kali was behind his suffering, he was very angry and annoyed. He shouted, "O Kali! Wait for a moment! I am Nala, the follower of good conduct and high principles. I will continue to follow the path of righteousness and I will defeat you." Nala was very angry and went to King Bhojarāja's kingdom and remained there as a horse keeper for a few years."

"Armed with the powers given to him by Dvita, Ṛṣi Bhṛgurāma advanced to conquer the increasing powers of the Kṣatriyas, the warriors. He came up to Niṣāda and saw the deeds of Puṣkara. He became furious and destroyed everything. He killed Puṣkara and went looking for Nala to give him back his kingdom, but he could not find him. Subsequently, he went straight to Vidarbha to meet Nala's father-in-law, King Bhīma and there met his daughter Damayantī. From her, he came to know in detail the sufferings of Nala in the forest and his disappearance. In order to find him again, he decided together with Rājā Bhīma to announce the remarriage of Damayantī. During this function, Nala came with King Bhojarāja as his charioteer. There, Ṛṣi Bhṛgu recognised him among the charioteers and told him that he should return as his kingdom now belonged to him."

"This was how King Nala managed to defeat Kali in the past. Now, O Janamejaya! Attack Kali with your arms and with the power of my tapasyā." At that moment, Kali appeared in front of them and announced in a loud voice, "O Janamejaya! I was waiting for this moment to bring about your end. I am now ready to fight with you, and to fulfil your long-term desire. Now that you stand before me, I shall satisfy your thirst of war."

Janamejaya was very happy to fight with Kali. He attacked Kali with his divine weapons and gave him a violent shove. Thus, started the long and deadly fight between Kali and Janamejaya. Finally, Kali overpowered Janamejaya and killed him. On seeing the result of the fight, Śukadeva left Indraprastha at night and proceeded straight to the Himalayas.

—

Chapter 9

EFFORTS OF THE IMMORTALS

Śukadeva saw that the death of King Janamejaya presaged the end of the established peace under the Pāṇḍavas and the eradication of their spiritual culture. He was concerned about the future of the earth and was very troubled on his way to the Himalayas. In the deep dark night, gloom weighed him down. Darkness intensified the silence around him and the loneliness inside him. He also felt oppressed as he could see the painful future awaiting the earth. He cried out, "O Brahman! I am always detached from earthly affairs and conscious of the Vedas. There is nothing for me now on this earth. I have offered all that I had in the fire of my tapasya and achieved detachment from everything. I have become part of Thee, all liberated. By the wish of my father, I became a Minister of King Parīkṣit and of King Janamejaya. I saw the misfortune that both the kings had to face due to the influence of Kali. I go with a heavy heart for the people of the earth. Why do I suffer so intensely? I weep continuously within myself for the future of mankind. I can see humanity suffering under the misfortune caused by the iron rule of Kali."

When two drops of tears fell from his eyes, he heard a voice within himself coming straight from the Supreme: "O Son of Vyāsa! I say to thee, go to Meghapurī, one of the highest peaks of Himalayas, and stay there in trance as long as I do not call you. Till that time, give up all thoughts of mankind and the earth and be peaceful within you."

With the voice of the Supreme, all pain disappeared from his mind. He was completely free and liberated from attachment. He felt no grief. He started to climb up to the peak of Meghapurī. Dawn was breaking and darkness leaving the earth. When he reached Meghapurī, he saw the blue horizon with sunrays glittering on the snow-covered peak. All around, he could see snow-covered peaks. In the white crystalline snow, the sunrays were reflected as if in a mirror and he could see a myriad other suns.

He observed silently the beauty of nature, and then entered in a cave. He sat down on a smooth marble stone with the voice of the Brahman resounding in his ears. Merging himself in a trance, he gave up all thoughts of past and future. With the power of the Supreme, he quickly entered into himself by collecting all his thoughts and the strings of outside consciousness. Then slowly, step-by-step, he withdrew his life consciousness from the five organs of action and the five of perception. The organs of action are larynx, hands, feet, anus and genital organs and the organs of perception are eyes, ears, nose, tongue and skin. Then he withdrew himself to his internal thoughts, apprehension and self-feeling. He observed his own body after the withdrawal of the outer consciousness. He sat immobile like a statue with no movement, without any heartbeat, circulation of blood, or breath. There was no movement in his organ cells. From that moment onwards, he left his thoughts and apprehensions, and existed in the eternal consciousness.

In this way, he remained several hundred years in a deep trance, his body cells preserved intact in the frigid ice, with no change or decomposition of the body. One day, four Immortals Hanumān, Vibhīṣana, Dhruva and Aśvatthāmā arrived in front of the snow-covered cave where he was seated and started to talk. They saw with their inner sight that Śukadeva was in a deep trance in the cave. They wanted to ascertain this fact.

First, Hanumān advanced towards the entrance. He gave a violent blow to the snow wall with his iron fist. The wall shattered into pieces and opened the way into the cave. When they entered, they saw that Śukadeva was seated in front of them on a marble stone and looked like a stone statue. King Dhruva went near Śukadeva, touched his forehead with his right index finger and said, "O Mahātmā! O Great Soul! The time has come for you to wake up. O realised soul, O detached one, take up your work again." On hearing the loud voice and feeling the warm touch, Śukadeva became at first aware of his organs of perception, his thoughts and apprehensions and then his organs of action. He opened his eyes with astonishment, and said, "O great Immortals of past Ages! Tell me why you all are here and why you are pulling me again towards action. After completing my work, I had withdrawn from the world and had entered into a trance. What is the emergency now that you wake me up?"

MEMORIES OF THE PAST

Aśvatthāmā replied, "O completely liberated son of Vyāsa! It is true that you had completed your work on the earth at an early age. You were moving like a liberated Brāhmaṇa who knew everything. Even your father Vyāsa was afraid to oppose your internal tapasyā of inaction. You maintained that your earthly duties were over. You also said that you had conquered all your earthly attachment even those connected with your birth. You had a controversy with your father regarding your experience of the inactive Brahman and the importance of action existing in the Vedas. You had to accept that in the knowledge of the complete Brahman both action and inaction were equally important. I do not know what further action you have accepted for mankind."

Śukadeva said, "You are correct. I had a profound controversy with my father. After a protracted discussion, I accepted the status of the complete Brahman, having at the same time, activity together with inactivity. Practically, I do not have a mission to perform. I accepted only that I stay in his house. One day I asked him a question. I asked my father to tell me the status of the activities of Brahman that are purely divine without any attachment. King Janaka had told me that he was always in action, but without having any attachment.

When I stayed with him for a few days, he told me that he had no children, only a daughter from the earth. He had no attachment for her and he offered her in marriage to the Divine Rama. I felt that Rājarṣi Janaka was a completely liberated soul. I could not say the same about my father."

I told him "Father, it was King Janaka who told me that you were a completely liberated soul on the earth like the Brahman. He also added that you are wiser and greater than him. If I had come to seek knowledge from him leaving you, then it was an illusion. However, I see that you, my father, are attached to your child, wife, houses and property. You also take care of them in every detail. Where is then your detachment, as you are always occupied in this world."

"When my father, Ṛṣi Vyāsa, heard my question, he smiled and looked at me. He said, "O Śuka! I see in you a want of inner knowledge. Try to follow what I say. Actions are done through external organs but the attachment is in the inner one. This is the place of illusion between knowledge and ignorance. As it is very difficult to find one's way in a forest, similarly it is difficult to differentiate between a man who is detached and the one who is attached. That is not possible without the experience of work."

"Spiritual knowledge is realised through meditation. Experience of work is realised only through action. One could work with great attention, but be wholeheartedly detached. The only aim is to bring out the divinity in action. In contrast, another could work for his own interest, to gain some benefits from it, the reason being that he was greedy and full of attachment. From outside, both these actions would seem the same. It is impossible to differentiate between them. One without attachment, who works with faith and concentration for the fulfilment of work and for the divine manifestation; the other who works with attachment and for his self interest, and is greedy to obtain the fruits of his efforts. O Śuka, have you not seen that the people are eager and interested for action only if they receive the benefits from that work. Otherwise they are disheartened."

"But the Karmayogin has no desire for the fruit of his work. His skill of work is only for divine fulfilment and sacrifice. In work, negligence is contrary to the divine sacrifice. He, who works strictly according to this principle, is a liberated soul. That is why I tell you, be desireless in your work. Do not work for your self-interest. Do not work to increase your own pleasure. In human society, working for divine fulfilment, is disinterested work. In such activity is the status of Brahman. In work, with the desire for self-interest, lies the danger of bondage with attachment. Work for the Brahman, by the Brahman is really doing the divine's work and that is the status of the liberated soul."

After saying all this he became quiet and I enquired from him, "Let me know, O Father! Is there anyone you know who is deeply involved in normal human activities but who is always in the totally liberated consciousness of the Brahman. I could, then, understand better a completely liberated soul." He replied without any hesitation, "Yes, my child, there is Vāsudeva Kṛṣṇa. He is Vasudeva's son and is completely involved with his big family, having many wives and children. You should go and see him."

I replied, "If he is at Dvārakā I will go and see him but first tell me more about the character and life of Kṛṣṇa."

"My father was happy to hear this from me. He told me about the life and character of Kṛṣṇa and I was amazed to hear about Lord Kṛṣṇa, so much so that I was drawn into divine bliss on hearing the account of Kṛṣṇa's life—Rāsalīlā. Then I went to visit Lord Kṛṣṇa at Dvārakā. I saw Lord Kṛṣṇa seated in his Royal Court surrounded by his queens, valorous heroes and wise Ṛṣis. When I arrived at the Court, Lord Kṛṣṇa got up from his throne, welcomed me by bowing down at my feet and said, "O liberated wise Śukadeva, son of Vyāsa, accept my regards and respects. Please take your seat and let me know how I can serve you."

"On receiving this warm welcome from Lord Kṛṣṇa's mouth, my heart was full of joy. I sat down and said, "O Vāsudeva! I have heard from my father about your childhood and your divine play with great joy. Now, I see your magnificence in the Court. I can observe how warmly you welcome a guest and how you treat newcomers who visit you. I am very eager to see your liberated condition." Lord Kṛṣṇa replied, "O Seer! See with your inner sight! Observe from within."

"As soon as I heard these words, I saw that the scene in front of him, together with all the Ṛṣis, the warriors, the queens with the royal court, disappeared and there appeared a vast void like the sky without any creative manifestation. From that eternal boundless blue sky, a voice came to me, "O Seer! In the eternity, see the eternal condition of mine, formless and unborn."

"After some time I saw a magnificent male figure (Puruṣa) with four hands, lying on a many headed snake with all the Ṛṣis chanting the Vedas around him. From the mouth of that figure, I heard the voice, "O Seer! See this form in the formless eternity. See this primal formation in the vast creation." After a while that vision disappeared and I saw a resplendent royal court studded with precious stones and jewels and ablaze in a golden colour. There, on a magnificent, glittering, pompous elephant throne was seated a male figure (Puruṣa), having many hands and heads with thousand eyes. He looked all-powerful and had Vajra in his hand. Around him were seated Ṛṣis, Gods and Goddesses. Before that Almighty's serious face, well-armed Gods, ablaze in different colours, were standing with fear and respect. The Goddesses were all seated quietly, very serious and fearful. The Ṛṣis were constantly reciting Vedas to please him. Now and then, Gandharvas and divine danseuses (apsarās) appeared in front of the Divine Puruṣa, singing an ode to him, to lighten up the atmosphere through singing and dancing. From that serious mouth, came a thundering voice, "O Seeker of Truth! Behold my appearance when I govern the creations. Before this power, all the creations shiver."

"I was astonished to see the Supreme Creator. Then the vision changed. A number of creations appeared, with innumerable figures, some good, others bad; some divine, others undivine. They started to quarrel and fight with each other. In this fight between good and evil, some were victorious and they started to punish the others. When the victors caused suffering amongst the vanquished, then the latter started to pray to the Supreme for justice. In that great catastrophe, a loud voice was heard, which frightened all creations. "O my people! Wait for some more time. I will then manifest on the earth to bring justice to the world."

"After this the vision changed, and I could see in front of my eyes the Lord of Dvārakā, Vāsudeva, seated on the throne, smiling and looking at me, surrounded by his queens, Yādavas, Ṛṣis etc. Then, King Vāsudeva asked me, "O Seer! Did you see me? You sat immobile for so many hours. Tell us some secrets of the knowledge that you gained."

I replied, "O Lord of the Yādavas! Thou art the Emperor of All Creations. Thou art the saviour of all. Thou art with all but Thou remainst above all. All my doubts have disappeared. Thou art the only God who can be worshipped. I bow down before Thee a thousand times." After saying this to Vāsudeva, I returned back to my father, full of joy. Then I studied the Purāṇas with my father, Ṛṣi Vyāsa. I accepted fully that my father was fully liberated. I asked him to give me some work. Ṛṣi Vyāsa replied, "When the time will come, suitable work will be given to you. At present, you should help in preserving the Purāṇas." I started working on the Purāṇas. I worked with other disciples particularly on the Bhāgavata Purāṇa dealing with the life of Lord Kṛṣṇa. Many years passed in doing this work and in discussions.

Śukadeva also told the Immortals about his experiences with the Kings Parīkṣit and Janamejaya, whom he had gone to assist on being asked by his father and his efforts in trying to stem the advance of Kali.

After telling the other Immortals about these events, Śukadeva became silent and then Aśvatthāmā started to speak. He said, "O Mahātmā, now the time has come where we all will have to suffer as we could not stop the spread of Kali.

Earlier, I myself had become the instrument of Kali to spread the darkness. After the battle of Kurukṣetra, the Pāṇḍavas were victorious. One night, I entered into the fort of the Pāṇḍavas with Kṛpācārya and Kṛtavarmā to take my revenge on Lord Kṛṣṇa and the Pāṇḍavas for killing my father, Droṇācārya. In the silence of the deep dark night, when all were asleep, I killed all of them. Not a single person escaped. At the very end, I beheaded five sleeping persons whom I thought to be the five Pāṇḍavas. I took those five heads in my hands and came running out of the fort, not paying attention to the heartrending cries of the queens and other women. With an unholy joy, I hurried to reach King Duryodhana, who was breathing his last. I told Duryodhana to take the five heads of the Pāṇḍavas and told him that he had become victorious at the last moment. With his last strength, he asked me to give him the head of Bhīma and he gave me the crown to rule this earth. With an unholy cry, I took out the biggest head, among the five. Duryodhana looked at it for a moment and then gave a blow to it with his iron fist. With a great sorrow and despair he uttered these words and died, "Ah! Aśvatthāmā, what you have done is not my victory, but my greatest defeat. You have killed the sons of Pāṇḍavas, those who were remaining on the earth to perform funeral rituals for us after our death. You cannot kill the Pāṇḍavas, where the Divine Kṛṣṇa remains himself to protect them. This will now be an impossible task."

After the death of Duryodhana, Aśvatthāmā thought that although he had tried his best to avenge the Kauravas; he had only received curses in return. He felt that he was extremely unfortunate. Then, he heard some strident voices. He looked up and saw Bhīma running towards him to kill him with a raised club in his hand. Arjuna and Lord Kṛṣṇa were also following behind. He remembered the incident of the previous night. What he had done for exacting his revenge was a horrible deed that no one would forgive. To save himself, he remembered the awe-inspiring weapon of his father, Dronacarya, that was extremely powerful. He wanted to use that weapon, but to protect the Pāṇḍavas, Arjuna took up another terrible weapon of his father. If these two weapons had been used, it would have destroyed the complete creation. To prevent the destruction of the creation, Brahmā appeared and ordered them both to control their weapons. Arjuna did so immediately, but Aśvatthāmā could not. The weapon went back to the Creator, by touching the head of Aśvatthāmā. He heard then a voice, "O Aśvatthāmā, so long as you are unable to establish on the earth that what you have destroyed, till then you will have to suffer from this pain." Aśvatthāmā then asked Śukadeva to rise up, look at the world, and see the condition of the earth.

Then Mahāvīra-Hanumān said, "O Son of Dvaipāyana! Look at the earth now. Now we have the kingdom of Ajātaśatru, son of Bimbisāra. He killed his father and wrested the throne from him. There is no one capable of dethroning him. The influence of Kali is everywhere. Everyone is forced to worship only the King Ajātaśatru, even though he is a patricide and a great sinner. Some people are unwilling to accept him but they are powerless. Inspite of the evil occurences, the earth is forced to tolerate it. There is no earthquake like the one that occurred because King Janamejaya had killed a Brahmin. Kali, after conquering King Janamejaya, has full sway on the earth. Through his influence, the one single united earth has been divided into many parts. Everywhere, ego is in power with selfishness reigning supreme. Together with these two, greed, passion, anger, jealousy and stupidity are spreading amongst mankind. The many states on the earth are developing in differing ways without any spirituality."

He told everyone that on seeing the spread of these anti-divine and devilish activities on the earth, he went to take birth in the family of devotees. He was called Vardhamān Mahāvīra and was born and brought up in the culture and environment of his parents. He also received his education there. He tried to disseminate the idea of spiritual development in society. He did a spiritual austerity and penance for a long time and continued his tapasya to show humanity clearly how one could rise above the Kali-dominated deeds, to become free from the devilish influence, and to rise up towards the divine consciousness and perform religious activities. At the time of Śiśunāga, he manifested himself on the earth. King Śiśunāga came under his influence and through him, he was able to spread the Sanātana Dharma throughout his kingdom. He explained that his creed was not to be attached to earthly enjoyment, and to be friendly and loving to all people of the earth, even to all creatures. Always one should remember to chant the name of the Divine and to think of the Divine. But with the influence of Kali, there came a division amongst his devotees. His teachings became distorted and his followers formed different groups. He was disheartened to see this development and then he left the earth.

After leaving this earth, Hanumān was thinking constantly what more could be done. He considered how best to control the situation now that Kali had given different interpretations to his teachings. While cogitating on this problem, he moved through the high peaks of the Himalayas. There he met King Dhruva and asked him, "O Dhruva! Look at the earth. Not even half a century has elapsed since I left the earth, but my teachings have been completely distorted by the influence of Kali. What can be done to counter this influence?"

Dhruva thought deeply about this matter and then addressed Śukadeva. He said, "Listen, O Son of Vyāsa! When Hanumān told me about his experiences, I was very disturbed and started to think about my duty to mankind. Then I decided and proposed to him that I would help to uplift mankind from vital derangement through my tapasyā. Look at the vital plane. There, Kali exists with his devil friends and other followers. From there, he is controlling the mental and physical plane. I can go to the earth now to do this work."

Hanumān was very pleased to hear this suggestion of King Dhruva. Dhruva went to the earth and took birth at Kapilvastu, as the son of King Śuddhodana with the name of Siddhartha.

There, he was born and brought up in royal surroundings and trained to become a king. He married a beautiful girl named Gopā and had a child called Rāhula. He loved his wife and child very deeply and was fully occupied with them. One night, Hanumān appeared in a vision to him to remind him why he had taken birth. Through that vision, Siddhārtha became conscious of his mission. Immediately afterwards, he left his wife and child in the royal palace and went into the forest. In the forest, he was absorbed in tapasya, severe meditation, for several years. Then, he learnt how to withdraw his consciousness from the vital plane and called that state—nirvāṇa.

His main task was to show mankind how to withdraw consciousness from the vital plane so as to be liberated from vital hostility. His advice to his devotees was, "Surrender to the Supreme Lord, surrender to the brotherhood, surrender to religious austerity, the ultimate goal being the nirvana." Through his teachings, King Bimbisāra was highly influenced. With the spreading of this idea, the number of his devotees and disciples started growing. He retired from other activities to show them the way to achieve nirvāṇa. To demonstrate to them how to be liberated from all bondages of the vital plane, he took complete nirvāṇa and left his mortal body.

After leaving his body, he came back directly to Hanumān. He was overjoyed to see that his principles and tenets could not be deformed through the influence of Kali. But, they observed, soon afterwards that Kunik, son of Bimbisāra, was coming under the influence of Kali. He wished to destroy his own father. In a dispute, due to a difference of opinion, Kunik killed King Bimbisāra. Under the influence of Kali, Kunik was motivated to change his name to Ajātaśatru. He thus established himself as King Ajātaśatru on his father's throne. The meaning of Ajātaśatru was someone who had no enemy, or one who had conquered all his enemies. Thus, King Ajātaśatru, the slayer of his own father, became famous amongst all people through the influence of Kali. All Siddhārtha's teachings were distorted and the condition of humanity deteriorated. The Immortals realised that under the iron rule of Kali, it was very difficult to protect and save humanity through spirituality, the knowledge of Vedas, the Sanātana Dharma and faith in the Gods.

Śukadeva heard quietly the past experiences of the Immortals. He then replied, "Hanumān and Dhruva, you both have done your best for the earth and humanity. But your teachings were deformed under the influence of Kali. Let us try once again. We must give knowledge of the self to mankind and to show them the path of Brahman and the eternity. O Son of Drona, Aśvatthāmā! O Vibhīṣaṇa! Let all three of us go to the earth in different places to make further efforts. I, myself, shall take birth in the East with the idea of detachment and ascetism. O great Vibhīṣaṇa! You take up this work in the West and give to mankind the idea of endurance and compassion, and O Aśvatthāmā! You take up the work in the centre of the globe in the place of your choice and give the idea of firm faith and determination to humanity. We all should have the same mission, to show humanity that the path to eternity is only through liberation from vital forces that are inimical to mankind."

They all agreed and proceeded from there to determine the time and place of their birth. Subsequently, Hanumān and Dhruva withdrew towards the high peaks of the Himalayas.

A MOMENT OF PERIL

A few centuries passed, Vibhīṣaṇa went towards Meghapurī to look for the other immortals. He wondered about those who had decided to go to the earth and others who were still in the Himalayas. He found none of them. He considered what steps still needed to be taken. In this way, he passed a certain period there, trying to remain calm and quiet. Then he saw from afar that Aśvatthāmā was approaching him. He looked very depressed. When he came in front of Vibhiṣaṇa, he stood up and clasped him. Then he asked, "O Aśvatthāmā, why are you so depressed." Aśvatthāmā replied, "O Vibhīṣaṇa,

I went to the earth for a certain purpose but I achieved exactly the opposite. Tell me, where is Śukadeva?" Vibhīṣaṇa replied, "I am also looking for the Mahātmā." Then Aśvatthāmā asked, "Where are the other two Mahātmās, Mahāvīra and Dhruva?" At that time they heard an echo from behind saying, "Here we are." They saw that the two, Mahāvīra and Dhruva, were coming down from a higher peak to join them. Both asked Vibhīṣaṇa and Aśvatthāmā about the goals they had achieved on the earth and the actions they had taken to uplift human society from the iron grip of Kali.

First, Vibhīṣaṇa started to tell the Immortals that he had arrived first. After a few years, Aśvatthāmā came, and then Mahāvīra and Dhruva also joined them. Still, there was no sign of Śukadeva. A few centuries had passed since they had separated from each other. Vibhīṣaṇa had gone to the earth to spread spirituality in the West.

He said, "While I was going through the sky, my body was blazing just like a moving star in the sky. The place chosen was Jerusalem. The father from whom I had decided to take birth was Joseph and the mother was Mary. I was born there and was brought up in a life full of struggle and difficulties."

Vibhīṣaṇa tried to stop the old methods of religious observances, which had become brutal. In that part of the world, which was predominantly under the influence of Kali, he introduced a new idea of eternity, as well as love for humanity and faith in heaven. He told the masses that the day would come when heaven will manifest itself upon the earth. He asked them to have faith that our Father who is in heaven takes care of them. God would guide them through all perils, and show them light in darkness, illumine their way so that they see, and give them food and drink to satisfy their hunger and thirst. He further added that their only duty was to remember their Father, who lives in heaven with the words—My father; I am thy child, helpless on the earth, surrounded by several enemies. I do not know what I should do. Thou art my father, saviour of all, save us in all perils.

He also performed some miracles through his power. Seeing this, the people were very attracted towards his teachings. A huge number gathered around him. They all were eager to accept and follow the new path that was spreading through his spiritual gospel, leaving the orthodox methods of religion. Those who followed the orthodox religion saw in his works a supernatural power. The blind got back their eyesight, the paralytics regained their natural movement, and the incurables regained perfect health. I told them that this was due to the power of the Father who was in heaven. If they offered their worship only to him, the day would definitely come when he would appear and manifest in front of them, and earth would become like heaven.

Vibhīṣaṇa continued, "The priests of the orthodox religion treated me brutally. They wanted to destroy me. When I came to know that, I hid myself amongst my disciples in a hilly forest. There, one of my disciples, under their influence, betrayed me. They came with Roman soldiers to my hiding place, arrested me and put me in jail. I was brought in front of a biased court, the judge was unfair and the judgement was unwarranted. To satisfy their spiteful hearts, and their brutal anger, they wished to kill me through crucifixion. They took me to an open place, where I found myself surrounded by a large crowd. Those who supported the orthodox religion, showed great hatred and wished to hurt me. They spat on my face, threw stones at me and wounded me in the head and body. They dragged me bleeding, with torn clothes and dust sprinkled on me to the open fields where I was then crucified. I saw from above that the people rushed towards me after the crucifixion. I thought that the heart of the people would change and they would give up brutality through my sacrifice. The influence of Kali and his devilish activities would subside and the iron rule would cease through the worship of innumerable people."

Vibhīṣaṇa waited a few years to see the effects of their sincere worship. But he was fully disheartened to find that the people had not understood the idea behind his gospel.

The only result was that they had formed a new religion to oppose the old one. To villify the Old Testament, they had written a New Testament and it was going from strength to strength. The effect of both the religions was the same. Only the activities seemed different. He was dumbfounded to see the effect of his teachings and for that reason he returned to discuss the failure of his teachings under the rule of Kali.

Vibhīṣaṇa remembered the time when he had implored his elder brother, Rāvaṇa, to return King Rāmacandra's queen to him, and not to wage war but to conclude peace; otherwise the whole family would be destroyed. Rāvaṇa had been very angry to hear this advice and had kicked his brother on the chest. Vibhīṣaṇa fell down on the ground. He got up, again warned Rāvaṇa and left him, to join forces with the Divine.

Similarly in this life, he could have saved himself from the crucifixion. Once more, Vibhīṣaṇa warned the people that they should look towards heaven. He added that God knew how to protect his child and that they were calling God's anger on themselves. On hearing it, the people became very angry; they spat on his face, tore his garments and threw stones at him. He surrendered himself to the Divine and left his body for crucifixion.

The Immortals were shocked to see this cruelty and brutality in human beings. They were surprised to see that the rational mind was under Kali's influence and unable to distinguish between good and evil.

After a few moments, Aśvatthāmā spoke, "I had been brutal and cruel in my past life, although I was the son of the wise Drona. I became like a devil under the influence of Kali. In this life, therefore, my mission was to spread the principle of brotherhood. It was decided that I take birth in Mecca. The parents decided for me were Mamud and Medina."

Aśvatthāmā took birth there and was brought up in their culture. He told people that they should have firm faith in the Divine. He said that a believer of Islam would enter into heaven and there would be no rebirth for him. A Moslem would be a purely spiritual figure on the earth. He had to meditate on the sky like eternity representing the universal self and thus be liberated from bondage to the body as well as attachment to life. Love, faith, light and consciousness were the main tenets of his teachings—to love everyone as one's brother, to have faith in one and in the divine existence, and to be conscious and enlightened of the eternity and cosmos. With this idea, his teachings spread and influenced millions of people. But, then he came to know that the son of one of his disciples would be the cause of destroying his teachings. He told that to his disciples and left the earth. From afar, he observed the happenings amongst his disciples.

To prevent such an event, he saw that the particular disciple, had decided never to marry. But then this disciple fell very ill and as a cure, the physician recommended that he have intercourse once with a woman. To ensure that no child was born, this disciple went to an eighty-year old woman. But through bad luck, the old woman conceived and a child was born. This man took great care that his son should be given the best and most proper education. Still, when the child grew up to become a youth, he became as if possessed by devilish forces. He killed many of the devotees. The teachings became distorted under this malefic influence. When Aśvatthāmā saw this he became very upset and returned.

A short period afterwards, Śukadeva arrived there and heard from the others about their experiences. Afterwards, he started to talk. "Listen, O Mahātmās! I will tell you my experiences on the earth. I went to the Malabar Coast of India, where it had been decided that I take my birth. I was born and brought up in a Brahmin family, who were devotees of Śiva. During my boyhood, I was disinterested in normal activities. I started meditation and undertook austerities, to be liberated from family attachment."

One day, Śukadeva was able to leave his parents and he proceeded to the Nilgiri hills to engage himself in his penance. There, he was absorbed in transcendental contemplation and entered in a trance. He spent four years there and realised the transcendental Brahman, the eternal existence. After four years, he attained the realisation that attachment to wordly affairs is the cause of all sufferings and unhappiness. It is an illusion that the family, parents, brothers, or sisters belong to one. Even it is false to think that the wife or children belong to one, and that in one's home one would find happiness or rest. The family's love and affection are neither necessary for the individual's growth, nor for his perfection and joy. It is only an attachment. Śukadeva told his disciples to be liberated from attachment and to merge themselves in the consciousness of Brahman and thus achieve their real happiness and ānanda. His mission was to tell humanity to be liberated from attachment and thus uplift themselves from the vital influence of Kali.

He managed to influence a number of people to follow his example. His further advice to the disciples was to detach themselves from worldly affairs and to merge themselves in the transcendent Brahman through constant meditation by uplifting the mind from the sex centre and by conquering all vital demands and desires. He wandered throughout India to approach people and to teach them the principles of "Sannyāsa" or renunciation. He managed to attract many married men to follow this way of life, particularly those who were completely confused regarding the nature of reality. However, he was very surprised to see amongst his disciples a growing hatred of the Vedic principles and particularly the existence of many Gods. He was disheartened to see the negative effect that the teaching of one Brahman, having transcendental consciousness, had on humanity. He was concerned that through this mistake, his disciples had turned against the Vedas. He proceeded then towards the foothills of the Himalayas and established some temples to the Vedic Godheads there. He left his body amongst the disciples and came here.

Śukadeva then became silent. All immortals started thinking what further steps could be taken at that time. Then

Hanumān proposed that they all proceed to the earth to look at the state of mankind and see how the spiritual ideas and ideals, they had propagated in different parts of the world, were faring. They wanted to see the conditions prevalent at that time. Śukadeva considered it a very good idea and said that afterwards they could decide which further steps could be taken to help mankind.

Dhruva had reservations about the effect of their teachings, as Kali was always present to distort and destroy them. Then Vibhīṣaṇa said, "Let us go and see once more if anything could be done. We must all remember that this is the period of Kali, a time when the Gods are resting, and they are inactive. Just remember, O Mahātmās, we all heard this message from the all vigilant, ever conscient Supreme Creator. His voice came to us—O Immortals of all ages, Kali will influence the creation, and a consciousness like the dark night will spread over the earth. This is the time when you, on the basis of your spiritual achievements, will have to provide some necessary help to mankind."

Aśvatthāmā replied, "We do not know what more can be done at this time. Now, the spiritual night is widespread and the Gods are resting. Instead of the Gods, the legions of Kali are influencing the vital plane of the human being. Our influence on humanity can only be through some outward activities or through some spiritual creeds and lectures. If Gods are not active, then mankind is either engaged in seeking outside enjoyment, or their consciousness is inert and dormant in spiritual matters. If this is the condition of mankind, then it will be difficult to make them understand spiritual values. They will be suffering through their vital demands as Kali will be all powerful." Vibhīṣaṇa replied, "This is true, O Aśvatthāmā, but we should still remember the message of the Brahman."

The Immortals then started their descent from the high peaks of the Himalayas. They went towards the South and then towards Vardhamān. There they wished to see the present shape of the teachings of Mahāvīra. They saw that the devotees of Mahāvīra were worshipping their Lord under the name of Jin. The worshippers of Jin called themselves Jain and they were spreading the creed of Jainism. They were surprised to see that at one place there was a quarrel between two groups of Jains. The contentious point was who were the real followers of Mahāvīra. The Śvetāmbaras were the Jains who wore white garments and Digambaras those who wore none. Both wanted to prove that they were the real followers, whereas both were far from the teachings of Mahāvīra. The Śvetāmbaras said, "O Digambaras, you have no culture. You remain in the forests like animals. If Mahāvira comes back, he will never accept you." The Digambaras replied, "You are all low creatures full of passion, O Śvetāmbaras. You have no idea about the creed of Jin. You have no compassion for small creatures. You have no affection for Japa of the divine name as given by him." The dissensions went on increasing on all these points and turned acrimonious between these groups.

The Immortals were very disappointed in hearing these dissensions. At other places, they found that although the devotees were chanting the name of the Divine, they were thinking only how to earn more money, how to exploit others, embezzle their property, and betray others. They were used to debauchery. On one side, they erected temples for the Godheads, built palatial houses for the guests and gave food to the poor people and the saints. On the other, they cheated other human beings in their trade, mixed poisonous substitutes in food that were injurious for human life, to earn more money. When Hanumān—Mahāvīra saw this, he became very angry and he wanted to punish them. He said, "O Mahātmās, I am very angry with these people. I want to destroy them. They have completely distorted my words."

Then King Dhruva said, "Be quiet, O Hanumān, Son of the Wind God, here we have come only as observers, as strangers, to study the present condition and to find solutions for the difficulties of mankind. We can do nothing with this religion." Hanumān became peaceful on hearing this and they proceeded to Kapilvastu and other places where they observed from afar those who were worshipping the Buddha. The followers said that their leader had been the son of a King; he had a beautiful wife and child. At the end of his life he achieved nirvāṇa. The devotees accepted the external life of Buddha as a model. Their idea of a holy life was to enjoy themselves fully with several women, having many children. They wished to attain nirvāṇa only at the end of their lives. Dhruva was very ashamed to see the degenerated condition of his followers.

Then they entered into a forest. There, they saw some people living here and there in groups. Some were alone. All of them were trying to achieve nirvāṇa. The Immortals appeared before these people like travellers. They asked them details about their life, what they were doing in the forest, why were they either living alone or in groups. These people replied that they were worshippers of Buddha and they were called Buddhist monks. They said that they were not leading a normal life; they were trying to attain nirvāṇa like their Guru. Dhruva told them that was very good. He asked them that if they were striving to gain nirvāṇa then why were they in a crowd and why were their families accompanying them. They answered that they had to take care of their families, as they could not stay anywhere else. Their families were of great help in their attaining nirvāṇa, and they were not a hindrance. Dhruva then reminded them that Siddhārtha had left his wife and child to take nirvāṇa. The Immortals then left and the devotees were left with astonishment. They went on wondering amongst themselves, who the travellers were, who had visited them.

The Immortals then proceeded on to Israel, then to Jerusalem, Bethlehem, and other places of concern to Jesus. They saw a number of people worshipping the cross to remember Christ, the cross where he had sacrificed his life. Then, they observed that the disciples of Christ, the Christians, had become more powerful than the Jews, the followers of Judaism. The Christians hated the Jews and looked down upon them. The Christians worshipped the cross, telling the world that Christ had sacrificed himself for redeeming the people of the earth. To avenge the crucifixion, the Christians took up the sword, and they shed much blood in his name.

When Vibhīṣaṇa observed this, he said with sorrow and deep pain, "O Mahātmās! Look at my followers; they are under the complete influence of Kali. Where are my principles—sympathy for people, brotherhood, call for divine grace, love and tolerance for all? Come with me." He took them to Golgotha, where he had been crucified. He told them that after Pilate's decision, his whole company had gathered around him, stripped him and then dressed him in a red cloak. Afterwards, they crowned Jesus with a crown of thorns and gave him a rod to hold in his right hand. Later, they mockingly bowed down before him and hailed him as the King of the Jews. At that time, they spat on him and taking the rod away from him, they hit him repeatedly on the head. Subsequently, they stripped him of the scarlet cloak, asked him to wear his own torn garments and led him away to be crucified. At the very end, Christ told his disciples, "Behold, I will be with you always till the end of the days, until the world comes to an end. Show your greatness through your modesty. If your enemy slaps you on one cheek, offer him the other. Conquer an enemy by being a good friend to him."

They saw that the Christians were always moving with an open sword. Vibhīṣaṇa mourned that his disciples had become more violent than the Jews, the followers of the Old Testament. When the Immortals were departing from that area, they saw in one place that the Christians were quarrelling amongst themselves. One group demanded that the cross should not have the figure of Christ, because it caused pain to the worshippers; while the others insisted that the cross should have the figure of the crucified Christ, as Jesus Christ possessed a body and the cross with the crucified figure reminded them of Christ's tolerance. Vibhīṣaṇa was very disturbed to see this clash amongst his believers. The controversy between his disciples was not only a small-localised quarrel. These conflicting ideas were spread as the one and only Truth from one part of the world to another, not only with words but also with the power of wealth, as well as arms and ammunitions.

After seeing this, the Immortals proceeded to Mecca and travelled through Persia and the Arab region. There, they were aghast to see that through the diktat of King Ejid, Islam had developed into a strange brotherhood, the brotherhood existing only for offering united prayers to the Allah—Allah allam Illately illala Allah. Those who repeated or shouted these prayers were Moslems; the others were non-Moslems or Kafirs. These should be either punished for not being Moslems or they should be ignored. The believers of Islam brought out the Koran Sharif as the gospel of Mohammed, the Prophet of Islam and they declared that a true Moslem would not be reborn. He would enter heaven at the end of this mortal life, and the non-believers would be banished to hell. With these words, they decided to spread Islam throughout mankind to transform the earth. They also adopted it as a State policy. They advanced from town to town with the slogan "Allah, O Akbar," and conquered new places with their arms and ammunitions. Seeing all these events, Aśvatthāmā exclaimed, "Look at my bad luck. My fate was always like that. I want to do good but the effect of my actions is always the opposite."

Then the Immortals proceeded to the Malabar Coast, to Vindhyācala, Banaras and other places to see the status of the principles of Śukadeva. They saw a number of people wearing saffron garments, living in forests under the trees, or inside the mountain caves, eating fruits, and cooked things begged from various houses, together with milk and water. Reading Pāñcadaśī and reciting Mohamudgara, they realised that family feeling and love and affection is Māyā (attachment). The relations between the individual and his parents, wife and children, and related responsibilities are an illusion. Śukadeva's advice to his followers was to forsake all relationships and renounce the world, to be free of all bondages, and to lead a liberated life. In this way, the followers of Śaṅkara preferred remaining under the open sky. Subsequently in one place, they saw that there was a quarrel between the Sannyāsins. Those, who wore saffron clothes and were begging from house to house, were inferior to those who were wearing just a lion cloth and living on fruits, water and food that they had begged. Śukadeva saw this development and was very disturbed. He said that, "I am the Śaṅkarācārya, the Guru of the Sannyāsins, and my teachings are all going to be deformed. I am so unfortunate."

Subsequently, the Immortals made their way back to the high peaks of Himalayas. At that time, Śaṅkarācārya saw two groups of Sannyāsins quarrelling and fighting with sticks on how to divide their begged food. Silently, in a sombre mood, they returned to the top of the Himalayas.

THE SPIRITUAL CATACLYSM

The Immortals remained silent for a long time and then Śukadeva said, "O Mahātmās! All of you saw with your own eyes the results of our activities. However, I still feel that we should protect those who are devotees of the Divine and those who ask for help. I knew the limits of my help when my father told me to go and protect the son of Parikṣit with my spiritual guidance. I could not help much as I knew that under Kali there would be no spirituality. Again, I asked him what would be the condition of mankind at that time. My father, Ṛṣi Vyāsa, replied that there would be a universal cataclysm. Spiritual consciousness would suffer heavily through the expansion of the vital plane, caused by the influence of Kali. With his hostile legions, he would enslave humanity and the earth and keep them captive. Through his influence, the world would be divided into many units. This would lead to the formation of many groups, parties and states, all following conflicting ideas, ideals and idealism. Kali's royal powers would spread over the earth through death, fear, famine, diseases and dissensions. Diversity will be the central theme in the Iron Age with quarrels exerting an immeasurable influence. Kali will also be furthering diseases. Through diseases, all creations on the earth will come under the control of death. The memory of immortality will be wiped off from the face of this creation. Now, we can understand, that whatever we did to help mankind resulted in the formation of different religions in various parts of the earth. These religions then fragmented further into groups. With these different creeds, theories and activities, people became victims of quarrels and disputes. Kali brought death to the world and banished the thoughts of immortality. With the influence of diversity and quarrels, humanity has become fully detached from spiritual consciousness and thus one can see the approaching spiritual cataclysm. The flood of the vital ocean has overpowered and covered the West and South of the earth, now the eddies of this ocean are approaching India."

Several decades passed and the Immortals were continuously observing the earth. They saw the Greek soldiers marching towards India. At that moment Śukadeva said, "Behold the effects of the vital attack. Mahāpadma and his sons etc. are merged in the flood. It seems as if they were all immersed in the vital ocean, fully occupied in vital enjoyment. Then they saw that Alexander the Great had reached the borders of India. The people of India had lost their bravery and their spiritual power. They had forgotton how to stop the advance of the Greek soldiers at the border of the river Śatadru. The sons of Mahāpadma remembered only the ancient idea of self-sacrifice for their country, without any spiritual power to support it. They sacrificed their life one by one in the battlefield. At last Purabanda arrested that advance, and then there was an armistice. The condition of the armistice was that he must not cross the Śatadru River.

But Candragupta, who was a commander in the Indian army, went secretly to the Grecian fort to learn their way of fighting. He was discovered and arrested in the fort and sent back to Purabanda. As Candragupta had violated the rules of the armistice, he was insulted and punished with dismissal from Purabanda's army. But in revenge, Candragupta killed Purabanda through Caṇakya's guidance. He became the

Emperor of India. Candragupta married a Greek lady and established friendship between East and West. With this friendship, he controlled the western flow from entering into India.

Then King Dhruva started, "See O Śukadeva! King after King, now Aśoka, the grandson of Candragupta, has come to understand that the waves of the western vital ocean would surely enter into India. He has made continuous efforts to build a further barrier against the West. He expanded his influence into the East and spread the Buddhist religion, to oppose the western flood. Thus he strengthened the eastern block called the Asian block as a counter to the West."

Aśvatthāmā added, "Several years passed under the protection of the Asian block, but through the pressure of the vital ocean coming from the West, there was an unprotected gap in the northern mountains. Jayacandra helped the vital forces to enter into India. Then the helpless Prithvīcandra was smashed and his kingdom swept away. Subsequently, Muhammad Ghori invaded India under the name of the religion established by me—Islam. These were followed by waves after waves of Moslem invaders. The ancient base of spirituality, the culture of the Ṛṣis, the Sanātana Dharma, the glory of the Aryans was betrayed by Jayacandra and was swept away by the Moslem invasion. The waves then started coming in to India faster and faster. After the Ghori dynasty came the Tughlaks, the Lodhies, the Mughals etc. and they spread all over India."

Then Mahāvīra started to speak, "Now we can see that India has been overwhelmed fully by the power of the Moslems. The invaders are imposing Islam on the Aryans of India through the force of their military might. The Aryans with their ancient Sanātana Dharma are shrinking under the onslaught of the vital ocean. Most of them are becoming submerged under the flood waves from the vital ocean. Some are taking shelter here and there to save themselves. The question now is, how do we save those who are still open to spirituality, from this all-destructive flood, particularly those who still have faith in Gods and the Vedas."

Then, Vibhīṣaṇa replied, "I remember an immortal Puruṣa who is remaining high above on the peak of the Himalayas. He is the only one who can do something for humanity at this stage."

Śukadeva was very curious and asked, "O Mahātmā! Who is that immortal?" Vibhīṣaṇa replied, "He is Prahlāda, son of the Demon Hiraṇyakaśipu. This Demon was an enemy of Lord Viṣṇu and had an intense desire to fight and kill him. In stark contrast, Prahlāda, his own son worshipped Lord Viṣṇu and was a very keen devotee. Then, a fight started between the father and the son. Hiraṇyakaśipu failed to kill his own son, even after numerous attempts. When he asked Prahlāda who his saviour was, he answered always that his saviour was Lord Viṣṇu. He claimed that with His protection, he had conquered death. Hiraṇyakaśipu asked him where his Lord Viṣṇu was. On Prahlāda's saying that He was everywhere, Hiraṇyakaśipu asked whether He was in the pillar. On receiving the answer, perhaps, he hit the pillar with his heavy club to crush Lord Viṣṇu. Then, Lord Viṣṇu appeared from the pillar, having the body of a man and the head of a lion, the figure of the Narasiṁha. Lord Viṣṇu thundered, caught Hiraṇyakaśipu, opened up his abdomen with his sharp nails, and thus killed him. All the Gods and Ṛṣis were trembling and Prahlāda sang odes to the Lord. By his prayer, Lord Visṇu quietened down and his violent mood disappeared. He became very soft and graceful with a divine smile. He placed Prahlāda on his father's throne and blessed him with the boon that he remain ever joyful, happy, and then disappeared. He is that immortal, who alone conquered the Demon Hiraṇyakaśipu. Through his devotion, Lord Viṣṇu appeared to save his devotee. His power of tapasyā is established on the constant japa of the name of Hari. Let us all go and find him."

All the immortals started to climb the highest peak of the Himalayas. With effort they reached the top, the ever-sunlit summit where the shadow of the earth never comes. No darkness was there and the light was everpresent. The Immortals were overjoyed to see the beautiful sight and the pleasant atmosphere, on the ever-glittering enlightened peak. They were advancing happily on the sunlit path when they heard a beautiful song. As that song charmed them, they followed the direction of the sound. After a while they saw the great Ṛṣi Kāṇveya Nārada, singing the song of Hari. Nārada had always been completely against Kali. He was absorbed in his tune, and with closed eyes was playing a lute and singing the song:

Hare Rāma Haré Rāma, Rāma Rāma Hare Hare
Hare Kṛṣṇa, Hare Kṛṣṇa, Kṛṣṇa Kṛṣṇa Hare Hare.

The meaning is: O Hari! Thou art Rāma, O Hari!
Thou art Rāma
O Rāma O Rāma! Thou art Hari,
Thou art Hari.
O Hari! Thou art Kṛṣṇa, O Hari!
Thou art Kṛṣṇa
O Kṛṣṇa! O Kṛṣṇa!
Thou art Hari, Thou art Hari.

They all became absorbed in this song. After some time, Nārada opened his eyes and saw the Immortals before him. He told them that he was also searching for a great soul to help mankind in the great anguish they were suffering under the iron rule of Kali. Out of great curiosity they asked Nārada himself, "Tell us, O great Ṛṣi, why are you so concerned about humanity when you are all liberated?" Narada replied to them, "Kali is my brother's son. He is anti-divine. I want to punish and destroy him but he has become very powerful through his worship of Rudra Mahākāla. He has obtained a boon from Rudra that for some time he has complete power over the creation. Now that time has come. The whole creation is under his devilish rule. I want to save those devotees who are still depending on the Divine. I approached the supreme creator, Brahmā and begged Him that He changes this creation where Kali took birth and grew up with an anti-divine attitude. I wished that Brahma would remove him and create a new Age Leader in his place. On hearing my appeal, Brahmā smiled and told me—Be quiet, O Nārada ! My creation cannot be changed. I can however do something helpful for you that could be against Kali. I replied to Brahmā that I, myself, did not need anything. But looking at the condition of the earth, where the divine devotees were suffering immensely under the iron rule of Kali, I would need his divine intervention for them. Then, Brahmā replied—O Nārada teach humanity that they should repeat the name of Hari who conquers the devilish power and add his human birth twice with it. That will be the mantra for the devotees to escape from the iron rule of Kali."

Ṛṣi Nārada again asked the Supreme Brahmā, "Why is the name of Hari by itself not enough? Why should the other two names of Hari from his mortal birth be added to it." Brahmā answered, "Chanting the name of Hari by itself is also enough. However, in Kali Yuga, there will be a number of personalities or avatars. Their devotees will try to prove that they are also incarnations of Hari. You should add the two names, Rāma and Kṛṣṇa, in such a way so that no other name can be added." On hearing this advice from Brahmā, Nārada composed this song and sang it in front of Brahmā, who was pleased. He said that this would be enough to save the divine devotees at the time of Kali and asked Nārada to spread it on the earth through a proper channel. Nārada then put the śloka in a proper tune. That was the song that the Immortals had heard. Now Nārada wanted a proper channel through which this mantra could be spread throughout the world. The Immortals said that they must find Prahlāda who was the right person to do this task.

They advanced further in the mountains and after a little while they heard "Harernāmaïvakevalam". Nārada was overjoyed and exclaimed that they had found Prahlāda. Then they saw him seated on a golden stool with closed eyes always chanting "Harernāmaivakevalam". They also joined him in his chanting. On hearing the name of Hari from others,

Prahlāda opened his eyes and saw them. Joyously he exclaimed, "O Mahātmās! You are all chanting the name of Hari. This has given me so much joy that I cannot express it in words. I am completely thrilled and am feeling the vibrations go through my entire body. I bow down to you all. Please tell me what I can do for you and how I can serve you. When anyone repeats or meditates on the name of Hari, Hari himself remains there. As you are chanting the name of Hari, you all appear like Hari to me. I am the servant of Hari." Nārada replied, "We are all servants of Hari, O Prahlāda! Observe the earth, where the devotees are suffering under the terrible rule of Kali. We want you to descend on the earth and give them the protection of Hari's name." Prahlāda agreed to do so and accepted this order as coming directly from Hari. He asked others about the directions where he should go. In response, Nārada decided that all should go down together to find the place and determine what needs to be done.

When they came down from the highest peaks of the Himalayas and approached the earth, they saw the activities of Kali in the period of the Moghuls. Sanātana Dharma was known then as the Hindu Dharma. The others were proud to call themselves Moslems. They were eager to convert Hindus into Moslems, and they used their power, and military might to this end. They did not even stop there. They also told those who were converted to Islam to hate and revile the ancient religion. Through these efforts, a strange kind of Moslem was created. They were Hindu by blood but had Islam as their creed. They were not real Moslems like the Mughals and the others. For example, if people had grudges against some Brahmins who had misbehaved against the ordinary Hindus, then those aggrieved people were converted into Islam and incited to take revenge against the Brahmins. Those who were honourable, very strict and wished to remain in their ancient religion, had to bear the brunt of the hatred of Islam. The Moslems tortured these devotees, through looting and burning of their houses, through kidnapping their women, through heavy taxes and through unfavourable conditions for them in trade.

Sage Nārada told Prahlāda, "Look, O Prahlāda! See the condition of the ancient culture and that of the devotees. They are suffering intensely. Go and save them now."

Dhruva added, "Listen, O Prahlāda! Kali has dispersed and distorted our efforts. There is no way that we can control this damage and protect our message."

Vibhīṣaṇa added, "Inspite of all my tolerance, the results of my activities are far removed from my teachings. There is no way to guard them."

Aśvatthāmā said, "All my faith, and my efforts to help have been converted into a rampant egoism, which is harming the divine devotees. O Prahlāda, all this evil has descended on the pure devotees like a flood and they are helpless in the vital world. Give them the name of Hari, which will prove for them like a raft to float on the flood of blind egotism. This only will save them."

Mahāvīra added, "O Mahātmā! Go and give them the name of Hari with the power of your Japa by which they can escape the flood of vital desires without sinking in them."

Śukadeva said, "This protection should remain until the time that Gods and Ṛṣis wake up again for their new activities. Until then, mankind should use this mantra, to save themselves in this hostile world. Look at Bengal in front of you. I heard from my father, Maharṣi Vyāsa, that this is the place where the dawn of Truth will take place. O Prahlāda, you can take your birth there."

Nārada supported the statement of Śukadeva and said, "This ancient history will always be repeated. Bengal is the place from where Truth manifested and the divinisation of the Earth will also commence from there. This is the eternal Truth that will continue to repeat always. Here at Navadvīpa, see the families of devotees. Amongst them, there is Śacī, a lady of pious heart. You can take birth there and commence your work. I myself will appear in front of you when you are a child. I will then give you the mantra as decided by Hari, and the exact words uttered by Him." Prahlāda then entered into Śacī to take birth there. The other Immortals returned to the Himalaya.

THE FUTURE VISION

A few centuries passed. Again the Immortals approached the earth with Ṛṣi Nārada to see the condition of mankind and the divine devotees. They also wanted to see what more could be done to help the suffering humanity. Discussing this, they reached the earth. Prahlāda started to tell them, "O Messengers of Hari! As decided upon, I took a human birth for spreading the divine message at this place. My name was Caitanya. After my birth, I spent a few years with my parents. During my early educative years, I was searching within myself, trying to find out why I had taken birth on this earth. For a few years, this question occupied me. With these continuous thoughts buzzing around me, one day, when I had gone into deep meditation, I saw Narada in front of me. He reminded me of my mission on this earth, namely to spread the name of Hari to assist the divine devotees and to provide support to them. After having regained the knowledge of my mission through my vision, I tried to find out how best I could perform my mission. On seeing that I was indifferent to family affairs, my parents became very worried. They started fearing that they might lose me to an ascetic life. In order to prevent my becoming a sadhu, they decided that I should get married soon. So they arranged that I be married to a beautiful girl called Viṣṇupriyā. I was married quickly. But the beauty of the girl could not charm and hold me. Instead, it pushed me further towards ascetism. I felt keenly the suffering of the people in the evil time of Kali. Everyone was caught in family life, waylaid by the charm of worldly affections. Then, all the souls were caught in the twirling of the Time Wheel. I felt it necessary to spread Hari's message by which they could escape suffering in this Age. Some other devotees joined me and we started reciting the name of Hari as composed by the Sage Nārada."

Hare Rāma Hare Rāma, Rāma Rāma Hare Hare
Hare Kṛṣṇa, Hare Kṛṣṇa, Kṛṣṇa Kṛṣṇa Hare Hare.

Prahlāda continued, "We went around with Mṛdaṅgas and cymbals among the neighbours. In the course of reciting Hari's name, it was amazing and gratifying to see more and more people joining our group. The crowd was increasing day by day. In this way, I was encouraged to move from village to village. I could see that a continuously increasing number of people were influenced. It happened that not only the illiterate and common people of the villages were joining us, but also the literate and educated group of people came under its spell. Of course, there were many oppositions and difficulties to be conquered day after day. Then I started moving throughout India, reciting the name of Hari in many places, one among them being Mathurā. In the place where Kṛṣṇa spent his early life, the famous Vṛndāvana, we started the worship of Kṛṣṇa; then I went to Puri to see the temple of Jagannātha. Then my work was done; and I dissolved myself in the Bay of Bengal. After the physical plane, I came to the ethereal plane and remained there for some time to see the effects of my work on the earth."

"I observed from there that my devotees were slowly becoming influenced by Kali. The result being that after a few years they started to quarrel and fight amongst themselves. The conflict was among the various groups in deciding who was purer and more authentic to practise and follow the path of Sri Caitanya. This was based on some external events of my life and my daily activities. I did only what was necessary at that time, but the followers took that as a rule of conduct for themselves. They considered these activities as the basis of their religion. They called themselves Vaiṣṇavas (followers of Viṣṇu). They were not willing to tolerate Śāktas (worshippers of Śakti, Durgā, Mahākalī etc.) and Śaivas (followers of Śiva). They have separated themselves from the others through food, clothes, etc., even in the flowers that they use for worship so that they can keep their separate identity. Like the others in the established religions, my followers also started quarrelling amongst each other through the effect of Kali. The Vaiṣṇavas were fighting within themselves as each group wished to be different from the other, having different codes of conduct and various other external and irrelevant rules. Each group was developing in a different way. They had a different name 'sampradāya' covering each of the various groups. I was very sorry to see that they were fighting amongst each other, instead of understanding my idea, which was to unite the whole world, so that it is one. They were fragmenting into an increasing number of smaller groups that would in the end destroy themselves. This is the real power of Kali, division and sub-division until total destruction follows. In this way, this negative force divided the devotees into smaller and still-smaller units so that they became isolated. At the very end, death would control them, which created a deep fear."

"The question now before us is how to control this ominous power of Kali, how to root out and remove the idea of division and sub-division from the human consciousness, which has entered there together with other inimical ideas. The only problem that exists before us is to tell mankind that the Truth about the Divine is the same for all. All religions have the same goal. The Godheads are the same and not different or inimical to each other. There is no separate goal for different groups, no separate Godhead or different heaven or hell for the departed souls. It is the same. All souls go to the same place and it is a false supposition that people belonging to different religions go to different places, which are either higher or lower".

Two drops of tears fell from Prahlāda's eyes. Nārada said, "O Prahlāda! This vicious period will come to an end with the rise of western culture. Look at the West. They are throwing off their old worn out garments of poverty. They are now dressed in a new costume, that of riches. They are becoming more powerful on the basis of material development, by neglecting the spiritual Truth. In this culture, only what the eyes see is the Truth, what remains unseen is Falsehood. They are trying to find out things or commodities, which will make life more comfortable. In this culture, seekers are busy studying the nature, and trying to determine to what use the elements of nature could be put. These elements are the earth, fire, water, air and ether. This material culture is coming to conquer the world on the basis of blind egoism. They, the British, the French, the Portuguese, and the Dutch etc., are coming one by one and are entering into different parts of India as traders. See, they are slowly conquering the Moghul Kingdom of India."

"Now comes the complete spiritual cataclysm of the ancient culture of the Ṛṣis, which was based on Divine Truth. The eternal Truth of the Vedas, the activities of the Gods in human beings, the culture of sacrificing to the Divine, the one united peaceful consciousness of the earth, all are being swamped by the flood of blind egoism and coming under the pressure of material Truth. In this approaching, overwhelming cataclysm by the onslaught of western culture, the divine devotees will be in a very weakened condition. The mantra on the name of Hari that you provided to them would be very difficult. This can collapse at any time. O Prahlāda! Let us go and find the Ṛṣis. Particularly, those who are already awake even though the dark Night of Kali is still not over. We can discover more of the ultimate Truth through these enlightened beings. The Supreme Truth will herald the divine dawn, conquer the dark forces of the Night and through its own power will dry up the flood of egoism and vital desires. From this cataclysm, the creation will rise up again and Kali, the Lord of the Iron Age, will surely be vanquished as I have heard from the mouth of the Brahmā."

The Immortals, realising that they had no other solution to help mankind, followed Nārada to the plane of the Ṛṣis. They were advancing further and further on the northern side of the Himalayas. Then they arrived at a place, which felt severely cold, although it was not covered by snow. All were shivering except Nārada. The Immortals asked the Sage,

"O Great Seer! Tell us please where we are ? We are feeling so cold and are shivering although we do not see the way covered by ice." The Sage replied, "This is the interior path of the Himalayas. Although there is no covering of snow, there is a deep compact silence. Through this silence, you all have started to shiver, which cannot be controlled by the external tapasyā. This is how King Yudhiṣṭhira ascended to heaven. On the way, he left his four brothers and wife, one by one, before reaching heaven. Due to this silence, these godly beings could not reach heaven. They also started to uncontrollably shiver. They could not walk further and fell down on the way. Now that you have started to shiver, you will not be able to proceed further. I will give you some secret knowledge through a mantra. With the power of that mantra, you can advance further."

The mantra according to Nārada was as follows: "I am the immortal soul. I have neither birth nor death, neither hunger nor thirst, nor health nor sickness. I do not feel cold or heat. I shall never be burnt by fire, dried up by the wind or decomposed by the water. No weapon can cut me. I am above all. I have no sin or virtue. I am the soul invincible. Nature cannot touch me with her attracting power. I am the soul immortal."

The Immortals repeated this mantra together with the Sage Nārada and regained the stability of their body. Without shivering, they advanced further on their journey. During their journey, they observed on both sides, many beautiful and attractive scenes from which they collected their strength. At last, they reached the bank of a very wide river. Nārada told them, "Look, O Immortals! Behold, here is the place where King Yudhiṣṭhira entered heaven, seated on the Divine Chariot of Dharmarāja. Now, look at your right. Under that tree is my chariot. Let us cross this river seated on my chariot." The Immortals then asked Nārada, "Do tell us, O Ṛṣis, how Yudhiṣṭhira managed to reach so far when his brothers and his wife fell down unconscious on the way. They were dragged in an unconscious state to heaven. How was it possible that he alone reached there in a conscious state?" Nārada replied, "Remember, O Mahātmās! When Yudhiṣṭhira was advancing towards heaven, he did not look behind him. At that time, a dog followed him all the way, protecting him from behind. On reaching the bank of the river only, he saw the dog, which was Dharmarāja in disguise. The knowledge and power that I gave to you all, he had developed due to his activities on the earth."

Then they all mounted the chariot of Nārada, crossed the river and reached a farther bank in front of the wide gate to heaven. They saw the gate of a beautiful city. Then Nārada started to speak, "Behold in front of us, we can see a big, glittering, beautiful city ornamented with jewels. This is the city of Kubera. On the left side is Gandharvaloka, the land of the Divine Musicians and Dancers and on the right is Yamaloka. From here you can see the sign and symbol of a pigeon, that is the palace of Dharma. The one with the symbol of the svastika, is the palace of the Viśvāvasu, who is the king of the Gandharvas. See all of them are in deep sleep. No one is awake so far."

Between the city of Kubera and Dharma, there is a straight road leading to the Tapovana, the land of the Ṛṣis. This land is divine and absolutely pure. "See, now, we have arrived at that place. Look at the beautiful forest of heaven; look at the fruits and flowers, which are not available on earth. These divine plants are quite different from those existing on the earth. Plants, trees, creepers, and leaves through their automatic growth and their position of standing and living with each other form the houses, boundaries and gates etc. They are all highly conscious, not inconscient like the earthly variety. They can understand the will of the Ṛṣis, as they know them very well. They talk with Ṛṣis as if they were devotees. They supply necessary fruits and cool breezes, which fan the Ṛṣis. They grow lovely in health through the smoke of the sacrificial flame of the Ṛṣis."

Then Nārada, together with the Immortals, entered and saw that all the Ṛṣis with their families were dwelling in different places. Some of them were alone. Some had separated themselves from their families. With some, the families were at one place and they at others. But all of them were seated in a comfortable position, with closed eyes and without any movement. The Immortals found it difficult to decide whether they were asleep or in a trance. But then Nārada explained that the Ṛṣis were resting, not sleeping. They were in a trance for rest and highly conscious, totally identified with the Brahman, and immersed in constant joy. But they were not aware of nor recognised the presence of the Immortals at the moment. Nārada told them that they would have to wait there until the Ṛṣis made a pause in their rest. They moved around near the gate. At one place they met the great poet Vyāsa. He asked them, "O Immortals, why have you come here? It is too early!" On hearing these words, the Immortals explained to Vyāsa the condition prevalent on the earth. Nārada, then explained the sufferings of the people of the earth, which was the reason that he had brought the Immortals there. They all appealed to Vyāsa to bring the sufferings of the earth to an end, as he had brought succour in previous times of distress. The Immortals said that if all the Ṛṣis were in the heaven, then there was no one to provide succour on the earth. They added that they had done all that they could. But their assistance resulted in the formation of many religions, which helped only in increasing the sufferings of the people during this Age.

After hearing this, Ṛṣi Vyāsa replied, "O great devotee of Viṣṇu! Accept my salutations. My contribution is not more valuable than the work of the Immortals on the earth, who have formed religions as a short-term help to the mankind. My work was also a temporary help to mankind. This has not arrested the advancement of Kali. Let us go to see Vālmīki, who remains near the other gate." While they were advancing, he continued, "A new dawn shall break upon the earth. Satyadeva, the Lord of Truth will influence the earth and disperse the darkness and sufferings of Kali by his own light. I do not, however, know when He will manifest."

At that moment, they arrived in front of Vālmīki. They saw him moving. Vālmīki asked the Immortals the reason of their presence. They described to him also the condition of the earth and humanity under the iron rule of Kali and asked for ways in which one could bring an end to the sufferings of mankind. The son of Ṛṣi Cyavana replied, "O Immortals! O Great Seers Nārada and Vyāsa! Of course, I have done a tremendous tapasyā for the descent of the Supreme. Lord Viṣṇu manifested then to triumph over the victorious Demons. In course of time, he conquered and established a divine kingdom upon the earth. Still, that was for a certain period. After that, Kali advanced again. To try the same method again would be of no use. My work had the same purpose, i.e., to help mankind in times of dire need. O Immortals! You established certain religions for mankind. O Vyāsa! You did a tapasyā for the Descent of the Supreme at a certain time. I also made a similar effort. Now nothing can be done. Let us go to see the Poet Bhārgava". While they proceeded in that direction, Vālmīki added, "I heard from my uncle, the Poet Bhārgava, that the period of Kali will be ended by the power of the Deva. When He will manifest is not known, nor where He is."

Then, they arrived in front of the Poet Bhārgava, who was at the other gate. He asked them, "Why are you all coming to me, O Immortals! O Nārada, Vyāsa and Vālmīki!" They replied, "We have come to inform you about the present condition of the earth. and the sufferings of the divine devotees during the period of Kali. What we did was effective for a short time. This did not reduce Kali's influence." After hearing the details of Kali's activities, Ṛṣi Bhārgava's face was very serious and he started to roar in his thunderous voice, "I remember Kali, the son of Pragatha, who neglected the Vedas. The Vedas were presented to the earth by me. Three different kinds of works are necessary, introduced in different ages to mankind. They are—the Vedas, Yajña and Dharma. Vedas is the knowledge, the knowledge of the existence of Gods and their activities. I introduced the concept of human work (karma) with knowledge. Kali introduced falsehood in human activities. Through his wrong activities, there came an interruption in the divine activities. For this reason, Satyadeva vanished from the creation. By the introduction of falsehood in the world, distance grew between human deeds and the Vedas, as the divine influence was missing. Insincerity and falsehood gave rise to egoism. This was due to Kali's baleful influence on creation. The Age of Truth finished at that time. Then all the Ṛṣis combinedly established the sacrifice (Yajña). O Caivana, you were the great poet at that time. You called the Supreme down upon the earth. With the power of the Supreme, the influence of Kali was temporarily removed.

Again falsehood, insincerity, egoism, desire and greed started to act combinedly on the earth through the influence of Kali. Sacrifice (yajña) disappeared from the earth. Introduction of jealousy and stupidity brought increasing violence in human affairs. You were the great poet at that period. O Vyāsa! You called down the Supreme upon the earth to establish Dharma—the Rule of Law, but that was again for a short period. Again Kali became all-powerful, the evil powers reigned over the earth. There was no Dharma. Let us all go to see Ṛṣi Mahācamasya, who retains the early memories of Truth. He is always at the other gate."

Then the Ṛṣis went to the fourth gate. They saw Ṛṣi Mahācamasya together with some other wise Ṛṣis having a small conference to unveil Mahas in the creation. There, Ṛṣi Mahācamasya described Mahas, the supramental plane and how it would be identified with Bhūr, Bhuvar and Svar, the other three planes. The Supramental would then guide them according to the tenets of Truth, as in the past.

When Kavi Bhārgava entered with the whole group, Ṛṣi Mahācamasya was glad to see them. He welcomed them with joy and invited the whole group to join the conference. Then Kavi Bhārgava said, "O great Seer, I have come to ask you when the Day of Truth will break upon the creation." He described the dire situation of the earth and asked what could be done to remedy it.

Mahācamasya replied, "O Divine Poet! I am unable to tell you more about the descent of Truth. The power of Time has taken away our previous memories. This secret is only with the Lord of Time "Mahākāla Piṇgala". He is the Divine Observer, Seer of all Seers, Poet of all Poets, Creator of all Creators, God of all Gods. Let us sing an ode to him and pray that He manifests here. He will tell us, when the Kaliyuga ends, the time when the Gods and Ṛṣis will awake and when the Day of Truth will dawn upon the creation."

All the Ṛṣis and Immortals sang an ode to Piṇgala Maheśvara, who appeared there and said, "O Mahācamasya! Kavi, Nārada, Vālmīki, Vyāsa and others. To bring about the end of the Night or the Kali Yuga and the Dawn of Truth, work is necessary. An immortal flame is remaining in the mortal cave. You will have to go there and bring it to this plane. Subsequently, you should gather in the house of Vasiṣṭha. Start a yajña for Satyadeva, the Truth God, in the house of Aṅgirā. Ask King Abhivarta to help in collecting together all the Ṛṣis. Through this Yajña, Gods will wake up, become active and join the Yajña. With the help of Gods, allow Vītihotra to identify with this Yajña. At that moment, Satyadeva (Truth God) will manifest. I shall also manifest there and open the way for the journey of the Gods to the earth, through the epic Devāyaṇa. Through this epic, the earth will become like heaven and the influence of Kali will be removed."

Piṇgala told this to the assembled Ṛṣis and then disappeared. They all recollected what he had told them. Mahācamasya said, "No moment should be wasted now. We should proceed without delay to the place of Vasiṣṭha. Nārada, go to the Creator Kaśyapa and Kavi, go to Ṛṣi Aṅgirā with Cyavana and Vyāsa."

In this way, they separated and went to their ordained places. Ṛṣi Mahācamasya presented himself before Vasiṣṭha and told him what Piṇgala Maheśvara had suggested. Vasiṣṭha arose from his rest with the twelve Vasiṣṭhas, when he came to know that Mahākāla had decided that this was the time to invoke the Truth. He directed Śakti (power) his son, to take Gauribiti with her aspirant flame, Vitihotra, to the house of Aṅgirā, to be identified at the Deva Yajña. Then, Śakti with the help of Mahācamasya took Gauribiti, with her aspirant flame, Vitihotra, from the earth to the Deva Yajña to be united with Satyadeva, the Lord of Truth. A huge ceremony was organized for the purification of the psychic being, where all were invited. Food was distributed to many different beings. The reason for this ceremony was to awaken the Gods and the Ṛṣiś from their rest in order to usher in the Golden Age. Then the Vasiṣṭhas and Ṛṣi Mahācamasya descended with Gauribiti, and the psychic aspiration into the human consciousness, into the human centre and surrounded it with human love. Since the fulfilment of the tapasyā by Gauribiti, the psychic being, the psychic flame is ever awake in the depth of the heart. This is the aspiration for the Truth Consciousness in the earth plane. Thus, the journey towards the Deva Yajña is the ascending movement of the earth consciousness for the Truth.

When the Vasiṣṭhas, Ṛṣi Mahācamasya and other Ṛṣis arrived at the house of Aṅgirās, they saw that all the Gods and Ṛṣis had arrived there before them. The sacrificial flame for the Truth was already burning and they were offering the clarified butter "havya", their pure will into the fire (Agni). Śaucikī, the son of Agni, was the Priest at that ceremony but Satyadeva had not as yet manifested. Abhivarta, the King of the Ṛṣis went to the Supreme Plane to invite the Higher Godheads to this purification ceremony. There he searched plane after plane to find Satyadeva, his missing son. Finally, he found him in the forest of Brahman and brought him back. Then Deva manifested in front of the sacrificial flame where the Gods and Ṛṣis were present. Before the Trinity–Brahmā, Viṣṇu, Maheśvara—he took his seat and Maheśvara started to tell the engrossing account of how he managed to conquer Kali to bring about the Golden Age. He told Satyadeva, the Lord of Truth, the details of the activities of Kali in the past two Ages as well as in the Kali–Yuga. First,

Maheśvara recounted the details about the period of Trita, then, Brahmā about the Ḍvita and Viṣṇu, about the period of Kali upto the full invasion.

After this, Satyadeva was encouraged to take up the work and he arose to conquer Kali. At that moment, the Creator Brahmā directed him to clasp Vītihotra, the psychic aspiration, and to create in Gauribiti, Uṣā, the Divine Dawn for the earth and Pūṣa, an unconquerable fighter for the heaven. Just when Satyadeva clasped Vītihotra, the psychic aspiration, in Gauribiti, the daughter of Śakti; Piṇgala Maheśvara appeared and proposed that during the present dark times on the earth, some illuminated beings should descend on the earth. They should tell humanity, that the Gods are coming to the earth, to bring about a new Golden Age. Mankind should be prepared to receive and to be identified with them. During the Kali influenced Night, people were always suffering with grief, repentance, and remained without hope, love or unity. The cause of their suffering was selfishness, and a quarrelsome attitude without any aim in life. As a result, diseases and death attacked them. To escape the iron hold of Kali, they have to welcome Satyadeva, the Lord of Truth and remain happy with the presence of Gods in the individual. They should have the right knowledge, love and peace and merge in everlasting joy with the Gods. They should aim to manifest divinity in this life and progress to the Life Divine, to become immortal and obtain immunity for themselves. They would then enjoy heavenly delight.

This proposal of Piṇgala was appreciated by all the Creators. They decided to take action amongst themselves. Kaśyapa, the Creator of Gods, took up the work with the other Creators. The seven Ṛṣis together with the Ṛṣis Kaśyapa and Aptya left the Yajña and came down to the plane between heaven and earth. From there Kaśyapa Ṛṣi directed Ṛṣi Aptya to the earth with these instructions, "O Aptya ! You go to the earth with your Śakti, and remain amongst the peoples of the earth. Educate them that this division in religion is an illusion. To think that one's own religion is somehow higher and greater than the others, is a myth. To have hatred for other religions and pride for one's own, is ignorance. The aim of all religions is the same. They wish to reach the same ultimate reality, the same truth and have the same goal. The aim of all those who are sincere and faithful is achieving purity and realisation. This is true of all religions. Unite all religions and demonstrate through your activities that there is one truth for all. All the prophets of the various religions are one in front of the Supreme. They have no conflict amongst themselves. However, by observing the conflicts, quarrels, disharmony, hatred and selfish egoism between the various religions, they are very sad and disappointed. They repent that they ever brought this message to the world. They are absolutely disillusioned to see the results of their divine message. They wonder why their followers have divided themselves into warring parties and groups. By the unification of all religions, they will be very happy."

To accomplish this mission Ṛṣi Aptya, came down to this earth along with his Śakti, Ambhriṇī and took birth in Bengal. He received the name Gadādhara from the family where he was born. He grew up with the ideals that had been previously chosen. He did not like the present education on the earth and had no interest in going to school. He lived according to his own principles. From his boyhood, he worshipped the power of the Mother–Śakti. He prayed to Mother Kālī through songs and meditation. Day by day, he developed a keen interest to see the Divine Mother Kālī. Sometimes, he spent nights at the cemetry in deep meditation of the Divine Kālī. He was busy singing devotional songs.

The parents and relatives became anxious about his future life. They were worried that he was going insane. To bring him back to normalty, they arranged his marriage to Śāradāmoni. However, he did not spend a single moment as a married person. He was selected as the Priest of the Dakṣiṇeśvara Kālī temple. There, through the adoration of the stony figure of Kālī, he entered into a deep trance. He attained universal consciousness and power and announced his divine accomplishment and the realisation of Mother Kālī. Then, he started to work under the name of Ramakrishnā by conquering passion, desire and greed as he decided that these were evils and the real causes of suffering of all mankind. He adored his wife Śāradāmoni with flowers, prostrated himself before her and called her the Mother.

By conquering passion and egoism, he entered into divine bliss. Then he practiced different methods of sādhanā, specifically those introduced by different religions. When he attained perfection in all, he announced the unity of all religions. He found that although there were many paths, many creeds and ways of looking at life, the goal for all religions was the same. There was no separate hell or heaven for Christians, Moslems, Buddhists, Jains, Hindus and others. One went to heaven or hell depending upon one's actions. All religions have the same ideal—to conquer disharmony, sins and sufferings, and to enter into divine peace.

On hearing these sayings of Ramakrishna, Kali, the Lord of the Iron Age, became furious and understood that Ṛṣi Aptya was working towards unifying the human society, which ran directly counter to his wishes. He ordered the evil forces to remove him from the earth. One of the sons of Arbuda, having the name of Kartaka, entered in Ramakrishna's body with his food and started to destroy his vocal chords together with the inner portion of the throat. When Ṛṣi Aptya came to know that it was not his work to destroy this evil power, he decided to leave this earth.

Ṛṣi Aptya, after leaving this earth, went to the other Creators and said, "As decided upon, I went to take human birth in Bengal to open a new path for the manifestation of Truth. I saw that the people of Bengal had competely forgotton their soul. They did not know themselves. They had lost their independent spirit, their Aryan culture and ideals after experiencing slavery for a very long period under the Moslems and the British. During my education, I learnt that the aim of education at present is to become a good servant for the British, to become a clerk in their offices and thus obtain their grades of honour."

"The Indians are taught by their foreign masters that they have no culture, that they are foolish and backward and that their forefathers were barbarians. They are taught that the Vedas were primitive as they worshipped the elements–water, fire, air etc., as Godheads, whereas the western education analysed these and made them serve mankind. The elements being worshipped, in ancient India, for want of superior knowledge, were now under the command of the West. They could control nature and its unruly elements and make them serve mankind. When I heard this incredible view, I remembered Rāvaṇa who had conquered the Godheads and, through his power, made them suffer. When Gods and Ṛṣis suffered, Rāvaṇa heaped insults on them. To punish him, there was a Supreme descent. I felt that there should be another descent of the Supreme to remedy the situation. I tried to unify all religions through my inner meditations and power. I developed this idea to some extent but time was against me."

Kaśyapa, the Creator of the Gods replied, "O Aptya, your activities were effective and beneficial for the earth. It is true that the division in religions is the cause of human sufferings. These divisions must be removed and the essential unity of all religions made clear to everyone."

Other Ṛṣis added, "O Creator! It is not enough to unite all religions in one way to achieve peace. Inner disharmony must be made evident. The actions of Gods and Devils must be identified in the human consciousness. Mankind must be aware of the power of inner guidance from Gods or Devils. They must know the power of the divine or undivine that is acting through them and manifesting."

Then Kaśyapa said, "O Creators, O great Ṛṣis, that is true! For this I must descend on the earth and take human birth. Not only to divide the power of divine and undivine in the activities of humanity, but to facilitate the birth of divine consciousness. People must become aware of their own divinity. Either they become instruments of Higher Gods for the divine play or they become aware of the divine birth of Godheads on the earth. This will lead to a transformation of humanity and change earth into heaven."

Thus, the Creator Kaśyapa came down from the higher plane together with the Divine Mother Aditi to this earth. The people of spiritual India had become completely enslaved under the materialistic culture of the foreigners and were under their guidance. It was decided that Kaśyapa would take birth in Bengal to redeem the spiritual consciousness from materialistic bondage, as Bengal was fully under the sway of foreign culture. Another goal was to make India conscious of her inherent spiritual values.

Mother Aditi would take birth, live in France, and work at sundering the materialistic bondage, brought about by the worship of material science, which was completely under the control of Kali. She would assist in uncoiling the Kālacakra (the Time Wheel) and prepare the earth for identification with the divine. Thus the Divine Creator Kaśyapa took birth in Bengal under the name of Aurobindo and the Divine Mother Aditi took her human birth in France under the name of Mirra Alffassa. They had their childhood in different parts of the world and thus grew up in countries with differing cultures and education.

In the meantime, the great Vivekānanda was inspired (from his guru Ramakrishna's plane) to give a lecture at the Chicāgo Conference, about the Message of Truth brought down by his guru. He told them in ringing tones that all religions had brought Truth to the earth and they should ideally be unified. Vivekānanda gave a lecture about the truth of all religions at a moment when a great dilemma confronted world religions. Through the powers of the Ṛṣis acting in him, Vivekānanda was able to impress and charm a huge number of people participating in the World Religious Conference. With this, Vivekānanda became very famous and received a large number of appreciative comments from Westerners. This he had not received in India. He returned to India as "the famous

Vivekānanda" an honour heaped on him by foreigners. Then he was also honoured in India.

This was the moment that awakened India presented her Truth to the world and the whole world was astonished to hear about her greatness. Before that, foreigners looked down upon India. Indians were reviled as foolish, orthodox, cowardly, ignorant, with a slave mentality. It was also claimed that they had no culture. Now, the West admitted that ancient India had a very high culture, which was demonstrated by the Vedas, Upaniṣads etc. The Western experts gave commentaries on these spiritual books according to their scientific knowledge. In fact, they were the real beginners. Not so the people of ancient India. In this way, India, which had been ignored and reviled, achieved some modicum of self-respect and fame through Vivekānanda. From that time, Indians have always looked towards the West to receive their support and commendation in order to feel confident about their own values.

Dr. K. D. Ghosh, Aurobindo's father, had his son educated in England from boyhood onwards, so that he could hold a high position in India when he finished his education. During his education in Europe, he had first–hand experience about the contemptuous attitude that the British had towards Indians. He returned to India without completing the Indian Civil Service Course, with the idea to uplift his motherland and work for her independence. He joined a political party and became a leader. He demanded full freedom of India from the British rule, to be achieved by any means, even violence. Before his arrival on the Indian scene, the other leaders, under the inspiritation of Vivekānanda, were actively trying to uplift the country. Some of them lent their support to Vivekānanda's work, carried forward under his disciple sister, Niveditā. Together with those leaders, Aurobindo Ghosh demanded full freedom for India. In his free time, he started to learn Indian languages, spiritual creeds with philosophy, and Yoga etc. Subsequently, he made a plan to achieve complete freedom for his motherland. Through his efforts, some people joined him, mostly in Bengal. They used all means at their disposal to kick the British out of India. As a direct result, he was arrested with his party and imprisoned. There, he realised that the Indians themselves with their slave mentality were a stumbling block to achieve liberation. In the prison, he wondered how a few individuals from Britain could come to India and rule over such a vast country. This could be possible only with the tacit support of Indians themselves. The Indians were fully committed in their service to the British Government.

He felt that it was necessary to bring about an inner change in the mind-set of Indians, to make them think about their unquestioned slavery to the British, to remind them of their deep cultural roots and educate them so that they could return to their ancient Aryan culture. As he had studied ancient Aryan religious creeds and philosophies as well as books of Yoga, he knew that the knowledge of ancient India needed to be practised. He started to practise yoga in prison and realised the universal soul. He came out of the prison with the voice of the universal soul telling him to spread the Sanātana Dharma and to bring about an inner change in the people and thus liberate them from foreign influence. He was convinced that without inner change it was not possible to advance further. He gave this advice to his party and he, himself, started to spread Sanātana Dharma through his many lectures. He also edited papers to spread information about his spiritual experiences. But he could not continue long.

The British Government had doubts about his work and considered it as another form of political movement. They made plans to arrest him. In the meantime, he became conscious of his true mission, which was to give spiritual knowledge to the country. For that, he required an isolated place, which would allow him to study and concentrate. With inner guidance, he selected Pondicherry. There he immersed himself in his quest for the Divine.

A few followers accompanied him but they were unable to understand his advanced ideas. After a few years, the Mother came to Pondicherry. Through her inner wisdom, she came to know that her present life's mission was with Sri Aurobindo, her Lord. On the other hand, Sri Aurobindo understood that the Mother had come to assist him and to explain the supramental knowledge in a practical manner to the followers. He gave up all responsibilities to her for the manifestation of supermind with a declaration that she was the Divine Mother, responsible for bringing the Gods on the earth, who will undertake the journey towards divinity. After this announcement, he isolated himself from his followers. He entered into the silence of his room, to discover the solution to the great problems faced by men, i.e. of birth and death.

In a few years, it was known to his followers that he was engaged in writing the epic Savitri, based on an ancient legend. The epic was about how mankind could fight death and the power of death to enter into immortality. When this theme came to be spread around, his followers assumed that Sri Aurobindo was immersed in a spiritual austerity for the uplift of the whole humanity into immortality, to transform humanity into the life divine through the manifestation of the Supermind. The people of India hoped that Sri Aurobindo through his sādhanā would find a solution to life's misery. Then, suddenly, he quit the earth and his followers were greatly shocked.

When Sri Aurobindo left the earth, he returned back to the Ṛṣis who were waiting for him with Ṛṣi Aptya between the higher and the lower plane. Sri Aurobindo said, "O Seers of all Creations! I went to the earth and tried to facilitate the supramental descent amongst mankind, to facilitate the birth of Gods, to open a way for the activities of Gods in human beings and to achieve a transformation of mankind so that life is divinised. I established before mankind the Divine Mother, as she is Aditi, the Mother of the Great Godheads. I was busy in this task discussed in my new epic, and was trying to conquer death."

Chapter 10

APPEARANCE OF THE DEVĀYAṆA

"At that moment, Piṅgala Maheśvara, the Lord of all Creations, appeared before me. He told me, "Look at me, O Creator of Gods! I am the Lord of Time, the Creator of all Creators. All creations are bound to be manifested by me. See the plan for the New Age, where I will manifest all creations in course of time. Cease your work and leave this earth now. Look at the people on the earth. They are not ready for this radical change. Your plan was to usher in the freedom of India and then to start work to manifest divinity on the earth, from the base of the independent spirit of India. Look at the leaders of India; they are not interested in the manifestation of the Divine. Their aim is to obtain political freedom. They wish that India acquires the same status as other nations, be respected among the comity of nations and receive the approval of foreigners. India should be honoured by other foreign countries. These leaders do not know the cause of the freedom of India, that this country is obtaining her freedom to disclose her Sanātana Dharma. With her spiritual power, she will usher in unity and peace for the whole of humanity. She will establish a divine kingdom on the whole earth. The earth will then be like one nation having one religion, one caste and one language for all and mankind will be in a constant state of happiness. By divine royal power, she will teach the secret of the Vedas, the reality of the existence of Godheads, their divine guidance in the human body to have a positive influence on human activities. This will enable mankind to rise higher and higher to reach into immortality in order to realise and usher in the Golden Age."

"When the leaders are not conscious about the hidden cause for the independence of India, there will be a very long waiting time for the manifestation of the new supreme drama. Let the Mother remain here to hold the threads of your supramental activities until I manifest the great epic, which is containing a new plan for the future. This would be the path unveiled by the journeys of the Gods, with the Supreme Truth, to humanity and journeys of men towards the divinity,—the Devāyaṇa. It will also describe the previous ages, how human beings entered into such darkness that they became unconscious and fell into the cataclysm. Again, how men will rise from there to attain the eternal divine consciousness and obtain immortality. Without the presence of the Divine Mother, it will not be possible to manifest this epic on the earth. I appeal to you again, O Creator, let her remain here doing the same work until I manifest the supreme secrets."

Sri Aurobindo asked Piṅgala Maheśvara, "In my absence, how long will the Divine Mother remain on the earth?"

Piṅgala Maheśvara replied, "She will remain on the earth until I complete my activities. In the meantime, O Creator, come to the supramental plane. From there, you will be able to push down the epic with the Supreme Truth towards the earth. And you have to be present there for my work until the descent of the epic is completed. I will come back again."

Sri Aurobindo said that after uttering these words, Piṅgala Maheśvara disappeared but he did not specify the exact time when he would return. After the disappearance of the Supreme Puruṣa, he closed his activities and after a few years he left the earth. He told the Ṛṣis that they should wait there until Piṅgala Maheśvara manifests again and discloses the secret path of the Gods. The other Ṛṣis replied, "This is the right procedure for the manifestation of the Supreme Truth. Where will be the place and who will be the poet?" At that moment they heard a voice saying that the place and the person will be decided now. Let us go to the earth.

THE CONTROVERSY

The Ṛṣis saw that Piṅgala Maheśvara appeared in front of them wearing a mass of matted hair, having three eyes like a lotus petal. His beautiful body had a golden red colour, a glazing moon on the forehead, and he was dressed in a golden cloth with a narrow scarf around the shoulder. He said in a resounding voice to the Sages, "Let us go to the earth, O Creators! Let us go for the manifestation of the Supreme Plan, the great epic, to open a new Golden Age." He said this and started to advance to the earth with all the Ṛṣis silently following him. They reached the place where the Divine Mother was still staying and maintaining the thread of her master's work for the manifestation of the supramental. A few of the illuminated souls appeared in front of her and the Creator Kaśyapa (in the form of Sri Aurobindo) said, "O Mother Aditi! I am here always for our esteemed work. I shall be with you until this mission is completed. Here is the Supramental Creator, Piṅgala Maheśvara, who has descended on the earth with a new plan to manifest a new creation, which will be the foundation and beginning of a new Supramental Race." The Mother looked at them and was very glad and full of joy. She expressed her joy with the divine utterance, "Finally, O Supreme Creator! You have descended on the earth. Now may I say that our promised work is fulfilled? May I announce this day as the day of the Supramental Descent?" At that moment all the luminous beings disappeared. Only a voice remained, "Yes, you can announce it."

But the Mother was in a dilemma by the sudden disappearance. She thought that she could not declare that the Supramental had descended without having a substantial proof. The vision had disappeared so suddenly, leaving no trace at all. The luminous beings disappeared and were searching the place for the manifestation of the great epic. After visiting a number of disciples chosen for this great task, they approached a small room where a young man was sleeping towards the end of the night. There, Piṅgala

Maheśvara paused and told the other Ṛṣis, "Behold, this is the person and the place that I have selected for the manifestation of my supreme plan." The Ṛṣis were surprised and asked, "O Supreme Creator! What special quality have you seen here?" Piṅgala Maheśvara replied, "See, I will show you all the inner receptivity. At every place that we have chosen, I have sung the Nāda, the sound Brahman "Om". The others were not conscious. For this reason, we left and searched further. Those who are incapable of hearing the Om, means that they have no faith in the inner divine existence. Once before when I visited the earth, I saw that this being was receptive but very weak to maintain it. Let us try again."

Piṅgala Maheśvara started to sing, "Om, Om, Om is the primal sound, the Sound Creator, Om is the root cause of all creations, all powers and ānanda; Om is the Lord of all, Om is the figure of the Nārāyaṇa with the four hands, who is the Lord of all beings; Om is the supreme soul and supreme being, who is holding all and staying everywhere; Om is to be worshipped daily as the supreme Lord." After singing this, Piṅgala said, "See the receptivity, the young man has awakened and is looking at us. But he is seeing us only; he has no power to express it. O Creator of Gods! Give him strength through the power of your tapasyā, which lasted for twenty-six thousand years. Now, let me describe the Nāda and its rhythm. The rhythm is the source of all creations." By disclosing the Oṁkār, the divine rhythm, the power of rhythm for the manifestation of the new creation, the luminous beings started to blaze like several suns at noon.

Piṅgala told the Creators in his highly resonant voice, "This is the place, O Great Creators. I have decided to manifest the epic here. I have chosen this young person, who is humble and open and does not consider himself wise, who has faith in the Gods, who has always had an aspiration for Vedic knowledge and is highly receptive. I have decided to make him an instrument to manifest the epic containing the supreme plan." Then he started chanting in the rhythm of the Anuṣṭubh. With His chanting the three creations trembled and the vast epic manifested. Piṅgala said, "O Creator of Gods, Kaśyapa! The Truth appears surrounded by a beautiful light. Look at the creation, where the wheel of time is turning. It is holding the meaning of the secrets and manifestation of Gods by unfolding the divine activities. Through the four Ages, the divine intellect becomes covered by the darkness of time. Then with the movement of the Time Wheel, the divine intellect again regains its glory and all the creations approach the Golden Age. From the Golden Age, the creation is proceeding towards the Iron Age. Look at the movement, O Creator! All the creations are again turning from the Iron Age towards the Golden Age. In short, the Creation is going from one Golden Age to the next, unfolding all the secrets of the creation. That is why I call this epic—the Devāyaṇa."

The Creators asked, "O Piṅgala Maheśvara! O Supreme Creator! You call this epic Devāyaṇa. Is there any special significance for this name?" He replied, "There is a special reason in the name. Devāyaṇa is a royal road from mortality to immortality, and from heaven to the earth. It provides a connection between the Gods and men. In this, one can see the journeys of the Gods towards mortality, to conquer death and diseases and other hostile elements with the divine power; and journeys of men towards the immortality of the Gods for the perfection of humanity, to manifest the Supreme Truth on the earth, by conquering falsehood and darkness existing on the earth."

The Ṛṣis added, "If the aim of the epic is to describe the divinised earth by the manifestation of the Supreme Truth with the activities of the Gods, then you could describe the future with some of the present occurrences. Why are you then describing the past in such detail, particularly that past which has already been described by the Ṛṣis Vālmīki and Vyāsa in previous ages? Perhaps this epic can start from the time when the previous two epics ended."

Piṅgala replied, "Devāyaṇa is not like the other two epics which described the activities of two Avatāras of Lord Viṣṇu with other Godheads, for achieving divine victory over the anti-divine. This is an epic, which invites the Golden Age on earth and seeks the divine light, and the power of Truth to conquer and remove the dark period of Kali. It manifests the peaceful period of Satyadeva in the creation. Everyone must be told how the creation came under Kali's control. Then, human beings could become conscious instruments of victory for the Supreme Truth. When everyone is conscious about the reason for their constant struggle, then this struggle will be successful. Human beings will then become living temples of Gods. They will then become a decisive factor for the supremacy of Truth. This epic does not aim to describe a great war between the undivine and the divine beings with the Supreme Truth, which would result in a divine victory. Nor does it aim to describe the human character of the Supreme and his miraculous activities as an ideal for all times for the human race. This epic describes an inauspicious evil time, which has covered the whole earth. During this time, Kali, together with his hostile forces comprising of ego, greed, anger, and jealousy etc., has been reigning supreme. Under the influence of such forces, human beings are bound to do evil deeds. At such a time, it is essential to recall the aspiration of humanity for the Divine. Furthermore, it would be necessary to prepare oneself for the advent of the Supreme Truth into the world, to remove Kali's nefarious deeds, and to re-establish the Divine. With the Gods becoming active in the human beings, the whole world will become transformed and humanity will enjoy immortality and immunity on the earth."

The Ṛṣis enquired, "Is it essential to describe the course of all activities of Kali, all those that were not told by Vālmīki and Vyāsa, the eternal beginnings of creation; the causes of the birth of both Gods and Devils; good and evil and not only its end? Vālmīki described in his epic Rāmāyaṇa the middle portion of the Silver Age. Then, a long period elapsed without any trace. Subsequently, Vyāsa told the tale of Mahābhārata from the middle to the end of the Bronze Age. Then again there was a long gap. Subsequently, we have the historical period, which stretches, from the middle to the end of the Iron Age. We can observe the manifold divisions of the world in many states, languages and religions. To show the eternal identification and the ever-recurring causes of division in the human consciousness, you have described the chain of events from the beginning to the end with a continuous description of the good and bad times for the creation. But during the narration of the continuous events, there are also prophets and incarnations. These have resulted in giving rise to diverse religions, which are maintaining their originality, by giving great importance to their rules and procedures. A great gulf divides these religions and there is a continuous controversy between them on the question of world unity. You have described for all religions a common source, which is based on the Vedic principles. These were the immortal souls such as Hanumān, Dhruva, Prahlāda, Vibhīṣaṇa, Aśvatthāmā, Śukadeva, etc. Thus Mahāvīra, Buddha, Christ, Muhammad, Caitanya, Śaṅkarācārya are the incarnations of the Divine for the different religions, whose faith and opinions are clashing with each other. How are these differing faiths going to accept that they have the same common source? How are all these beliefs going to become one so that the whole earth has one religion, one language? How will mankind enter into a peaceful state?"

Piṅgala replied, "In fact, there will be very few people who will accept this idea. Only those, who are inwardly connected with Truth and are conscious, will believe. Most will completely and violently reject it. Some of them, who are under the complete influence of Kali, might even become violently opposed to the whole concept. All this has no significance. By the advance of Satyadeva, Kali cannot but retreat and withdraw from this creation. At the very end, the condition of the earth will become alarming. Divisions will be due to religion, caste, and languages. There will be an ever-increasing number of states in this world. Under these conditions, there is bound to be terror and fear. To escape this condition, human beings are bound to search for a way to achieve unity and peace. At that moment, they will realise the truth of this idea."

Then, Kaśyapa, the Creator of Gods, said, "O Piṅgala Maheśvara! The epic that you have shown and described to us appears to be very lengthy. I think it is really impossible to manifest. Nowadays human beings have a very short life. I think that this epic requires at least a hundred years to manifest. Then tell me, O Piṅgala! O Lord of the Poets! How can a human being receive this epic in such a short life"

Piṅgala replied, "Listen, O Creator of Gods! I have decided to compress time so that the 12,000 pages of Devāyaṇa that you have seen with your own eyes, can be completed. For manifesting this epic, take ten pages daily and with your power of words bring them into existence. If ten pages are possible in a day, then in a month, you will be able to realise three hundred pages. By the same calculation, in three months and ten days, you will have brought down a thousand pages. If you multiply this by twelve, then we can see that the manifestation of Devāyaṇa will need only three years and four months."

Kaśyapa replied, "Time has now been shortened. But I still think that it is difficult for a human being to sit quietly at one place for three years and four months. It is difficult as men are dependent on food, and they have to face constant attacks of hunger and thirst."

To this, Piṅgala answered, "O Creator of Gods! You have achieved a great power through your long tapasyā at the beginning of the manifestation of creation. Through your power, empower this instrument so that he is able to receive this vast epic. He will become an adequate channel to allow the constant stream of the eternal epic. He will not tire even for a moment and there will be no suffering for him as long as he sits quietly during the writing of the epic. Instead, he will be glad and joyful in his heart when he will receive the epic. He will become stronger day by day."

Again Kaśyapa said, "O Lord of the Poets! In this epic, only a few words will not suffice. As this epic is twelve times longer than the other epics, twelve times more words will also be required."

The Poet Piṅgala responded, " That it definitely will. Also, there will be many disturbances, obstacles, and impediments mainly put there by the Lord of the Iron Age and through the ignorance of men. So I am calling upon the Democrat God, who is the Lord for all peoples to bring perfection in their lives; who is elephant headed and the giver of accomplishment. By his presence and influence, all will be solved. He is called Brahmaṇaspati to manifest the creation of Brahman, he will remove all opposition to the epic."

Then he called upon Pārvatī's son, the Rider of the Rat, who appeared there. Brahmaṇaspati (Gaṇapati) asked Piṅgala, "O Supreme Creator! Why are you calling me, tell me what can I do?" Piṅgala answered, "Listen O Gaṇapati! Son of Pārvatī ! Here is a vast new epic, a message from the Supreme for a new creation, a new Age and a new race, which will be manifested. Your work is to assist in the collection of words, to present it in the right form and to express these words in rhythm." To this Gaṇapati replied, "Amen! O Lord of Time."

IN THE COURSE OF MANIFESTATION

Lord Gaṇapati told Piṅgala Maheśvara, Lord of the Poets, "O Piṅgala Maheśvara! I am ready to work on this epic. Please let me know the subject matter of your epic."

Piṅgala replied, "Look, O Gaṇapati at the subtle form of the epic, which is containing twelve thousand pages. I have decided that daily ten pages should be manifested."

At his instruction, the son of Pārvati, the elephant-headed, took his place in the young devotee below the brain and above the first cervical vertebra behind the throat. The devotee was astonished to see this vision, and was like a spectator. The Creator of Gods, Kaśyapa, took his place on the occipital brain and Piṅgala stood on the frontal brain. From there he made a bridge with the Eternal Supreme. Kaśyapa was providing support to the mortal instrument with his power of tapasyā, so that the human being did not become overwhelmed with excessive joy and constant thrills. He could then start the work of the manifestation of the new creation.

Gaṇapati then started to pull down and called upon the eternal power his mother, who remains in a dormant state at the "Mūlādhāra" in each human being. From there, this power guides all human beings in their activities. "Mūlādhāra", a psychological centre, which the Yogis have told us, is located in all human beings at the bottom of the body. The exact location is the small place between the anus and the genital organ. Inside there lies the mother of all creations. As the Yogaśikhopaniṣad says, "This is the power that maintains and guides all creative powers with their creations, who lies dormant at the "Mūlādhāra". This power is called Mahāmāyā or Maheśvarī, she is Mahālakṣmī, she is Mahādevī or Mahākālī, and she is also Sarasvatī. When this centre awakens, the Yogis see before them a flash of illumination with beautiful colours and they hear the sound of "Om" inside their body with the movement of the awakened power (śakti). The Nāda comes from the Mūlādhāra centre at the bottom; this sound comes up to the navel centre roaring like a cloud. When it enters the heart centre it gives forth the tune of a beautiful bird song." By the pressure of the power of Kaśyapa's tapasyā in that human instrument, the eternal power with a beautiful blue-white colour awakens and he hears the nada, the great sound with the subtle akṣaras. Then the individual saw this power rising up to the navel centre and heard the nada with astonishment. By the call of Gaṇapati, this power made a connection with the higher consciousness existing at the region of the heart. With this connection, the individual's needs, desires and activities went into the background and the action of the higher consciousness became automatic.

This young man thus became an instrument for the Divine. To manifest a new creation, the Divine Mother took the individual's mind to give it a mental shape. All his thoughts took form through her divine knowledge. His vital force and the movement of his work were also under her direct control. Subtle creations were taking shape through individual thoughts as she was forming the shapes. The psychic became the instrument for mechanical activities with the pressure of the vital force, as the Universal Mother was manifesting the epic. Gaṇapati put her divine rhythm into poetic metres. The Lord of the Poets, Piṅgala Maheśvara, received the idea, the subtle form of the epic. He was the one who gave the epic a material shape for mankind, without any changes or twists. In this way, this epic, Devāyaṇa, is the direct action of the Divine on the earth and the young man a mere medium or instrument for this great manifestation.

During the course of the manifestation, Gaṇapati put questions and Piṅgala responded. He described how in the eternal void, the creation appeared. Then followed details of the coming into existence of the great Godheads to the smallest creatures. Subsequently, there is a description of the manifestation of this world with the earth, the planets and the creation on the earth. Evolution, with the human race at the end, comes next. The epic then describes the spiritual history through the Ages. In the beginning, there is a short description of the Golden Age. Also, mentioned is how humanity proceeded from there to the Iron Age, passing through the other two Ages. Finally, follows a description of the ayana, from the Silver Age through the historical period up to the present condition. Then come the details, how humanity will again enter into the Golden Age from the Iron Age with a detailed description of that Age.

Chapter 11

TRANSIT TO THE GOLDEN AGE

After describing the activities of Kaśyapa in this world for the manifestation of a supramental age, the activities of Gods in human beings and divinity in mankind, Gaṇapati asked how this would come about. There was neither change nor any transformation in the human society. How would the human society accept divinity?

Piṅgala answered, "Listen, O Son of Pārvatī! I have until now disclosed the past with the present. Now I will describe to you the present with the future. After finishing his mortal work, Kaśyapa, the Creator of Gods, will withdraw to the higher plane with the other Ṛṣis. Those you see here will remain in the world, until this epic has manifested. As these Ṛṣis had been busy in the Deva Yajña, they decided to return there. This Deva Yajña had commenced a long time ago on the immortal plane for the manifestation of the Truth (Deva). There is a description of the early life of Deva and his boyhood activities in the family of the Ṛṣis. When the Deva was preparing himself with the power and knowledge of Ṛṣis to take up the work of creation, and to hold the Kālacakra, at that time Aptya and Kaśyapa with other Ṛṣis came to this world to prepare the ground for the advent of Truth. Now, they have returned to the immortal plane to take part in the Deva Yajña. At the Conference, outside the Deva Yajña, there will be the union of Deva and Gauribiti, the aspirant power for the Truth, who was also at the Yajña together with the Ṛṣis. With this identification, which took place with the help of the Ṛṣis, the stage has been prepared for the descent of Truth in this creation. The desire for calling the Truth back to the earth had always remained in the human consciousness. This was due to the tapasyā of Gauribiti. This endeavour was protected by the Ṛṣis and given the name of Vītihotra during the absence of Satyadeva."

"O Gaṇapati! Look at that plane from here. Kaśyapa and the other Ṛṣis have reached near the place where the Deva Yajña was taking place and where the others had been waiting for them. As soon as the Creator of Gods, Kaśyapa reached there, he gave his consent to the other Ṛṣis for taking Gauribiti before Satyadeva. They explained the purpose of the Deva Yajña to Satyadeva and Gauribiti. After receiving the approval of the higher Godheads they brought about the union of Satyadeva and Gauribiti. On this occasion, all the Gods were very happy and they held the ceremony of ambrosia. The Lord of Ambrosia, Soma Devatā, the Godhead of Joy and Ananda entered into the Ocean of the Brahman (the Kṣīrasamudra) and brought a golden pot of ambrosia. Satyadeva, the Lord of Truth, distributed it amongst all the Godheads and Ṛṣis. After drinking the nectar, they were overwhelmed with joy. Then Deva drank the Soma and clasped Gauribiti into himself. She received through his embrace, the power of joy to develop in herself the creation of Truth. This had been the aim of the ceremony as all Godheads and Ṛṣis wished to release the earth from the bondage of Kali, and manifest Deva on the earth.

ADVENTURE OF DAWN TOWARDS NIGHT

The aim of this Deva Yajña was to bring about a new Dawn of Truth after the end of the deep dark Night of Kali. This would complete the old cycle and start a new one. This would also bring about a new race, a new rule and order in the activities of the human being. Through the aspiration of Truth, and the power and light of Truth, the closed path between immortality and mortality, would now open. The path that had been closed when the deep darkness of Falsehood spread over the world, prevented the human being from feeling or understanding the presence of the immortal world.

To open the closed path, called the Devāyaṇa by the Vedas, the journeying of the Gods and the effort of the Ṛṣis started. Through Devāyaṇa, the mortals would realise the Truth existing in themselves, recognise the activities of Godheads in their bodies, and accept the thoughts and knowledge of the Ṛṣis as their own. Thus Devāyaṇa is the royal road to divinity, which has started from immortality to mortality, to allow the journeys of the Gods to men or the journeys of men to the Gods. This is the road of the supramental secret, which is completely unknown to human beings at present.

This secret path will be opened through the power and light of Truth. Satyadeva, the Lord of Truth, will approach the mortal world with his divine troops. They are well equipped with divine weapons to conquer death and diseases. They will drive out Kali together with his anti-divine forces and remove completely their influence on human beings. After removing Kali's influence from the mortal world, Satyadeva will spread his light and power and give the sense of immortality to humanity. Now I will tell you, O Gaṇapati, the secret concerning the manifestation of Light and the Power of Truth, in a figurative form, that is the coming into existence of Uṣā and Pūṣa. Listen carefully to this secret. I have told you, how the aspiration of mortality attained the Deva Yajña and was identified with the Truth. Gauribiti is the aspiration for Truth that rises from the mortal world to the Supreme. She received the light and power of Truth in her womb through her union with the Satyadeva. In her womb the light and power of Truth developed and took two different shapes. The light took form as the daughter, Uṣā and the power took form as the son, Pūṣa. Both came into the world as twins. The Ṛṣis and the Godheads were very pleased to see the birth of Truth Light and Truth Power. They were the ones who, according to their secret knowledge, gave the twins, the names of Uṣā and Pūṣa. They announced that the two children would connect mortality with immortality. Uṣā and Pūṣa grew up in the home of Ṛṣi Abhivarta with all the Ṛṣis around them. They received the secret knowledge of the Vedas during their childhood for their work for the Ṛṣis, for the Deva and for men. When they grew up and had fully manifested themselves with the Light and Power of Truth, they were told to start their mission and they advanced toward the mortal world.

The Seers directed Uṣā to enter into the house of Nakta, the Lord of Tāmasa, where Rātri, the Night, the daughter of Ṛṣi Bharadvāja was kept captive. Uṣā's goal was to release Ratri from her imprisonment. The Ṛṣis said, "O Uṣā! Go and enter into Nakta's house and appear before Nakta and Rātri with your extremely bright light. Charm Nakta with your bright beauty and revive the past memories into the mind of Rātri, the Night. As she is the daughter of a Rṣi, she has to come back. Make her your friend and ask her to mount in your chariot. Charmed by your beauty, Nakta will try to follow you to catch you. At that moment, you start dancing with the full Power of Truth. Through your dance, Uṣā, a portion of the dark forces of Nakta will be destroyed. Nakta will then become very angry and try to punish you. Pūṣa will then advance to protect you and will fight with Nakta and conquer him. Then, O Pūṣa, you will have to command divine troops numbering over nine million. You will march behind Uṣā to the border of the upper and lower hemisphere. When Nakta becomes angered by Uṣā, his troops will try to arrest her. At that moment, you will have to fight with Nakta and try to conquer him together with his troops. After that you march up to the level of the human beings."

Uṣā started her adventure towards the Night in an automatic chariot lead by Saramā, who is the daughter of Svara Bhūvana, heaven. She is one of the Chiefs of the Intelligence Department. That Department keeps the records of all the secret activities of the enemy. There is information such as deployment of enemy troops, their weak points, how to enter in these areas, as well as information about the jail in which the daughter of Ṛṣi Bharadvāja was held captive.

Uṣā advanced towards the house of Nakta in the chariot of Saramā to release Night from his power. Behind the chariot of Uṣā, Pūṣa advanced together with the divine armies. The other Godheads and Ṛṣis were also accompanying him.

When Uṣā arrived at the door, she saw Tāmasa the Commander-in-Chief of the huge army of Nakta. Tāmasa saw Uṣā before him, a young golden girl having a dazzling white halo around her. When he saw this beautiful golden girl of heaven, he was charmed and attracted by her beauty. He invited her to stay in their house together with Rātri, the daughter of Ṛṣi Bharadvāja. She could remain there without hesitation and with all her honour. As this was also the aim of Uṣā, she accepted the proposal happily.

RELEASE OF "RĀTRI", THE NIGHT

When Uṣā arrived at the palace of Nakta, she entered into the place where Rātri remained alone in great sorrows. She was living in complete solitude because she refused to accept Nakta. Uṣā reached there and whispered into her ear the news of the arrival of Pūṣa, with the huge divine army. She also added that her father Satyadeva, with all the great Godheads and Ṛṣis, was conducting this whole operation to release her from bondage under the dark forces. On hearing this, Rātri felt overwhelmed with happiness and tears of joy started to shower from her eyes. After a moment, she asked Uṣā, what should she do at this auspicious moment. Uṣā told her to get up very quickly and enter into her chariot, which Saramā would then lead to their goal. Following this advice, Rātri jumped into Saramā's chariot. She turned the chariot towards the Deva and whipped the six horses so that they galloped fast.

Tāmasa was standing a bit further away and was observing the intimate coming together of Uṣā and Rātri. He was astonished to see that Uṣā, a very beautiful girl, was also very brave. He could not believe that she would be so courageous as to take Rātri in her chariot and try to run away with her in front of him. He shouted, "O girl of heaven! Do not try to go any further, do not try to escape; stop right there and come back again". Uṣā replied, "Tāmasa, this is the decision of the Ṛṣis. They have told me to release Rātri from her imprisonment under Nakta. Inform your Lord Nakta, who is seated asleep on his throne, covered with layers upon layers of darkness, of this decision taken by the Ṛṣis. From here, I would take the Night. I am Uṣā, the Dawn, heaven born, the daughter of Satyadeva. Behind me, my brother Pūṣa is coming to pierce and split your dark dormant kingdom. He will bring Truth to you, which will bring doom and punishment for your dark activities."

As soon as he heard the words of Uṣā, Tāmasa became very angry and excited. He started gnashing his teeth and shouted, "This is a challenge, O foolish girl. You are unnecessarily vaunting your courage. I command you. Come back yourself and save your honour. Otherwise you will be insulted and forced to come back." Uṣā replied to these harsh words with her own challenge, "Try and stop me if you can." The chariot was rushing forward at full speed. Tāmasa saw that Uṣā and Rātri had reached near the boundary of the area under his control. He ordered his troops to capture the chariot of Saramā. On receiving this order from their commander, the dark troops of Tāmasa surrounded the chariot of Uṣā. It appeared as if dark clouds had covered the dawn. The whole creation sank into gloom. As mentioned in the Vedas, Ṛṣi Kutsya and others on seeing this started to chant in a resounding voice.

"O Uṣā, thou art the daughter of heaven. Thou must reach the earth to awaken thy Lord Viśvadeva, the unconscious world soul. Thou canst not allow yourself to be detained on the way of your journey by any opposition. Thou must kick them off. Dance, O beautiful daughter of Almighty Deva, you are dressed in pure white. Rātri, the Night is your friend. Release her from the clutches of Nakta, the Lord of Darkness."

In this way, the Ṛṣis reminded Uṣā of her duties at that moment. She understood their command and started to dance. Her dance was so dazzling that she could escape from the clutches of Nakta's troops. Through her dance, she kicked and scattered them and thus opened a passage to escape. She ordered Saramā to drive the chariot out from this passage to escape from the innumerable troops of Tāmasa. When Saramā drove the chariot and brought it away from the forces of darkness, Uṣā during the course of her dancing, suddenly jumped inside the chariot. Thus both of them, Rātri and Uṣā, escaped the surrounding troops. The troops of Tāmasa followed the chariot, but then they had to face Pūṣa, the Power of Truth, who was advancing on them accompanied by divine troops. Then followed a great battle between the two armies, in which the divine troops defeated those led by Tāmasa. After that, Pūṣa and Tāmasa fought, and Pūṣa won.

The tremendous noise of this battle woke up Nakta who watched it from afar. When Nakta saw the defeat of Tāmasa, he attacked Pūṣa with his most powerful weapons, which created a lot of thunder. The fight between Nakta and Pūṣa lasted a long time and left eternal memories in creation. It was very difficult for Pūṣa to defeat Nakta. At that time with the help of Satyadeva from behind, Pūṣa conquered him. Pūṣa pushed these forces out of creation towards the west. When Nakta was running away with the dark-forces, at that moment, Kali appeared, the Lord of the Iron Age. The dark coloured Kali, having three eyes, ornamented with snakes, was surrounded by various kinds of snakes, also those that were many-headed. He shouted, "O Gods and Ṛṣis! Do not advance a step further. These three creations are under my control. I am the representative of Rudra Mahākāla."

In response to this, all the Gods and Ṛṣis replied, "O Kali, son of Pragatha! Your time is over now. We do not want you in these three creations. You can go to hell now. Look, here is Satyadeva. He is the Lord of the Golden Age for the three creations and is the representative of Piṅgala Maheśvara."

Satyadeva advanced towards Kali and spoke in his thundering voice, "You are Kali, who has been the cause of extreme suffering in the three creations. The Gods, Ṛṣis and the other beings do not like you. I order you to leave the Kālacakra, the Time Wheel to me and apologise for all your evil deeds." On hearing these hard words from Satyadeva, Kali shouted in a roaring voice, "You are not my Lord that I should beg your pardon. O Satyadeva, together with other Gods and Ṛṣis, depart from here or enter here with your own strength." With these words, Kali attacked the Deva with his powerful weapons. Satyadeva destroyed the weapons of Kali with his force and weapons and gave him such a violent push with his Javelin that Kali whirled and whirled and was pushed out of the creation.

With Kali and Nakta having been expelled with their tāmasic troops, the passage to the mental lower hemisphere was opened. Uṣā and Pūsa entered together with their divine troops in that mental plane, a part of which is connected to the higher mental sphere. In this plane, the power of death, demonic forces, diseases, disbelief and other hostile powers had surrounded and influenced Viśvadeva—Jagat Sūrya, the world soul and held him captive, unconscious and dormant.

THE WORLD SOUL (VIŚVADEVA—JAGAT SŪRYA)

Viśvadeva lives in the pure mind. When the purity is sullied through the influence of hostile or demonic forces, then he becomes unconscious and lies supine in his palace. Uṣā or the Dawn is his power. She left him at the end of the previous Golden Age. He, who was robbed of his own power, came under the influence of negative streams of consciousness and became unconscious.

Viśvadeva—Jagat Sūrya gives guidance of purity in thoughts, in meditation, in the active human brain and in the nervous feeling. His power illumines the human consciousness with a divine light and gives us joy of purity, when he is connected with Uṣā, the Daughter of Heaven. When he is unconscious, being under the domination of lower forces, then human consciousness becomes darkened and heavy. This causes the feeling of depression, which gives constant pain and sorrows through impurities in life. When Viśvadeva, the giver of purity, slept unconsciously in the mental plane, Uṣā entered there together with her brother Pūṣa under the guidance of the Ṛṣis. They said, "Behold O Uṣā! In front of you there is a place where a Puruṣa is lying unconscious. He is your Lord. Awaken him through your worship. Drive the negative powers out and occupy your legitimate place."

As instructed by the Ṛṣis, Uṣā entered into the room and approached Viśvadeva, the unconscious World Soul. She confronted the negative forces and they were outraged on seeing the Divine Uṣā. They felt that this divine power had come to disturb their peace. They told Uṣā to leave as they were providing a restful sleep to their Lord. Uṣā replied, "This is not your place but mine. Don't you know that this is my home where I live with my Lord for eternity? Now, I will wake him up so that he could do his tasks as ordained by the Ṛṣis." Then, a struggle started between the two opposing powers. Uṣā, with the help of other divine powers, managed to drive the negative forces out.

In the meantime, through this disturbance, Viśvadeva woke up. He observed their quarrel. When Uṣā won after driving out the hostile forces, she came in front of him. At that moment the Ṛṣis came nearer and spoke to him, "O Sūrya! See in front of you, Uṣā, the heaven-born daughter of Satyadeva, your partner and your friend. Accept her and clasp her". With the words of the Ṛṣis, Sūrya remembered his past, how he had married Uṣā, how she had disappeared when she heard that Vaiśvadevī, his sister came back from heaven. Then, the relation between heaven and earth was severed. She quit this earth and proceeded towards heaven and went to the sea of Brahman to dissolve herself. However, in the sea of Brahman, that is impossible.

When Sūrya remembered all that with the words of the Ṛṣis, he got up and with an ardent love clasped Uṣā, the Divine Dawn. Then he saw Pūṣa in front of him. He eagerly advanced a few steps, clasped him to his heart, and said, "My lost brother, my heaven-born brother, my sweet-divine brother." Pūṣa uttered with his very sweet voice, "I have come here from heaven, O brother Sūrya, to offer you my sister, Uṣā."

Jagat Sūrya replied, "I must present something to you, come with me." Holding Pūṣa's hand he went to an adjacent room and knocked at the door. Vaiśvadevī opened the door and saw her beloved Lord. On observing Pūṣa so unexpectedly, she felt such a pressure of joy that she could not speak nor invite him inside. Jagat Sūrya told Pūṣa, "Here is my sister Vaiśvadevī, my present to you. Accept her with your great kindness."

When Pūṣa saw Vaiśvadevī, he remembered his past and recognised his beloved wife. She had to depart from heaven and come to the earth and thus they became separated. This was due to the time. Now he went to her and embraced her. At that moment, Satyadeva appeared there with the Ṛṣis to bless them and told Jagat Sūrya, "Hear O Sūrya! O Immortal Son! The time has come for me to take control of the three creations. Now you call a conference of all the Godheads and Ṛṣis to decide on your future work. Sit on the throne of your kingdom with Uṣā to spread your influence over the creation. Occupy the mental, physical and life planes on the earth. Establish my rule and remove the influence of Kali, the Lord of the Iron Age. Vaiśvadevī will accompany Pūṣa to heaven."

According to the order of Satyadeva, Jagat Sūrya called a conference in his royal court. All the Ṛṣis and Godheads took their seat with Satyadeva, Jagat Sūrya and Uṣā were seated on their former thrones through the guidance of the Ṛṣis. All the Godheads were willing to speak about their former existence and the activities of other Godheads. First of all was Taranta, as he was the son of Jagat Sūrya from the previous Kalpa. They decided to call him back again to have the same existence with Uṣā, to give a new birth to the King of the earthly mind. As suggested by the Ṛṣis, they did the Yajña for creation. Then there was the birth of Uṣā's son, and the Ṛṣis gave him the name, Taranta. It was a great pleasure for Jagat Sūrya, the Ṛṣis, other Godheads and Satyadeva to see the newborn's growth and play. The child Taranta received his education from the Ṛṣis. When he was fully grown up, he was established as the ruler of the vital plane. Śaśīyasī, the daughter of Vāyudevatā, who had been the queen of the vital plane, was lying hidden in a secret vital cavern. When Taranta entered the vital kingdom by conquering his opponent Pumān, the Demon Queens, Viradā and Devatī awakened Śaśīyasī. These were the two queens of Pumān. They were instrumental in hiding the Divine Queen Śaśīyasī from the fiery greed of Pumān. In this way, Taranta met his own Queen Śaśīyasī. He gave the two demon queens proper respect and allowed them a passage to leave. After their departure, he established his suzerainty on the vital plane with the power and influence of Truth and with the help of the Ṛṣis.

PURE VITAL EXISTENCE (TARANTA)

Taranta came to the vital plane with the regiment of Bhavayayavya. These were preceded by the higher divine troops with Viśvadeva or Jagat Sūrya, Satyadeva, Ṛṣis and other Godheads. Taranta fought valiantly with Pumān and conquered with the power and influence of Satyadeva. At the end of the previous Golden Age, Taranta had been defeated by Pumān. This had occurred due to the withdrawal of Satyadeva from the creation. Thus, he had to leave the vital plane, his kingdom, and take shelter and remain in the forest of Brahman (Brahmāraṇya). Now he has returned to take up his work to serve the Truth. Taranta is an ardent worshipper of Truth. His work is to manifest Truth to counter vital Falsehood. He aims to banish the treacherous ego to achieve a sincere peaceful vitality. Finally, he defies egoistic arrogance in the face of ignorant and helpless vitality. He together with Śaśīyasī (daughter of Vāyudevatā) and with the help of the Ṛṣis established their Kingdom of Truth on the vital plane.

When Taranta established his power on the vital plane, the truth of vitality manifested at that moment. Then the Ṛṣis suggested to him that he start a sacrificial flame for his creation. Under the instruction of the Ṛṣis, he together with Śaśīyasī started the sacrificial fire, in which he called upon his son to appear through the Yajña. Śaśīyasī had also been conceived through the sacrificial flame and in the same way she delivered two children. The Ṛṣis gave the name of Vaidadaśvī to the elder and Purumilha to the younger. Both were having very strong and powerful bodies as they were born and brought up with the power and purity of Divine Truth. Śaśīyasī is the embodiment of the energy and purity of the Divine Wind. She exists in the human vital as a power of the purity of five winds and brings pure enjoyment in the human being. Another Godhead had descended as well during the period of Taranta. He was the son of Pūṣan called Bhagadevatā.

EXISTENCE OF PURE JOY (BHAGADEVATĀ)

Bhagadevatā came down to the vital plane from the great heaven. He stayed with Taranta, the pure vital existence, and acted as the Commander-in-Chief of his forces. He took care of the enemies of the pure vital and gave guidance to the three powers in the world, namely to Hunger, Thirst and Sleep. Bhagadevatā is the eternal bachelor. He himself incorporates divine joy and through his presence, beings become joyful. His appearance provides fulfilment in life and his disappearance emptiness in life. The word "Bhoga" is enjoyment. From this root his name "Bhaga" has been formed and it means joy. He is the embodiment of pure joy and by his contact and presence; human beings can enter into divine enjoyment. He is pure like the blue sky. He is the purest among all the creations; no one can equal his purity. He is pure joy. He is simple like a child. No one can keep him in self without his will. He acts in being after being throughout the whole creation. He gives them satisfaction from hunger when they eat. He quenches their thirst when they are thirsty.

He gives them rest in sleep when they lie down. All feel fulfilled by the presence of Bhagadevatā. He gives constant guidance to physical existence for achieving an ever-youthful beauty and a life long immunity. He manifests divine play and enjoyment in action and maintenance of life on earth. Through this effort, human beings become like Gods on the earth and this transforms earth into heaven.

EXISTENCE OF DIVINE BEAUTY AND IMMUNITY (VAIDADAŚVI AND PURUMILHA)

Vaidadaśvī and Purumilha were born through the energy and purity of Divine Truth. They represent physical strength to human beings. They were guided by Taranta and Bhagadevatā to the physical plane and they followed the other Godheads, Ṛṣis and Satyadeva. They destroyed innumerable enemies of human beings, through which they were in constant suffering. These enemies were physical illness through diseases (vyādhi), the signs of old age (jarā) and death (mṛtyu), which implies the departure of consciousness from the body. These hostile forces are under the constant control and the command of Kakka. Vaidadaśvī and Purumilha entered into the physical plane through the command of Bhagadevatā.

On entering the physical plane, they encountered all those negative forces, which were driven out from the vital plane. These forces remained in the physical plane to maintain their strength and cause harm to the human body. The result was that the divine forces had a longer and more violent conflict on the physical plane, than on the vital. At last, victory came and Vaidadaśvī, Purumilha, Bhagadevatā with Bhavayavya and other divine troops drove out all the enemies from the vital and physical planes. When the forces which were responsible for causing physical suffering were driven out, Vaidadaśvī took up the task to establish the rule of truth, peace of purity and joy and opened the divine beauty in the physical body with the help of Bhagadevatā. At the same time, Purumilha became busy in hunting out the enemies, who perhaps had taken shelter in some nooks and crannies of the being. Through his activity, he came near the prison where all the body builders of Truth had been arrested by Kakka and kept imprisoned for a very long time.

When he opened the prison of the physical sheath, he saw among the prisoners Bāla (childhood) and Yuvā (youth). These are the chief architects in the physical functioning of the body. Bāla remains very sincere and simple. Simplicity is his beauty and sincerity his character. He is very affectionate to all beings. Through his influence, affection grows for all mothers, for all people, even for all brutes. He is very soft, soft as a blooming flower, soft as foam, as butter. Through his softness he creates affection for others. He fully influences all newborns and protects children through his softness. Through his influence, children take up the quality of softness. They appear simple through his simplicity and sincere through his sincerity. When Bāla comes fully under the influence of Bhagadevatā and Vaidadaśvī, at that precise moment, the physical existence enters into immunity.

As long as the connection with the Truth is non-existent, so long there is no contact with Yuvā (youth), who has the strength to fight with innumerable diseases and defeat them. But Jarā (old age), who is leading the disease regiment, fights with Yuvā (youth) after all diseases have been defeated. The fight continues for a certain period until Yuvā is defeated. Then Jarā (old age) enters into the body with diseases. Day by day, the health deteriorates as Jarā drives out Yuvā, and then death can enter into the body. This is the eternal fight between youth and old age.

Yuvā (youth) is the God of Beauty. He is pure love and he spreads his charms through the eyes. Any person looking at him even once would be charmed. By the sole presence of youth, love emanates between beings to attract each other. It promotes the identification between lives. One soul touches the other by conquering diversity and separation. It dissolves hatred for others, discards the shame of littleness, casts away fear or cowardice by breaking the boundaries of limitation and accepts universal wideness. This force attaches life to life through physical appearance. That is the reason behind human beings becoming friends, lovers, comrades to each other – man to man, man to woman and woman to woman. Yuvā remains as strength, love, beauty and hope for an individual as well as for the universal life. In the physical plane, Vaidadaśvī reigns all supreme as long as the Age of Truth lasts. Purumilha remains the Commander-in-Chief of the Vaidya army to control old age, death and diseases. Bāla and Yuvā are given full power during this Age to allow the human beings to have their constant play in themselves. Through this play, the physical sheath or the body remains always flexible and light for constant change through the manifestation of the Divine Truth.

TRANSFORMATION AND DIVINE VICTORY

All these internal developments and the furthering of the Divine Truth on this earth means that Satyadeva, the Lord of Truth, is influencing this earth with his legions to make it ready for the Golden Age. Viśvadeva, Taranta and Vaidadaśvī control the thoughts, life movements and physical activities. Whatever has been described until now have been subtle changes that one could feel through the nervous sense. However, the transformation of the world for the final divine victory is not only of thought or feeling, but has to be seen by the external eye. The Divine Truth has come down as well and touched the physical plane but still the human being cannot understand or believe in the descent of Truth. The reason is because the human beings are sentient creatures who are particularly conscious about their existence in the gross physical body. We can divide the physical body into two parts, the inner and the outer physical body. Whatever has been mentioned so far was for the inner physical plane, for the individual, as well as for the universe. In the inner physical plane, Satyadeva established Vaidadaśvī. In this plane, remains the physical unity and diversity.

For the creation of the physical body, there is Sinibalya with the power called Sinibali. From the physical universality, he takes a portion of the whole physical substance to give it the shape of an individual figure. He is called "Garbhakartā", meaning the creative force in the mother's womb. Once one can understand the inner physical then the outer physical will be clear to differentiate. Universality of this force is so closely connected with the individual that at times it causes confusion and then it becomes difficult to understand. Between the inner and outer physical, there remains a great gulf. According to the general understanding of human beings, the outer physical body is a complete entity and entirely separated from the others. No connection is felt between individuals. A feeling of understanding comes through nursing a being or providing nourishment, becoming aware of each other through a friendly conversation, through a touch, a clasp and a kiss. During the period of Kali, human beings have relations based on this outward perception. Love, intimacy, friendship are always dependent upon outer activities. Work and action are the only basis for relations through which love comes into the life of human beings. Love, devotion or affection can only be shown through service, because Kali has destroyed the bridge, the connection between the inner and the outer physical. There is a big gulf in between where formerly Satyadeva had built a strong bridge.

Due to this great gulf, human beings, aware of only the outer physical, find it impossible to know the condition of the inner physical on the other side of the gulf. That is why in our scriptures, the wise men say that the attachment to the world, Māyā, has to be sacrificed through tapasyā—penance, through one's own efforts, in order to know the inner world. Many great souls, who came to the earth, tried to fly over this gulf with their disciples. A few of them were successful but none of them have yet tried to build the bridge over the gulf. They had no idea whether it was possible or not.

When Kaśyapa came to give the message of Truth, he demonstrated the connection between this separation, activity and inactivity. The inactive condition means the unmanifested state and the active condition is manifestation. On the physical plane, the activity consists of taking a form from the unformed condition. These activities could be for the divine purpose of self-fulfilment or to have a transformation. This point needs to be considered deeply. Transformation of the physical would mean a change in all of our activities—the senses of sight, smell, touch, taste; and the actions of working, walking, swallowing food, evacuating, generating etc. It would therefore be important to know first who we are during this period of Kali. We live through an illusion that the ego is the master of these activities. We say that we see, hear, smell, taste, touch, work, walk, swallow food, evacuate, generate etc. We are the masters of these activities. Kali establishes the ego, through his influence of the dark Falsehood. When we transform the word "I", that is the divine victory.

Here the Vedas reveal that the individual being is eternal, being the abode of several Godheads. This knowledge is achieved only through transformation. For example to realise that—I am not seeing, but it is Sūrya, the Sun God who sees through these eyes. I do not hear, it is Rudra or Digdevatā who hears through these ears. I do not smell, it is Vayudevatā who smells through this nose. I do not taste, it is Agni who tastes and talks through this tongue. I do not feel, it is Vanaspati who feels. I do not work, it is Dakṣa who works through these hands. I do not move or walk, it is Mitrā-Varuṇa who moves through these feet. I do not swallow food; it is Yajña who swallows food through this mouth. I do not evacuate, they are Aśvinīs who evacuate my bowel and bladder. I do not create through my genitals; it is Puṣkarasraja with Sarasvatī and Sinibali who give birth to children through these genital organs. The five organs of senses are controlled by Sūrya, Rudra or Digdevatā, Vayu, Agni or Vanaspati. Dakṣa, Mitrā-Varuna, Yajña, Aśvinī and Puṣkarasraja influence the other five organs of action.

Finally, there are three subtle senses. I do not think, it is Candra who thinks through the mind. I do not judge good or bad, divine or undivine, pure or impure, it is Bṛhaspati who judges through the intellect. Then "I" becomes the representative of the unmanifested Brahman, to govern the three creations and contain all the Godheads in it, who would destroy the falsehood of ignorance, the ego. "I" who is Idandra or Indra am identified with all the eternal Godheads without any gulf separating them from the divine illumination. This is the transformation of "I". The Vedas express it in other words—I am Indra, Candra, Bṛhaspati; I am Jagat Sūrya, Rudra, Agni, Vāyu, Vanaspati; I am Dakṣa, Mitrā-Varuṇa, Yajña, Aśvins, Puṣkarasraja. That man is perfect, divine or superman who has completely identified himself with the Godheads who are in an individual, functioning from mind to the physical senses. That is the transformed condition of "I" through an identification of all the eternal Godheads in their outer physical senses.

WHY THE DIVINE VICTORY IS VARIABLE?

Because the anti-divine forces, the Asuras settled themselves on the individual ego, the "I" became very powerful by individual effort or tapasyā. The power of tapasyā takes us to the highest level of consciousness from where the individual can say, I am all. "I" is the lord of all—I judge, think, see, hear, speak, smell and feel; I perform my activities, I walk or move, I taste or swallow, I evacuate and I create my race. The Godheads, who exist in the different senses, are bound to serve my order; they are my slaves. This powerful ego stands against the divine victory, which is identification with all Godheads. This is a submission to all different activities that are his out of nature. Meekness is anathema to the ego. This "I" with its desire and greed stands on a high status and remains in the creation for a certain period of time. It brings great sorrows, misfortune and wretchedness for the whole earth.

Subsequently, the Supreme Creator established Indra, the Supreme Divine Existence as "I". This "I" identifies with all Godheads, and conquers the asuric ego through the instruction of the Creator. In this way, the Divine Victory became varied. Truth and Falsehood conquer each other according to the decision and boon of the Supreme Creator. The Ṛṣis described in different times and forms, the fights between the Devas and Asuras inside the individuals as well as in the vast universe. The Purāṇas are very rich and glorious with these descriptions. Through their efforts to discover the Truth, the Seers of ancient times came to the conclusion that human beings remain separated as long as the egoistic "I" is there but when the "I" is purified through the identification with the universal Godheads, then individuality disappears in the universality.

OPENING THE WIDE GATE OF IMMORTALITY

When this individual "I" is identified with the universal Godheads or dispersed in the universality, then the gates of heaven open before an individual. When the person is connected with the flow of the universal streams, his power of activities, knowledge and love become a current of eternal movement. Through this experience, he feels the same streams and currents as in other individuals. This signifies that he realises the eternal consciousness, light, love and power acting through all the varied individual beings that are under the one order, law and governance. When some realised souls reach this stage, they discover that everything, all individuals are under the control of the Supreme Creator. Even a leaf cannot fall from a branch without his consent. This is the realisation of the eternal consciousness for an individual being.

Here our concern is not for an individual to realise supreme consciousness. Our aim is not also to be only liberated from ignorance. We do not strive to be in the eternal movement of activities, surrender to the Divine or even enter in a full trance. Our final aim is that all individual beings realise the Supreme Puruṣa and become active instruments of the eternal movement, where we may realise immortality in mortal life. How to do that or reach there, is the difficulty faced by us at present. It is difficult, but we know that we could realize divinity in life, by becoming conscious of the many Godheads of the Vedas in all of our life activities and in our active senses. Instead of realising the one Supreme Being, we have to realise the work of the divine beings in our sense organs and activities. This is the secret knowledge of the Vedas. Through this path, this earth can enjoy divinity in life or life can be transformed into divinity.

SACRIFICE OF SIMPLICITY AND SINCERITY "BĀLAKHILYA YAJÑA"

Only a simple mind or a sincere heart can understand that the eternal Godheads with their greatness and strength are acting together in an individual being to bring about the dissolution and dispersal of the egoistic "I" which limits him. It is not easy to understand or visualise that all the great Godheads together with the Divine King are working in the limited area of a small living body. It is dangerous to know or disclose in one self where the ego is fully established that the Divine Empire is the human body. There, the Divine King Emperor Indra is ruling over his kingdom with the other Gods—Jagat Sūrya, Candra, Mitrā-Varuṇa, Agni, Bṛhaspati, Dharma-Yama, Aśvinī, Bhagaryama etc.; all working in different parts of the body as well at the universal level to open the gates of immortality. These individual divine empires form altogether the universal body, having similar activities. Such actions are going on in all bodies just as in one single body. This is a powerful and simple thought, which a sincere heart could grasp. For the manifestation of the Universal Divine Truth upon the earth, to conceive and to understand that the whole Divine Empire is in a single body—is an idea that may seem childish and simple to the worldly-wise people of the earth. This is an idea, which would bring a smile to some people's face. The Truth is that Bālakhilya Ṛṣis were simple-minded people having a sincere heart. In nature they were still boys, but they were wise and had achieved eternal knowledge. They took the responsibility to draw Lord Indra, the universal King Emperor, to take a human birth in the limited human form. This looks an impossible task to all reasonable minds even to the universal mind.

There is an interesting story on this in the Purāṇas. Seeing the activities of the Bālakhilyas, Lord Indra started to laugh and then ordered them to stop such activities. However, before the power of sincerity and simplicity of the Bālakhilyas, Indra was helpless and even he could not stop their work. So he evolved to take this small shape through their sacrifice of simplicity and sincerity. Thus the whole universality, the Divine Empire is in the limited form of a single individual and the one individual is an expanded form of the universal action. This is the knowledge of Bālakhilya, one identified with the universal and the universal contained in one. Eternity has moulded itself into a limited individual and the individual has expanded into eternity. On the basis of this Bālakhilya knowledge and sacrifice, the Divine Emperor Indra took a human shape on the earth with the name of Darbhya.

Chapter 12

ADVENT OF THE GOLDEN AGE

Through the simple and sincere sacrifice of the Bālakhilya Yajña, the supreme soul was drawn to take birth in the limited human form. There were divine births even amongst common human beings. The supreme light from the divine beings filled some keen, pure, simple and sincere hearts which then proceeded to take birth in the human mother's womb. This was then followed with a sheath of māyā covered with the ignorant love and affection of humans. The Divine Māyā of the supreme beings entered in the human sheaths just as a sharp sword penetrates in its leather sheath. These divine births would take place at the present time of the Kaliyuga. Those beings would be self-manifested. Their activities would cause the change and turn humanity towards the Golden Age. These supreme beings would take an ordinary human birth.

DIVINE BIRTH IN THE HUMAN IGNORANCE (DARBHYA) THE DIVINE KING

They would take human birth under the names of Darbhya, Kirtya, and Yauvanāśva etc., who actually would be Indra, Candra, Sūrya and other Godheads in different parts of the world. Darbhya took birth in Bengal as an incarnation of Indra. He was educated according to the modern methods, the scientific method of education—where the scientist does not experience the spiritual knowledge of Truth. Knowledge depended on the scientific method of discovery, where one learnt nature's rules and activities, based on ignorance. He had discussions with his professors on this point and they had no answer to his questions. He spoke through his inner knowledge and the professors had to admit defeat. They were initially angry on hearing his arguments but he quietly managed to demonstrate to them the truth of his beliefs. They were very impressed and started believing in the Divine Truth. During the course of these discussions and through the pressure put on him by the questions of the professors, he was forced to disclose his divinity. These professors were astonished to hear and see the divine manifestation in a human form. Soon the other students came to know about it. Among the students, a few appreciated Darbhya's lecture immensely and recognised it as their own inner Truth. They went to see Darbhya and thus came to know about their own inner divinity. Through this inner divine knowledge, they established physical relations between each other through marriages. Darbhya gave his sister to Kirtya, Kirtya gave his sister to Yauvanāśva and Yauvanāśva gave his sister to Darbhya. Subsequently, they had communications with their countries and the leaders of their countries willingly offered their state governance to Darbhya.

They wanted Darbhya to establish himself as an emperor and tell the world about his divinity. There came some opposition from anti-imperialistic thoughts. Some people after having bitter experiences of governments formed by the people—democracies—came to join Darbhya. For this reason, they were interested in establishing a spiritual empire on the earth for perfect peace and world unity. On the way of establishing a divine kingdom, there was a great fight between the two great parties—one being the anti-imperialistic communist party and the other the imperial idealistic democratic party.

The rising India stood up with the divine message for a peaceful settlement. The anti-imperialistic party did not accept this solution although they praised it in theory. When they tried to wield their influence over India, they were instantly rebuffed by her soul power. Even the leaders of India were astonished to see her immediate preparation by collective identification. The peace proposal of the leaders was turned down. Then they had to think about their defence due to the attack of the anti-divine non-imperialistic party. In the clashes, they had to learn to advance further towards divinity. Some of the opposing parties were crushed and some learnt from the difficult way by taking the false path. They all submitted after understanding their mistake.

Darbhya started his works at this moment. He started to think of dissolving the separation of the world states and bringing them together into one ideal divine kingdom. At that moment, Piṅgala Maheśvara appeared before him and told him that he himself was divine. His work was to establish a world state. However, he could not solve the problems faced by the present state. Kalki, the incarnation of Viṣṇu would manifest and solve the problems. He would appear in a state sacrifice or Yajña. To this end, he should start the world state sacrifice.

Then Darbhya started the Yajña of the States by worshipping the Divine Imperial King with the Vedic hymns of Indra. At the end of that Yajña, Kalki manifested himself before Darbhya as an ordinary human figure. Others could not recognise him. Only Darbhya and Kalki were able to recognise each other and conclude a friendship. With the guidance of Kalki, all the ideas of separation were removed. They brought about an identification of world states on the basis of knowledge of God's activities as they were being carried out in an individual being through the various sense organs. Similarly, this was enacted on the global level. The Presidents and Leaders of different States were being influenced and guided by the various Godheads and Darbhya was established as the Supreme Ruler to bring about his divine rule upon the earth. Then came Vasukra, son of Indra as the son of Darbhya. He was born and brought up as a divine child and trained fully in the divine culture. He was announced as a divine man upon the earth and was under the full influence of Kalki and Satyadeva.

CONQUEROR OF IGNORANCE "KALKI" INCARNATION OF VIṢṆU

Kalki took birth in a poor family. All around him was poverty. He led a very simple and ordinary life. He lived unnoticed among the neighbours, friends, and relatives. He did not go through the formal earthly education and did not obtain a foreign degree. Due to this, he did not receive any importance among the people. He was completely ignored. He came to the state sacrifice without invitation as a servant accompanying a famous leader who was cordially invited.

At the end of the Yajña, all were seated and absorbed in the calm, quiet and divine atmosphere of the sacrificial "Udgītha" songs of Vedic hymns to Lord Indra, when suddenly in the blue sky appeared a big circle of beautiful pure dazzling white light. The sacrificial fire from below rose progressively higher till it was touching the big circle of light. All the spectators were thrilled and spellbound when they saw the Divine Vision. At precisely this time, Kalki went to Darbhya and told him that he himself was an incarnation of Viṣṇu. They established their eternal friendship with a stream of never-ending love flowing between Darbhya and Kalki.

They discussed how to dissolve the stubborn ignorance from the earth and to manifest the eternal knowledge. They conquered the dense egoism, which enveloped the human consciousness and separated it from divine consciousness. Darbhya and Kalki managed to remove this separation and thus opened up the gulf between earth and heaven. Then followed the birth of Vasukra, son of Darbhya, which was the divine birth on earth that had been announced by Kalki. They made a programme for world unity and peace, which would finally lead to a divine kingdom in the world. To establish a divine empire and to govern this earth by a peaceful divine ruler, they selected an emperor. It was Vasukra. For his coronation, they invited Indrasnusha, the power of Vasukra to act as the Divine Empress upon the earth. For the Divine Coronation, they invited all Godheads and Ṛṣiṣ to manifest upon the earth. At that moment, they made a bridge over the gulf to make a connection between the outer and the inner world and Devayāṇa manifested so that the guests from heaven could come directly to the earth.

A TRANSITIONAL PERIOD

When Darbhya drove out Arbuda from this creation under the guidance of Kalki, then men could understand their own shortcomings, and then only were they able to realise their own self. They learnt in their existence to depend on divine forces, to develop themselves or to maintain their daily affairs for the manifestation of the Divine. They realised that the divine forces were acting through the different human senses and doing their work, which was influenced by the Godheads. Human beings realised that as different Gods were doing their daily activities; they did not have to do anything.

After reaching that stage of development, they became seers and witnesses or "Sākṣi-puruṣa" to the divine activities being done by them, and they enjoyed the fruits of the Divine activities and became a "Bhoktā-puruṣa". Calling for Divine activities to open a new chapter by finishing one action after another they became an "Anumanta-puruṣa."

These are the three faculties that remained with the human beings—to see, to call and to enjoy the effects of the divine activities. Thus they became liberated from all sufferings, repentance, grief and illness. They enjoyed heaven on earth, lived and behaved at all times like Gods and Goddesses. That is the new divine or supramental race that will live on this earth. It will consist of human beings who have realised their divinity and who live accordingly.

Chapter 13

THE GOLDEN AGE

When the false egoistic "I" was removed from the earth, then Truth manifested. It was as if the clouds had been dispersed by the appearance of the Sun. Similarly, the Lord of Truth, Satyadeva appeared before the people and the clouds of the egoistic "I" disappeared. The truth-enlightened people of the earth were very glad to see the great conference. This was an astounding meeting with the countries of the world being represented by groups of people together with Godheads, Goddesses, Ṛṣi̇s, Ṛṣikās, Kings, Queens and Heroes from previous ages.

The Ṛṣis indicated which country, represented by its culture, education, arms and ammunitions, would be allocated to a particular Godhead. They indicated which Godhead would rule through their self-knowledge. In this way, the Ṛṣis made a classification of the various countries. After arranging the divine status of each country, they were able to make a united empire of the world. The various Godheads of Heaven with their individual activities exist in a divine accord under the Supreme Divine King Indra. Similarly, peace and unity on earth was established with the Heads of States – Presidents, and Kings under Darbhya. A peaceful unity without any diversity was formed. The Ṛṣiṣ also separated and assisted the particular Godheads to remain vigilant and to maintain the united consciousness amongst the peoples of the earth.

CORONATION OF VASUKRA

Then the coronation of Vasukra commenced to establish him as a Divine Emperor of the whole world that comprised all world states. With this step, heaven came down on earth—with its simplicity, sincerity, immortality and immunity; by spreading pure joy, love and ananda and by removing birth and death to begin the Golden Age.

Vasukra, son of Indra, came to the earth when Darbhya invoked him through his Yajña. He entered into the womb of Kṣeti and took his human birth on this earth. He developed himself on earth in his divine consciousness by frolicking as a young boy. Then he was educated by the Ṛṣiṣ through his inner vision and guidance and was taught to use divine arms and weapons by Skanda and Vāyudevatā. At the moment of his coronation, the crown and garland came from heaven. His Empress, Indrasnusā, his own power, came to this earth directly without passing through a mortal mother's womb. She came to the earth having a shape of condensed ether. She appeared on the earth in a thin transparent ethereal body, her enlightened soul glittering with light, love and joy. Her body could be changed at any time by her own will. In this divine formation, she got the name "Ūrnavatī" by the Ṛṣis. She brought with her heavenly ornaments, jewels, garlands and crown. Among these jewels, a few offerings were also from the earth. A Ṛṣi became the Priest and took responsibility for the coronation ceremony and all the involved auspicious events. Thus this great ceremony was completed with the hymns of the divine kingdom.

GOLDEN AGE MANIFESTED

After the coronation of Vasukra, Darbhya and Kalki stayed for a short period on the earth. Then they left for heaven to go to their own place. At that moment, the people of the earth were fully enlightened with the divine light, consciousness, love and ānanda. They were able to understand their own divinity and their work on the earth. They realised that they had an immortal existence, and that they had manifested from immortality. They were in reality sons of immortality "Amṛtasya Putrāḥ" as the Veda says. They became conscious that the Creator had created this universe with its nature, wealth and food for the enjoyment of the people, in the course of a continuous dramatic play of love and ānanda.

The Divine King Vasukra did not collect wealth or taxes to establish or enrich his treasury. He did not levy taxes on the wealth earned or collected by the people. Under the rules of his divine government, the food or wealth that had been earned or collected, by the citizen's own labour, would be for them only. There would be no income tax and people could use that wealth as they wished. Property and land needed by the people could be acquired. There were no taxes on the land. However, land that was of no use to them or had been unnecessarily acquired was considered a crime and for that people received punishment. There was no valuation of the land, bought from the other party. Under his rule all would have equal claim on the land. People through their birth received a right to their motherland. All the property, wealth of earth and nature belonged to their father. Thus, their father enriched the people. The mother earth gave equal authority to all her children on her treasury. She provided them with the feeling of need, power of activities and intelligence to collect the riches. She divided her riches by her own will according to the necessities of her children. In this way the people on the earth enjoyed the bounties of the earth according to their needs, power and intelligence.

The only rule that existed was that the unused portion of the properties and wealth that the people earned or collected, was to be offered willingly to the state government. Without any pressure or imposition from the government, the people had to donate what they did not need. This was a very gentle form of government. The main income of the Government was from places where generally people do not go or cannot go. These were the forests, mountains, rivers, lakes and oceans, seas etc. The Government could collect all wealth from such areas. Production from under the ground, namely operation of mines for the production of precious metals, stones, coal etc., would be under the Government. However, the government must not try to conduct business in these areas. People could help themselves and take whatever they required; the rest would belong to the Government. If any state had deficits in certain materials, they could exchange them with another state that had a surplus. Only such trade existed in the divine government.

The main activity of Vasukra, through the divine governing body, was to arrange to provide inner protection to men and women from attacks of the negative forces. Under the divine government, not much importance was given to arrangements, rules and regulations. Instead, there was full freedom for the people. They could regulate and control themselves. The King's powers and forces were engaged to locate and plug any loopholes, weak areas, faults, mistakes or defects, through which negative forces like passion, anger, greed, stupidity, egoism, jealousy, disease, old age, fear of death etc., could enter into the atmosphere. These forces had been very active during the Age of Kali. Darbhya drove them out of the world in the beginning of the Age of Truth with the help of Satyadeva. Vasukra's troops were engaged to stop these evils from reentering into the earth atmosphere.

Under his instruction and guidance, the people of the earth came to know how to protect themselves against the attacks of the evil forces. They also learnt how to protect themselves by allowing the free play of divine power within them. Vasukra had the authority to command the Divine Powers on earth, like Lord Indra in heaven, so earth too became like heaven.

Vasukra, in one of his functions, controlled completely the functioning of death, whether willing or unwilling. Death was forced to leave this earth and to give up her control over the longevity of all beings. Vasukra banished death completely from this earth. Instead he made a connection with Yama-Dharmarāja, to allow human beings to leave this earth willingly. Men could live as long as they wished and when they wanted to go to heaven, they could call on Dharmarāja to open the doors of heaven. Vasukra left this earth after completing his tasks and proceeded directly to heaven with his transformed body.

KINGDOM OF VASUS AND PERFECTION OF DEVĀYAṆA

Vasukra remained for one thousand years on this earth to establish his reign. At the end of his life, he called his son Vasukrid from heaven to give charge of his divine kingdom to him. Vasukrid descended, along with his power Vasusaṅga, directly on this earth with their illumined divine bodies. Vasukra enthroned Vasukrid and his power Vasusaṅga. He left Urnavati on this earth to change the method of human birth on the earth. From that time, human beings could manifest directly with divine bodies. Then Vasukra went directly to heaven without undergoing any change through mortal death. This is one of the very important signs of the Golden Age. This is in contrast to the Iron Age, where each and every person takes birth through the mother's womb. Even an incarnation of the Supreme, would leave his mortal body on the earth and then proceed to the other plane. Here we have Vasukra who took birth through his mother's womb, then went on to manifest his divine consciousness by conquering the dark forces of death. He transformed his mortal body into immortality. Thus he was able to violate the rigid rules of the Iron Age and he opened a wide passage for the people of the earth.

Vasukrid enabled the souls to manifest upon the earth directly and the problems faced during ordinary births were removed. He himself came directly from heaven and thus avoided the secret path through his mother's womb. As his divine mother was on the earth in a divine body, she could invoke her son and called him to manifest through her directions. From the time of Vasukrid, the problems regarding birth and death were removed even for the ordinary beings. They were connected with the immortal world and mortality was banished from the earth.

During his reign, human beings enjoyed earth like heaven. In health, they achieved immunity from all diseases. They remained in a constant youthful condition and had a divine beauty. They became completely liberated from sexual thirst and other desires. They achieved their natural vital fulfilment and remained in unceasing joy and happiness. They had no reason, chance or wish to allow the negative feelings of anger, greed, passion, jealousy and stupidity to enter into them. The base of all these negative feelings was ego and that had been completely destroyed through the influx of divine forces in the earth atmosphere. Through this change, humanity was enjoying divinity. There were no difficulties, which had to be solved, no dilemmas to be clarified. There remained no hidden problem that had to be solved in the future.

Vasukrid remained for a thousand years on this earth, and then he invoked his son **Vasukarṇa** and enthroned him, and gave him the whole responsibility and departed for heaven.

Vasukarṇa descended with his power Vasupriya on this earth like his father. His main activity was to show, how a soul could take the shape of a body without entering into the mother's womb. Whether to take a big formation or a small one was a secret, which remained with him. This is one of the divine secrets, which has remained hidden from those who have not received immortality. The Demons and Asuras sometimes came to know this secret through their power of severe penance. Sometimes the yogis or sages can learn this secret through their yogic austerities, which is an accomplishment of their yoga. That is true in other ages. When in the Golden Age, Vasukarṇa came down to the earth; he himself opened the secret of the physical transformation of the earthly people by which they can have a body like god. Persons could appear and disappear according to their own will. Vasukarṇa remained for a thousand years on this earth and then he called his son Vasurocisa, put on him his own throne and returned back to heaven.

Vasurocisa came down to the earth with his power Vasukānta and gave clairvoyance to the human beings. The normal eyes of the human beings became clairvoyant instruments to see events in the distance, not only in any part of the earth, but also in other worlds. In some Yoga Śāstras it is said that some sages through their own efforts and practice of yoga have achieved this faculty. But King Vasurocisa gave it to all people for common use, through which they could see events everywhere. They did not have to travel to these places to see them. This power remained on the earth till the Age of Truth or the Golden Age remained. At the end of the Golden Age, this power was withdrawn. Vasurocisa remained on this earth for a thousand years, then he called his son Vasuśruta, enthroned him on his own place, handed him all the responsibilities, and went to heaven.

Vasuśruta, like his father, descended on the earth with his power Vasuvara. He gave the power of distant hearing, existing in the universal nature, through which people can hear talks from any part of the world, whatever conversations or messages they wished to listen to. This power was not only restricted to sounds emanating only from this world. They could also hear from other worlds, even the conversations between Ṛṣis and Gods. They could hear all conversations in heaven just like the Gods can hear the hymns of the people of the earth from the heaven. Through the activities of Vasurocisa and Vasuśruta, the concept of time and space vanished. People could talk with and listen to other people from near or from the farthest end of the world or from heaven or earth. People and Gods could see each other and talk without any barrier. This power remained on the earth till the Golden Age remained and then it disappeared. Vasuśruta remained on this earth for a thousand years shouldering his responsibilities and then he called his son Vasuyuva, gave him his throne, and returned to heaven.

Vasuyuva descended on the earth with his power Vasulata. While his father gave the power of listening to the people of the earth, he brought down the power of all pervading love. This had an impact on the behaviour of individuals in gesture, posture and conversation. He gave to the people the divine rhythm as well as art and beauty for their expression. By his influence and in his reign, everyone felt like a united body in spite of being separated in innumerable bodies. There was no diversity, no misunderstanding or any hint of discord in their expression. Not the least depression could enter into the atmosphere. People were constantly happy through their conversations and their understanding. This was the divine blessing upon the earth. This power he kept until the end of the Golden Age and then it disappeared. He remained also for a thousand years and then went to heaven. After him followed his son Vasuna who had also come directly from heaven.

Vasuna came with his power Vasundharā on this earth. After his father brought to the earth all pervading love, rhythm, art and beauty; he brought down the power of divine wealth and riches. Under his reign and influence, the earth grew richer in all aspects. She became more fertile, generated more flowers, fruits and plants. The earth also grew richer and accumulated more jewels, stones and metals, oils and coals etc. The earth and the persons living there became very rich in all respects. There was no poverty. Beggary vanished from the face of the earth. Greed, passion and jealousy could not enter into the earth atmosphere. This power remained until the end of the Golden Age and then it withdrew. Then came Vasumana, Vasuna's son from heaven, after a thousand years of his rule.

Vasumana came to the earth with his power Vasumatī. He protected, preserved and increased the wealth and riches of the earth. Whatever bounties the former Vasus had provided, he maintained and increased them. As he was the last Vasu on the throne and had no child, whom he could invoke to come and take his throne, he started a Yajña, a sacrifice for obtaining a child. On worshipping the fire before water, the Aśvadevatā manifested from the water as a young boy having a red colour, fully armed. Vasumana called him Rohidaśva, left him in full charge of the earth, and retired to heaven.

EXCHANGE OF VASU RACE

Rohidaśva ruled over the earth for five hundred years. He remained a bachelor. The divine powers that were active on the earth took care of him as a mother. He worshipped these powers and worked under their guidance. He did not possess divine powers, but he was their child. He did not develop anything new nor did he allow any capability to be lost. He protected all that had been achieved by his forefathers. As instructed by the divine powers, he also organised a Yajña to obtain a child from the sacrificial flame. This Yajña continued for a long time until he was able to draw out the seed from the eternity in to the sacrificial flame. From there a male being came out who was just like a young boy. Rohidaśva gave him the name Traivrişnu and gave him his throne, left him in charge of all the responsibilities and withdrew to heaven.

Traivrişnu was a manifestation from the eternity just like the Creator at the beginning of creation. He manifested the power from himself to manifest his creation. The Creator engaged his power for the creation but Traivrişnu engaged the power for his activities. He (Traivrişnu) was a passive personality on the earth, but his power was added to the powers of the Vasus. At that moment, Arbuda, the evil power, was gloating from afar and watching the condition of the creation and planning how to enter into the earth atmosphere again. He observed that the powers were active in the universe but the male force was passive. He saw that the earth was full of divine riches and wealth, he was very eager and greedy to enter there and desired to possess those divine forces that were acting through the creation.

Traivrişnu remained for five hundred years and he had no child to continue the divine race. He did a Yajña for a son. Through the power of the Yajña, three powers manifested, who together would manifest the son of Traivrişnu. They are "Kāmarūpavihaṅgama" or birds that could take any shape or formation whenever they wished. Their names were Aruṇa,

Ariṣṭnemi and Tārkṣya. These three powers made one formation that came out from the Yajña like a young boy. Traivriṣnu gave him the name of Traiaruna and handed his throne to him.

A TRANSMUTATION, KINGDOM OF TRAIARUNA

When Traiaruna came to power, he wanted to enjoy himself as a divine king upon the earth. He wanted to use the divine powers, those who had come to this earth from heaven, for his own enjoyment. However, these divine powers were unwilling to tolerate such imperial edicts, which caused a discordant note in the divine plan. They, then, made a complaint to the Supreme Court.

Urnavati complained to the Divine Empress Śacī, who had left the earth for heaven, as she had been disgusted by the activities of Traiaruna. In heaven her name was Indrasnusā. She appealed to the Divine Queen, as she was her daughter-in-law. Śacī, the Divine Empress, was the Empress of all divine powers. She said, "O Mother of Heaven! O Empress of all Divine Śaktis! Listen to the present condition of the earth. We were all working under your guidance. You decided that we have to work on the earth as we were working in heaven. At present, the Vasu race is completed. Now a male being has come from other sources. He cannot be our Lord." To this Śacī replied that he could not rule over the divine powers.

CURSE OF SACI, APPEARANCE OF ARBUDA

Indrasnusā added, "I have left the earth for this reason and have come to stay in heaven. Please allow me to stay. Vasusaṅga is also appealing through me for you to allow her to leave the earth." Śacī asked her to wait there, took an earthly dress and went to see for herself the conditions on the earth. She saw the doings of Traiaruna and was very displeased.

She confronted the earth, Pṛthivī, and told her, "O Mahī, I am sorry to see you in your immortality. You have allowed the divine powers to function under the dictatorship of

Traiaruna. These divine powers have complained to me about the state of your immortality."

At that moment, Pṛthivi, the earth, was not so conscious of the fact that the power of the sacrifice of Arbuda was influencing her. She replied, "This is not true, O Śacī! You are always jealous about my immortality. You wish to take it away. For this reason you have come to tell me about these false claims. There is no such imposition on the divine forces." Śacī replied, "O Mahī! Thou art always disobedient and stubborn with thy peculiar nature. That is why this immortality will not last." With this curse from Śacī, the earth became very depressed and angry. She told Śacī, "If I am disobedient and stubborn! Let me be like that. I do not want to remember you." Śacī left the earth with Vasusaṅga and informed the Divine Emperor, Indra, about the condition of the earth.

When the Divine Empress Śacī disappeared, Arbuda appeared before the earth and told her, "O Mahī! Why art thou fearing the threats of Śacī? She is very proud that is why she is cursing you. Look towards me and I shall protect thee. With my power you will be a creatrice like Śacī." Pṛthivī looked at him and saw that Lord Indra was in front of her and she prostrated at his feet. "Thou art my lord, my saviour, thou hast a great compassion for the earth, and I prostrate before thee."

THE SUPREME ERRAND

When the earth was bowing in front of Arbuda, at that moment she heard a sweet but loud voice, "O Mahī ! I have come to help you. You are suffering from Śacī's curse. Do not be repentant. I shall relieve your pain. Look at me." She looked behind herself and saw the Lord of all creations, the King of Gods, Lord Indra himself, who a few moments before had been in front of her. Both had the same appearance, dress etc. She started wondering who was real. She put a question, "Are you the same Lord, to whom I was bowing? Were you standing in front of me a few minutes before? Then you disappeared and came from behind me and called me."

The Lord Indra replied, "No, You have not seen the same being, both are quite different. I am the King of Gods, I am Indra. The other being to whom you were bowing is Arbuda, the King of the Demons." Again she asked, "If he is a Demon King, then how could he appear like you as the Divine King." Lord Indra replied, "This is through his power of tapasyā. He did an intense penance to become the Divine King and immortal. The Creator did not agree that he be a Divine King. However, he did acquire the boon for immortality and thus will exist eternally. He demanded that he receive a similar status as mine for his activities. The Creator told him for a part of the 'ayana' he would have influence similar to mine but only on the earth, not on heaven. O Mahī! That is the reason why he could take my appearance and come before you." The earth then asked with fear, "O Lord! How can I differentiate between both of you, real and unreal; divine and undivine?"

Lord Indra replied, "Look at me, O Mahī! Here is my unique weapon Vajra that is not for others, neither for the Gods nor for the Demons. This power cannot be achieved by any effort or through any penance; this is my unique power, through which I govern the Gods and Demons together with all the creations. I was elected among the whole creation by the Creator Brahmā to hold this unique power and position; no one can achieve that state. See on my arms the signs of Vajra, for this I was called by the Ṛṣis "Vajrabāhu". Before my colour was like raw gold but by the burning of fire the colour has become burnt gold. Is it not enough to differentiate me from the others?" The earth stated, "I have understood that, the anti-divine influence had created this illusion in me. I have bowed before Arbuda as I thought you had manifested before me, O Lord. Tell me how I can save myself from this illusive influence? Now, I also understand why Śacī cursed me. She saw the dark influence of illusion on me."

Then Lord Indra, the Supreme King said, "Be quiet, O Mahī! I will explain the cause of this illusion. When Arbuda received the boon for immortality from the Creator, he demanded again to have my position but the Creator refused. The Creator repeated, "The position of Lord Indra you can never attain. I can only say that in a Kalpa, time will be divided in two parts, real and unreal, Truth and Falsehood, Deva and Kali. At the period of Kali, you will influence only the earth, just as Indra, but not the other planes." Then his Yajña came to an end. He was however not entirely satisfied. He was disappointed to be the Lord of the earth only for a divided portion of the Kalpa with me, he wanted to have the earth for ever." By hearing this, Pṛthvī started to shiver with fear and said, "He wishes to be my Lord for all times?"

Lord Indra replied, "Be quiet, O Mahī! He did not achieve his wish. Then Arbuda prayed to Śiva, to be your master forever. Śiva instead of granting him this boon became furious with him and told him, "O Arbuda! For a portion of the Kalpa you will be Lord of the Earth and the Divine Indra will not be able to conquer you. But in a human form, he will conquer you and drive you out from the earth. Then the Divine Indra will be the Lord of the Earth for a portion of the Kalpa."

"This was the arrangement made by Mahākāla Rudra. O Mahī! You will be bound to worship Arbuda as your Lord and to remain under his influence for a certain period of time. This is not an illusion only. There is always Truth behind the illusion otherwise the illusion cannot be effective. For this, Śacī became angry with you and cursed you. You were bowing to Arbuda, so she understood that Arbuda will be coming to influence you."

Again the earth asked, "That is the tapasyá of Arbuda and the boon given by Lord Śiva but my heart will always belong to you, O Supreme Lord! How will I spend this long time of separation from you?"

Lord Indra replied, "For this reason I have come to see you, O my beloved Mahī! Always your heart will remain with me. Whenever you suffer from hostile forces of Arbuda, when it becomes too much for you, then I will come to release you from your sufferings. With me, my eternal friend, Lord Viṣṇu will come to provide succour. Because Arbuda will not allow my manifestation at this period, you will have to worship Lord Viṣṇu. I will manifest each and every time that he descends on the earth. There will be a period at the end of Arbuda's activities when there will not be even one kingdom on the earth. At that time, my influence will be non-existent. Even the idea of a kingdom will become abhorent. Then only, I shall decide to come down on the earth in a mortal body to conquer Arbuda, to replace and to re-establish my unique kingdom, which will extend over the whole world. This will be done by dissolving the false illusive ideas of state, and by removing all isms. Then my divine rule will manifest to fill you once again with peace, unity, knowledge, love and joy."

"This will be the moment when there will be a confrontation between Arbuda and myself to rule over you. I will be with all the Godheads and Arbuda will be with all the anti-divine forces and Devils. Keep this secret in your heart. This is not a mistake or an illusion, but an eternal movement called the "ayana" by the Ṛṣis. Do not be disheartened. I shall always be with you when you remember me." Then Lord Indra disappeared. The earth understood that sombre times were approaching, and that she will be coming under the influence of the negative forces, and she will have to make efforts to fight against these forces.

Chapter 14

END OF THE GOLDEN AGE: A TRANSITIONAL PERIOD

With the passing away of the Vasu, slowly the end of the Golden Age approached. Humanity still enjoyed perfect bliss and harmony but slowly and surely in the course of a couple of thousand years, some powers gained during the Golden Age become lost. These became evident only under the reign of Traiaruna when the conflict between Divinity and Humanity began.

BEGINNING OF EFFORTS IN NATURE

According to the orders from the Supreme, Indrasnuṣā withdrew two great powers from this earth, one who replaced sexual birth with the movement for self manifestation in a divine body and the other controlled death, and thus allowed human beings to go directly to heaven with their divine body. These two powers were Vasusaṅga and Vasupriya and they left the earth. So Traiaruna had to worship the lower nature for bringing children into the world and for maintaining the Vasu race alive on the earth. He got married and had to make great efforts to have children. He had no other problem. The result was that he had hundred children. They were called Paurasha because they came to this world only through the human effort, by the 'Puruṣakāra' effort.

This was the first tangible sign of the influence of Arbuda on the earth again. Traiaruna spent five hundred years on the earth and then departed for heaven after leaving his body on the earth, i.e., he had a natural death.

COMMENCEMENT OF FIGHT IN NATURE (PAURASA OR CAITRA RACE)

Among the hundred Paurasas, Purukutsya was the eldest. He was the heir to the throne. He came under the influence of the hostile forces and suffered from hunger and thirst.

Furthermore, hunger gave rise to anger and thirst brought passion. For that reason he became greedy for his creation and was angry if he faced any opposition to his wishes. He became passionate and excited during his works. For that reason two more divine powers were not able to stay on this earth and they departed for heaven. The effect was that the people lost their faculty for seeing and hearing everything.

He begot many children, amongst whom, Tryasdasyu was the eldest. He was a very brave and effective fighter. Purukutsya, his father, gave him the throne. Purukutsya lived for five hundred years on this earth and then he departed for heaven leaving the charge of the activities on the earth to Tryasdasyu.

At the time of Tryasdasyu, there was a great battle between Devas and Asuras on the earth. The Devas were lead by Tryasdasyu and the Demons by Hiraṇyakṣya. Hiraṇyakṣya was more powerful than Tryasdasyu. So he killed Tryasdasyu and his was the first death on the side of the immortal beings on the earth. At this time, to help mortal men defeat evil. Lord Viṣṇu came to this earth as a wild boar and killed him. When his younger brother Hiraṇyakaśipu came to know that Viṣṇu had killed his brother, he was full of hatred against the Lord and wished to take full revenge and punish him. However, he could not find him. Then he decided to conquer all the divine beings along with the earth and the heaven.

Thus Hiraṇyakaśipu attacked King Citra, son of Tryasdasyu and the war lasted several hundred years. Finally, Hiraṇyakaśipu killed King Citra. The fight with Hiraṇyakaśipu continued with one king after another. At last, King Venya was defeated by Hiraṇyakaśipu. He lost his empire and withdrew to the forest to take shelter.

CONQUEROR OF DEMONS REARRANGEMENT OF DIVINE KINGDOM (SAGARA DYNASTY)

With the defeat of King Venya, the Demons had gained the upper hand and there was a demonic kingdom throughout the land. Hirṇyakaśipu conquered heaven and drove out the Godheads from there. He became like Lord Indra. Hiraṇyakaśipu, after conquering heaven and earth, was still not satisfied because he had not defeated Lord Viṣṇu. He was looking for Lord Viṣṇu through the earth and heaven but was unable to find him. When someone desires to see Lord Viṣṇu from the depth of his heart, whether devotee or enemy, this wish is always granted.

Hiranyakàsipus' son, Prahlāda, was a devotee of Viṣṇu. This resulted in a long and continuous clash between father and son. Hiraṇyakaśipu, in spite of repeated attempts, was unable to kill Prahlāda because Lord Viṣṇu always protects his devotees. Finally, Hiraṇyakaśipu was killed by lord Viṣṇu in his Narasiṁha (Lionman) avatāra. Lord Viṣṇu gave his throne to his son, Prahlāda.

At the period, Pṛthu, son of Venya was gaining in importance. Both of them joined their forces together because both were devotees of Viṣṇu. Prahlāda was very pleased to see the work of Pṛthu. He gave his kingdom to Pṛthu as he knew the previous history and then he withdrew. By the amalgamation of his state with Prahlāda, Pṛthu became the ruler of the whole earth. His new capital was called Venya Purī or Vaṅga Purī.

Pṛthu did a great sādhanā to please Viśvakarmā to form a new capital and collected all the materials. According to the request of Pṛthu, Viśvakarma made the most beautiful capital for him. This city was as beautiful as Vaijayanta, the capital of Lord Indra with its beautiful divine garden, "Nandana Kānana." Similarly, in front of the new capital a beautiful garden was made which was given the name of "Sundara Kānana." As Vaijayanta become glorious with the beauty of the garden "Nandana Kānana", similarly Vaṅga become marvellously beautiful with the beauty of "Sundara Kānana".

Pṛthu's son Sagara wanted to have a lake in front of the glorious garden "Sundara Kānana" to enhance the beauty of his father's garden and capital. He had hundred sons. Therefore, he asked them to build a lake in front of the garden. They dug the earth for building the lake, but they could not complete their task, as there was no water. To obtain the water they decided to do an Aśvamedha Yajña, a horse sacrifice ceremony. They lost that horse, as Lord Indra did not wish that they should have a more beautiful place then his in heaven. Human beings could not surpass heaven. They tried to locate the missing horse, which had disappeared without any reason and found it near the Āśrama of Kapila. They thought that Kapila was the thief and they insulted him. However, Kapila was in deep meditation and had completely identified himself with the Brahman. By their disturbance, his trance was broken and he became enraged. Through his anger, the hundred sons of Sagara were turned into ashes.

Only one descendent of the Sagaras remained and his name was Asamañja. On hearing of the destruction of the whole family, Sagara (the grandfather of Asmañja) was greatly shocked and he left this earth. After witnessing the havoc and catastrophe in the royal family, Asamañja left his child Bhagīratha to continue the royal family and withdrew himself to the Himalayas to do penance.

His son Bhagīratha came to the Himalayas to look for his father and to know more about his work. Seeing his father in a trance, he had to wait several years. Then Asamañja opened his eyes and told his son, "Bhagīratha! We still have to complete the work that was not finished by my father and grandfather. My forefathers dug up a lake but it remained empty and dry, as there was no water. I did sādhanā to bring down the holy Gaṅgā from heaven to the earth to fill up the lake. However, my impure body cannot reach the Supreme world. Bhagīratha, you are a bachelor and have a pure body. Enter into heaven and bring Gaṅgā down to the lake." After speaking these words, Asamañja left this world.

Then Bhagīratha sat on his father's seat and did a long penance, which continued for several years. His aim was to bring Gaṅgā down to the earth. At last, he entered the Supreme Abode. He sang odes to the Supreme Lord and received his boon and his permission to bring Gaṅgā down to the earth. Then he met Gaṅgā and prayed that she advance towards the earth. She agreed and started her descent towards the earth. When Gaṅgā reached the lake by the side of Venyapurī or Bangapurī, then the whole scene looked as if it could compete with the heavenly city of Vaijayanta at the bank of the Mandākinī. When Sundara Kānana was reflected in the waters of the pure Gaṅgā, it was seen as a wonder in the whole creation. Bhagīratha gave the name of Sagara to the lake to keep the memories of his forefathers alive. In course of time, the water of the lake was mixed up with the Indian Ocean through the great floods. However, the memory of Sagara of Baṅga still remains and it means the Bay of Bengal.

King Bhagīratha had a son named Sohana, an incarnation of Hayagrīva. After Bhagīratha, he became the ruler of the earth. He stayed in the Elysium Baṅga Puri, which reminded him of heaven surrounded by the pure water of the holy Gaṅgā. It had an elusive beauty with Sundara Kānana reflecting in the Sāgara. Through the work and influence of King Sohana, human beings enjoyed the heavenly happiness on the earth. Without any hostile forces on the earth, there existed under King Sohana a peaceful and united mankind throughout the earth. Even Virocana, son of Prahlada, surrendered his demonic race and kingdom to him. In this peaceful way, five hundred years passed, then Sohana left his son Suratha in charge and departed from the world.

During the period of Suratha, the Demon Bali, son of Virocana felt humiliated to be under the divine rule maintained by human beings. He hated his father Virocana's activities and wished to extend his kingdom when he came to power. Bali conquered the whole earth for himself and Suratha continued to lose his kingdom bit by bit. Even from Venya Purī, he lost portion after portion. At last he was able to protect a small portion of Venya Purī on the border of Gaṅgā for himself. When Bali became busy in a great sacrifice for doling out gifts for obtaining greater fame, at that time Suratha established his small kingdom in the small area and gave it the name 'Kola Purī' but his ministers betrayed him. They were negotiating with Bali without keeping any contact with Suratha. One day, they surrendered. When Suratha came to know about his position, he had to leave his kingdom and go into the forest. There he took shelter in Medhas āśrama and worshipped the Divine Mother under the guidance of Medhas Muni and received her boon to get back his kingdom.

At the same time, Bali received his punishment from Vāmana, the Avatāra of Viṣṇu. From the other side, Māndhātā (brother-in-law of Suratha, who married his sister Surathī) arose to conquer and drive out all the Demons from the earth. When Suratha came back to his capital 'Kola Purī', he saw that Māndhātā had become victorious over all the Demons, successful in driving them away from the earth, and extremely powerful through this victory.

He decided to give the charge of the earth to Yauvanāśva, son of Māndhātā and Surathī. On an auspicious day he declared Yauvanāśva his successor and withdrew from work. He fully dedicated his life to spread the news about the character, activities, greatness and glory of the Divine Mother. With Suratha, the Golden Age came to an end.

From Māndhātā to Harit is the transitional period from the Golden to the Silver Age. Yauvanāśva, son of Māndhātā, came to power as the ruler of the earth. Māndhātā had organised his whole empire very well and established unity and peace. He made his capital at Ayodhyā to keep the memory of his father Māndhātā, who had no enemy to stand opposite to him. Yauvanāśva conquered all opposition to his rule through arms, organised the outer world and then did a great tapasyā to organise the inner world of the human beings. Yauvanāśva remained on the earth for five hundred years and then went to heaven.

Harit was the son of Yauvanāśva. Yauvanāśva enthroned his son Harit in his place and gave him the responsibilities of the ruler of the earth. From the rule of Māndhātā to Harit there was no change on the earth. Harit gave his throne to his son Hariścandra and then departed for heaven.

From the period of Hariścandra, there was a great change on the earth, which has been described earlier. That is the moment when the Silver Age started. Thus the whole human cycle of 26,000 years started again.

CONCLUSION

We have tried to give a concise and clear idea of Devāyaṇa, as it is a very lengthy and voluminous Epic. It is a spiritual and evolutionary story of the whole world and is the history of mankind during the four Ages. Still many questions will arise, when the readers become familiar with the part covering the future, especially queries about the names and places where the Divine Beings or Godheads and Ṛṣis will manifest on the earth. They will think that if they manifest, there might be a Golden Period. But then doubts will surface in their minds about their existence? Another relevant question is, whether the names will remain the same in future? The fact is that the divine author declared the names only as the eternal Vedic existences. They could have different names on the earth. In the course of birth and rebirth, the souls are taking diverse shapes in different places with changed names in the course of their lives and activities. That is why he deals with the characters and functions of the different existences in an eternal movement in different epochs.

He gives a clear and broad picture of the play of the Supreme Drama. He says for each Kalpa with four Ages, the Supreme Creator has a new idea. This earth is a stage to enact the drama. Birth and death are the two opposite wings for the players to enter and exit. The eternal existences are players, those who are manifested here and those who are waiting behind the stage; to play their parts in different times as selected by the director of the drama. The director of this cosmic drama is the great time 'Mahākāla' and the audience are the seers, the liberated souls etc.

For the complete drama he gives the name 'ayana'. In the course of this drama, we all are players. From the supreme incarnation to the ordinary beings, everyone is playing their own part according to the script. The success of this drama depends upon the Nature, that has three elementary functions: Sattva, Rajas and Tamas. The prompter is the lower nature 'Aparāprakṛti' and the dresser is the higher nature 'Parāprakṛti.' Mahākāla is the director of this drama. To organise the drama, the director made four great divisions by dividing the time into four ages, each age having a number of scenes. Who understands this drama, enters into everlasting joy, and conquers birth and death.

In the course of this play, there is a certain period for each and every ordinary being, Divine Existences, Gods and Ṛṣis. They manifest for their activities. These are four classes of ordinary beings, those who are suitable for the particular ages. We can classify them thus:

First class beings are similar to the Godheads with their natures and functions. They are eager to worship Godheads and Ṛṣis, as well as the idea of a divine kingdom, and follow the rules of Truth without any deviation. They manifest during the Golden Age with all the Gods and Ṛṣis on the earth and make earth like heaven. In this Age, the Vedas, the great spiritual authority, the perfect and direct knowledge, are revealed. In addition, there is divine happiness, ānanda, immortality, and immunity. At the end of the Golden Age, a certain number of Asuras manifest with the second class of beings.

The second class beings have no similarity with the Godheads. Their nature and functions are a little mixed up with the divine power of existence: they like to worship Godheads and Ṛṣis, but they also mix Truth with Falsehood. They have to fight always for Truth because a portion of them is also open to the dark forces. They manifest in large numbers at the time of the Silver Age, when the Vedas disappear, but their memory remains. Then the Upaniṣads and the Epics are revealed. They develop minor Vedas such as knowledge of medicine, art of archery or military power, music, art and architecture. They remain true to the proven knowledge; they maintain sacrificial ceremonies to further happiness, peace, and unity. They live together with death and diseases. At this period, a few Gods, Ṛṣis and first class beings, as well as Asuras, Rākṣasas and the third class of beings, take birth.

The third class of beings mostly lean towards undivine existences with their nature and functions. However, there is some tendency to inquire about Gods, Ṛṣis and ultimately they want to go to the heaven. They wish to do many activities on this earth so that at the end of their mortal life they can go to the heaven and be with the Gods and Ṛṣis. They manifest in large numbers at the period of the Bronze Age when the Upaniṣads disappear but their memory remains. The Purāṇas and the Epics are revealed. They give their cultural impact upon the minor Vedas and they achieve specific knowledge, surrendering happiness, joy, love, unity, and peace, for death, diseases and other lower forces. At this period, very few Gods, Ṛṣis and the first class of beings manifest. But there are also a few Asuras, Rākṣasas and fourth class of beings who exist then.

The fourth-class beings are directly opposed to the divine existence. They announce that there are no Gods, Ṛṣis or Heaven. All this is only due to our imagination. These anti-divine beings are influenced by the un-divine and asuric forces. They do not want to accept any subtle power except death. For them a divine gospel is to be mocked at. They think that those worshipping Godheads are fools. They think that they are very wise and knowledgeable. In reality, however, they are not as wise as they consider themselves. That is why they compel the divine devotee to follow them and try to be practical. They appreciate only scientific truth that is practical and can be utilised. They manifest in large numbers at the period of the Iron Age, when the Epics and Purāṇas disappear. However, the memories of the Epics and Purāṇas remain. They write imaginary poetry with the description of nature's activities. They are fully dependent on the minor Vedas; achieve scientific knowledge and historical happiness. Passion, jealousy, anger, greed, diseases and death with other lower forces control them. At the end of the Iron Age, the numbers equalise and then gradually the first class beings increase, those who invite the Golden Age to manifest, together with Gods and Ṛṣis.

Appendix I

SHORT SUMMARY OF THE EPIC DEVĀYANA

The great Epic Devāyaṇa has been manifested in three Kalpas such as:

1. Brahma Kalpa (3 volumes)
2. Viṣṇu Kalpa (4 volumes)
3. Rudra Kalpa (5 volumes)

The complete Devāyaṇa is in twelve volumes. These twelve volumes are divided into thirty-two Maṇḍalas.

SUMMARY OF EACH MAṆḌALA

1. Deva Maṇḍala

A few words on the commencement of the epic, how Dr. Hajari became a channel to manifest this Epic. A conversation between Piṅgala Maheśvara (Lord Śiva as the Divine Poet) and Siddhidātā (Lord Gaṇeśa) on how best to manifest this epic.

The influence of diversity in the eternal unity.—A description and the cause of fight between the Gods and the Devils, the good and the evil. Both had the same father but different mothers.—Their position in the Oneness.—The sense of greatness and demand of supremacy.

A clear description of all the creations in the universe.

Description of the birth of Truth, who is the guide and manifester of the Golden Age with the name 'Satyadeva'. He took birth in the family of Aṅgirā Ṛṣi who came out from the mind of Parabrahman. The childhood, boyhood and play of Satyadeva (the Lord of Truth) and his meeting with Nārāyaṇa Ṛṣi and other events.

2. Ṛsi Maṇḍala

A description of the Ṛṣi Vasiṣṭha and the destruction wreaked by the Ṛṣi Viśvāmitra on the sons of Vasiṣṭha. The eldest son of Vasiṣṭha was Śakti.

A fight of the Parvatas (mountains—the material consciousness) with Lord Indra (the Supreme Divine Power). Conquest of the material rigidity and life's disobedience of that higher force.

Establishment of Vītihotra (the psychic flame) as an aspiration for the Eternal Truth by the Ṛṣis with the help of the Creator and the Greater Godheads.

3. Yajña Maṇḍala

Satyadeva saw the effect of the negative forces in this creation and felt revolted. He disappeared from the earth and went under the golden veil. So the Ṛṣis started to establish the "Deva Yajña" (sacrificial flame for the Deva, to manifest the Unmanifested Satyadeva).

The Ṛṣis asked Agni, the Lord of Fire, to become the communicator between the Unmanifested Truth and this creation.

4. Biti Maṇḍala

The meeting of all the Goddesses (Powers of the Divine Deities) for the identification of Vītihotra (psychic being) with Satyadeva (the Lord of Truth), a marriage ceremony on a universal scale. All the Divine Deities were present at the sacrificial flame (the Yajña) where the Ṛṣis were invoking the Godheads through the power of Agni. All came and took their high altar. Then comes the description of the purification of Vītihotra (psychic being). She becomes ready for identification with the Truth.

Before this ceremony, all the manifested beings from the various worlds and planes came to participate in the food ceremony organised by Gauribiti, where food was supplied to them with the help of Ṛṣis and Godheads.

Then occurs the manifestation of Satyadeva (Lord of Truth) at the sacrificial ceremony, in the presence of the Trinity—Brahmā, Viṣṇu and Maheśvara—where all the Ṛṣis and Godheads, as well as other beings of the creation were present. Piṅgala Maheśvara asked Satyadeva to take control of the Time Wheel from Kali, the Deity of the Iron Age. With this action, the creative being will enjoy the joy of immortality and be surrounded by Truth.

5. Pragatha Maṇḍala

When Satyadeva asked Maheśvara for details about Kali, Maheśvara started to inform the Gods about Kali, the son of Pragatha Ṛṣi. Here is the description of the marriage of Pragatha (son of Kaṇva Ṛṣi who manifested from the mind of Brahman) with Gathinī, the daughter of Kuśika (grandfather of Viśvāmitra). With the influence of Saturn (Śani) and the Teacher of Saturn 'Śukra' a part of the greater darkness (Nakta) was born as Kali.

Description of Kaṇva's family. There are twenty-seven sons of Kaṇva—Among them Nārada (one of the sons of Kaṇva), as well as the others, were very displeased on seeing Kali and his behaviour. Only the love of Kaṇva protected Kali, who grew up with his evil deeds. Even his parents were very unhappy. With the help of Śani and Śukra, he grew up to become anti-divine and the biggest enemy of Ṛṣis. He became the Deity to the Asuras, the Demons, the Evil Beings, the Snakes etc. When Kali held the Time-Wheel, Truth disappeared from the creation.

For the manifestation of Deva, the Ṛṣis kindled the sacrificial flame on the altar in the centre of creation. This was to remove the power of Kali and to enable Satyadeva to re-enter in the creation.

A description of the birth and activities of Trita and Dvita, the sons of Aptya Ṛṣi, who helped in reducing the influence of Kali and limiting his unbridled power only to one-fourth of the time span allocated to the dark forces.

6. Trita Maṇḍala

First came the Kings of the Solar Dynasty. The life of King Hariścandra known for his strict adherence to Truth. How he successfully passed the various tests Ṛṣi Viśvāmitra placed in front of him to emerge victorious. His life and reign has remained as an example even today.

Then came King Rohitāśva, the son of King Hariścandra. Here is shown how the son tried to maintain the strict standards of his father in his kingdom.

King Ikṣvāku, son of Rohitāśva, described here is his knowledge, kingdom, the events of his reign, his piety and culture etc.

King Dilīpa, son of Ikṣvāku, his kingdom, power, his rules of conduct etc.

King Raghu, son of Dilīpa, a description of his life, his kingdom, knowledge, power, ethics, culture etc.

King Aja, son of Raghu, a description of his life, knowledge, power, kingdom, dharma, culture etc.

7. Rāma Maṇḍala

The life of king Daśaratha, son of Aja, with details of his vast kingdom, his desire to have an heir and the efforts he made for it. How he finally attains that wish. The birth of his four sons, Rāma, Lakṣmaṇa, Bharata and Śatrughna.

The life of King Rāma described by Ṛṣi Vālmīki in the Rāmāyaṇa, in seven chapters written in beautiful poetry.

8. Lava Maṇḍala

Lava, son of Lord Rāma was made the king (after the disappearance of his mother, Queen Sītā into the earth) under the guidance of King Janaka. A description of his life, kingdom, knowledge etc.

A conversation between Lord Rāma and Janaka where Lord Rāma describes the various paths of yoga – Rāja, Haṭha and Bhakti Yoga to King Janaka and the ways to obtain complete self-realisation. Furthermore, Lord Rāma imparts the knowledge of the Upaniṣads to King Janaka in a very forceful and understandable manner.

Meeting of Ṛṣis with Lord Rāma, manifestation of one hundred seventy two Upaniṣads.

Passing away of Lord Rāmacandra—The early deaths of Lava and Kuśa through snakebites. The responsibility of keeping the name and memory of Lord Rāma alive was given to Hanumān, who remains an immortal being.

9. Bhṛgu Maṇḍala

The complete destruction of Kṣatriyas (the warriors) three times by Ṛṣi Bhṛgu (the second son of Pragatha, a brother of Kali). Then Bhṛgu undertook a prolonged penance for the purity of the earth.

The story of King Nala and Damayantī—his well known fight with Kali—his great suffering and how he finally became victorious.

The events in the life of Dyumna, "son of Lava, grandson of Lord Rāma" his life, his kingdom, etc. And his fight with King Śalva and King Madra, these two brothers belonging to the Candra-vaṁsa (Lunar Dynasty). King Dyumna died in the battlefield.

His son Dyumatsena—A description of his life, his wars, details of his kingdom and his fight with King Aśvapati (son of Madra). After this fight, Dyumatsena lost his kingdom and escaped to the forest where he remained in hiding. The birth of Satyavān took place in a little hut in the deep forest.

Then there is the description of the Kings of the Lunar Dynasty and their rise as the rulers of the earth. These are the Kings Ruru, his son Aśvala and sons of Aśvala, Madra and Śalva. Aśvapati is son of Madra.

10. Rājarṣi Maṇḍala

A description of the world conference of knowledge. There is the famous discussion on the various Upaniṣads between the Ṛṣis before Rājarṣi Janaka. In Devāyaṇa, thirty-nine Upaniṣads are included.

11. Sāvitrī Maṇḍala

In this Maṇḍala, there is a description of King Aśvapati's kingdom, an earth ruler. He became a victorious king in the only kingdom upon the earth. Still he was not happy, because he had no child. He went to do spiritual austerity to have a child to continue his family. He did penance for several years and received the vision of the puissant Mother Divine—Ambhrinī and received the boon of a child from her. Then with the Divine Mother's blessing, her power entered into his body. This power then took birth as a daughter of Aśvapati. After birth, she cried, on the lap of the queen, with her divine voice asking them to name her Sāvitrī. Sāvitrī grew up to become a very beautiful girl. She also took the place of the son that her father never had. She learnt how to use arms and became very valiant. Then her father asked her to go on a long tour to find her own life partner.

In her journey, she saw Satyavān, son of Dyumatsena, in the forest and found him to be her soul-mate. So she gave him her love garland and returned to her father's royal chamber to tell him about her decision. King Aśvapati initially tried to change his daughter's mind as Dyumatsena had been his enemy, but on seeing that her mind was fully made up, he gave his approval.

Opposition came from Ṛṣi Nārada. He said that the life of Satyavān was very short, only a year more. There was an intense discussion between the King, the Queen, Ṛṣi Nārada and Sāvitrī. But she remained firm. She decided to go to Satyavān's place; and while there she did an intense tapasyā for a year. On the day of the death of Satyavān, she went with him to the forest to save his life. When Lord Yama (death) came before her, she had long discussions about life and death. Lord Yama was pleased with her and gave her the boon that Satyavān would live for a hundred years, have his own kingdom and that his parents would regain their eyesight.

Next morning, Aśvapati came to the forest, took them to his palace and gave the kingdom to Sāvitrī. So Sāvitrī became the Queen of the Earth, and Mother to all. She had a son named Nahuṣa. As all the warriors were killed, she trained a female regiment—composed of those women, who were valiant warriors. They removed the demonic influence from the earth, under the command of Sāvitrī.

After the kingdom of Lava, the Trita Age finished and up to the kingdom of Savitri, it is said to be the transition period from Trita Yuga to Dvita called 'Sandhyāṁśa'.

12. Dvita Maṇḍala

This is the beginning of the Dvāpara Age.

King Nahuṣa, son of Sāvitrī ruled upon the earth. He became famous because he defeated the Demon Kambu, who had been troubling the Gods for a long period. Lord Indra was very pleased with Nahuṣa and he invited him to come to heaven and live there. There, one of the divine danseuses, Nivavari, fell in love with Nahuṣa and Lord Indra arranged the marriage. After the marriage, Nahuṣa made a tour of heaven and he visited the various worlds. Here are powerful descriptions of the various worlds. Then he returned to the earth with his Queen.

—A description of the events in his life, his marriage, the status of his kingdom, etc. As the earth had become depopulated and was without any warriors, he had a hundred sons, their birth, early life etc. They were then sent to various parts of the world to repopulate these areas.

Eldest son of Nahuṣa, Yayāti, became the king and ruled upon the earth. Yayāti married Devayānī, the daughter of Śukrācārya, the Mentor of the Demons. Here is a very strange story. Once when Śukrācārya was displeased with Yayāti, he cursed him that his youth would vanish and he would become old. Later on, he relented and said that Yayāti could regain his youth if one of his sons' wished to donate it to him. Out of his four sons, only the youngest son, Purūravā agreed to this proposal and Yayāti decided that only Purūravā would be the heir to his throne.

King Purūravā, son of Yayāti, married Urvaśī, a divine danseuse who left him to go back to heaven—an account of the events in his life, his kingdom etc.

King Duṣyanta, son of Purūravā, married Śakuntalā, daughter of Viśvāmitra and Menakā (a divine danseuse). Menakā had been sent by Lord Indra to disrupt the meditation of Viśvāmitra. When Menakā had achieved her task she returned to heaven and deserted her newborn baby. Later on, Kaṇva Ṛṣi, found the baby girl and brought her up. There is a description of the events of King Duṣyanta's life, his kingdom etc.

13. Bharata Maṇḍala

King Bharata, son of Duṣyanta, his glorious character, his knowledge, his spiritual acitivity, his early life, his marriage with Mādhavī, the daughter of King of Kāśī Pratardana, his kingdom and rule upon the earth.

Then followed King Bharata's descendants. Ajātśatru, son of Pratardana, Kuru, son of Bharata, Hasthi son of Kuru, and Pratīpa his son. King Śantanu, son of Pratīpa. A description of his life, marriage with Gaṇgādevī (a divine power) and how she threw her children immediately after birth into the river. She destroyed seven children, immediately after birth. When she went to immerse the eighth child, King Śantanu stopped her. So she smiled and reminded the king that he had promised not to question any of her actions. If he did, she would leave him. She gave him the last child and disappeared. Later on, he married Satyavatī (daughter of a fisherman) on the condition that his son Bhīṣma would not ascend the throne, but Satyavatī's son would be his heir. Bhīṣma had to also promise that he would not marry at all. Satyavatī's sons were: Vičitravīrya, Čitravīrya and Čitrāṅgāda. Čitrāṅgada died at an early age. The other two married and Vičitravīrya got the kingdom. But both the brothers died without any children.

14. Bhārata Maṇḍala

Son of Vičitravīrya, the blind king Dhṛtarāṣtra, and son of Čitravīrya, the king Pāṇḍu were both fathered by Vyāsa. Here is a wonderful description of the war of Mahābhārata in eighteen parvas (chapters) as composed by Vyāsa, son of Sage Parāśara. This also includes the Bhagavad Gītā.

15. Parīkṣit Maṇḍala

Here is a narration of the life of Parīkṣit, grandson of Arjuna (third Pāṇḍava) and son of Abhimanyu. Also, the depiction of events in his life, his moral stature, his knowledge, etc. There is also an account of the situation prevalent in India and other places of the world (those that were spiritually influenced). There is a concise description of the state of the world after the battle of Kurukṣetra (the world war).

16. Kṛṣṇa Maṇḍala

Parīkṣit cursed "by a powerful Brāhmaṇa" was waiting for his death that was predicted after seven days. These seven days he passed in a spiritual atmosphere guarded by several Ṛṣis and guided by Śukadeva (son of Vyāsa). Śukadeva described the life of Lord Kṛṣṇa, his divine play, his actions, his kingdom, his warfare etc. Hearing the Bhāgavata Purāṇa facilitated the ascent of Parīkṣit's soul to a higher plane after a snake called Takṣaka bit him. There is also a short description of other Purāṇas.

With the passing away of King Parīkṣit, came the end of the Dvāparayuga (Bronze Age).

17. Auhi Maṇḍala

An account of the power wielded by the snakes and their works, the action of Takṣaka and why Taxila was remembered.

There is also an account of the life of Dillika, great-grandson of Lord Kṛṣṇa. King Janamejaya constructed a city, Dillikanagara or Dillinagara, in the memory of Dillika.

As a revenge for the death of his father, Janamejaya organised a snake killing sacrifice (Yajña) where all the snakes were burnt. Ṛṣi Āstīka managed to stop the sacrifice and saved only the snake Takṣaka. There is also a short account of the life of Ṛṣi Āstīka.

Also described is Janamejaya's famous horse sacrifice ceremony (Aśvamedha), which was left unfinished. He thus failed to bring peace to the world. When a Brāhmaṇa laughed on seeing his failure, he became upset and killed him.

18. Kali Maṇḍala

Then begins the uninterrupted influence of Kāli on the earth. King Janamejaya, who was very sad and dẹpressed after killing the Brāhmaṇa, listened to the complete Mahābhārat as a penance. Subsequently, follow the details about the reign of King Kuśambhi, the eldest son of Janamejaya. He built a new city called Kauśambhi Nagara. Then follows an account of the life and reign of King Kumbhika and King Nikhumbhika, the direct descendants of King Janamejaya

Subsequently, there is a description of Sanatkumāra's work in the Naimiṣa forest. He wrote down the Upaniṣads, Purāṇas, Mahābhārata etc., to keep the past memory and history for future generations. These are the books that we read even today.

19. Arbuda Maṇḍala

From Jarāsandha's dynasty, King Bṛhadratha became powerful with the influence of the snake king Arbuda. Then follows the account of the life and kingdoms of his direct descendents Śiśunāga, Bimbisāra, Ajātaśatru and Darśaka. During this period there was no spiritual or divine influence on humanity. The spiritual world was too far from human activities. During the Kaliyuga (Iron Age), the Gods rest and are dormant just as we rest at night. The Age of Kali is like the deep night for divine activities. However, during these dark times, some immortal beings ensure that humanity does not completely come under the dark influence of Kali. These were the immortal beings, who had done great penance in the previous three Ages. These were Hanumān, Vibhīṣaṇa, Dhruva, Prahlāda, Aśvatthāmā and Śukadeva. Their taking birth in the world during these dark times led to the formation of various religions, which however did not have their basis on direct divine knowledge or spirituality.

During the reign of these kings, Mahāvīra was born as an Avatāra of Hanumān and he founded the Jain religion at the time of Śiśunāga. Śākyasiṁha (Buddha) was born as an Avatāra of Dhruva and he founded the Buddhist religion at the time of King Bimbisāra.

In this Maṇḍala, there are short descriptions of history of these religions.

20. Laya Maṇḍala

In this Maṇḍala, there is a short description of Jesus, his actions, the events in his life and his painful crucifixion. There is an account of the spread of his teaching and the formation of Christianity. Jesus Christ was an avatāra of Vibhīṣaṇa of the Tritayuga, the close friend and devotee of Lord Rāma.

Also an account of the life of Muhammad, his actions, his character, the mode of his sādhanā, his last moments, the motives of his disciples and formation of Islam. Muhammad was an avatāra of Aśvatthāmā (the immortal Aśvatthāmā, son of Droṇācārya, the teacher of the Pāṇḍavas and the Kauravas).

These were the periods when the descendents of Darśaka were powerful in the Indian Kingdoms. They were the Kings Nandivardhana, Mahānandi, Mahāpadma, Candragupta, Bindusāra, and Aśoka. Their lives and the events of their reign, their activities, their policies etc., are all described in this Maṇḍala.

In their reign, Śaṅkarāčārya, an avatāra of Śukadeva, manifested. There is an account of his life, activity and the formation of sanyāsism. Subsequently, follows the description of the Pula kingdom with a short sketch of the situation of Indian culture, religion etc., up to the time of King Pṛthvīrāja.

Then comes the invasion by the Moslems (the Gauri dynasty) and a short account of the Moslem kingdom and the spread of Islām. Also detailed is the condition of the various Indian religions under the impact of Islām, deterioration in the cultures, together with a description of the general humanity and the condition of the masses.

During the Mughal period, Śrī Gaurāṅga was born in Bengāl as an avatāra of Prahlāda, who spread Vaiṣṇavism in

India. A short account of his life and its impact on different parts of India.

Then came the end of the Mughal rule and the invasion of the British, French, and Portuguese etc. At that time, the Indian soul was completely lost and was influenced by foreign culture. The World Soul was entirely unconscious; the dark and hostile forces were fully in control of life and were thus guiding the whole humanity. Thus Naḳta, Śukra, Śani and the snake king Arbuda were acting together with Kali and promoting the dark forces in the nature of human beings. On seeing the pitiable condition of humanity, the immortals tried to save the creation and to awaken the Ṛṣis. To awaken the Gods after their rest, the Ṛṣis started their meditation.

21. Pratiṣṭhā Maṇḍala

The Ṛṣis started to kindle the sacrificial flame with the Gods to invoke Satyadeva (Lord of Truth) to begin the Golden Age. At this period, in divine association with some powerful Ṛṣis, the Creators took up the task to lead the humanity towards divinity with their powers. To manifest Truth from the higher world, they descended from the Supermind to bring down new impetus, power, light and joy of the supramental plane.

22. Aptya Maṇḍala

Ṛṣi Aptya, the Creator and father of Trita and Dvita, responsible for the Two Ages, the Silver and the Bronze, descended with his power "Ambhrinī" as Ramakrishna Paramahaṁsa and Saradamoni. Their lives, their sādhanā, their work is described in this Maṇḍala. Among his disciples, Swami Vivekananda was influenced with the power of Dvita. There are details about his life, his works and also a discussion between him and his disciple Nivedita.

After leaving this mortal world, Ṛṣi Aptya (Ramakrishna) appeared in front of the Creator Kaśyapa and described his work amongst humanity and also the situation prevalent at that time. On hearing this, the Creator Kaśyapa decided to come to the mortal world himself and take humanity towards the divine light.

23. Kaśyapa Maṇḍala

Subsequently, Kaśyapa, the Divine Creator (father of all the Supramental Godheads) descended with his power Aditi. There is a description of his descent and the choice of the place for his manifestation in the external world. There is an account of the birth of Sri Aurobindo (an avatar of Kaśyapa, the Divine Creator) and a sketch of his mortal life, his education, marriage, political activities, imprisonment and realisation of the Kṛṣṇa consciousness in jail. Subsequently, came the cessation of his political activity, his sādhanā at Pondicherry and his efforts to bring down and establish the Supramental on the earth. After completing his work in the world, he returned back to the higher planes to push the Divine Dawn towards the earth. The world would in this way escape from the Dark Night of Kali and experience the Divine Dawn upon the earth.

In this Maṇḍala, there is a description of how India achieved independence and the work of the Indian Leaders.

24. Aditi Maṇḍala

Aditi is the Mother of all Supramental Godheads—Indra, Candra, Mitra-Varuṇa, Bṛhaspati, Vāyu, Agni and Sūrya. She is therefore called the Divine Mother. Aditi descends to open the path so that the Supramental Godheads could come back to the earth. Her work in the mortal world is to clearly differentiate between the divine and the undivine and show humanity, the path of immortality. She is the only power, who holds the activities of the Supramental Godheads in her eternal nature.

She takes birth as a human being to guide the humanity towards the divine, to become prepared, to accept the Truth and to enter into the Golden Age where the human being achieves the immortal life, the life divine.

She chose to take birth in Egypt in a family, where her father was Turkish and the mother Egyptian. Later on, the family migrated to France and she developed spiritually on the basis of eastern tenets. There is a short description of her birth and early life in Yoga before she met Sri Aurobindo and accepted his sādhanā. She took up the responsibility of his work to manifest the divinity in human nature through the formation of the Sri Aurobindo Ashram in Pondicherry. She was constantly fighting the hostile and negative forces to manifest herself as the Divine Mother in order to facilitate the entry of her Divine Children, the seven Supramental Godheads, into the mortal world.

There is a detailed account of her immense work, although to the human mind, she remained in a limited area. Her work is for the whole humanity. But the human beings did not understand it. It is like the sick or sleeping child not realising the deep love that the mother bestows upon him while she holds him in her lap. Similarly, the Divine Mother is nursing the whole humanity. One day, the humanity will become conscious, see the marvellous Mother and enter into divine bliss.

25. Uddyama Maṇḍala

In this Maṇḍala, there is a vivid description about the manifestation of the present epic—Devāyaṇa and how Piṅgala Maheśvara decided to bring it down. There is a discussion between Kaśyapa and Piṅgala about the necessity of the epic and its quality, scope, rhythm and language. For manifesting the epic Devayāṇa, three great personalities divided the task as follows:

a) Piṅgala took the work of bringing the poetic flow towards manifestation. The flow of words had the same force as a waterfall from the mountain to the earth.
b) Kaśyapa, with his great power, controlled the flow so that a human consciousness could receive it and guide it slowly towards expression.
c) Siddhidātā facilitated the expression of the epic, removed all deformations and difficulties in the expression.

After the completion of Devāyaṇa, Kaśyapa withdrew again to the higher plane, where the sacrificial fire had been kindled before. He started the ceremony of Ambrosia or Amṛta, the divine wine. There is a superb description of the ceremony of Amṛta (the divine nectar) with the participation of Satyadeva together with all the Godheads and Ṛṣis. At that ceremony several Ṛṣis sang immortal songs for the Soma Devatā.

After drinking ambrosia, Satyadeva, or the Lord of Truth became prepared for the new creation. With the guidance of the Ṛṣis, he clasped to himself the Vītihotra (humanity's aspiration for Truth). With this identification, the Divine Dawn opens before the astonished mortal world.

26. Uṣā Maṇḍala

Here is described the birth of Uṣā, the Divine Dawn and her brother Pūṣa, the valiant warrior who is responsible for the manifestation of Uṣā in the world. Pūṣa conquers the dark forces of Nakta, Kali, Śani, Śukra, and Arbuda etc. Stories are included about their early days, play, education and the commencement of their journey towards the world. By the touch of Uṣā, the World Soul, Viśvadeva, awakens from an unconscious deep sleep in the humanity. A ray of Vedic light touches the humanity.

27. Ákhyāna Maṇḍala

Some unmanifested secrets of Vedic Truth, which are going to manifest at the time of the Golden Age. Here are some descriptions of the two daughters of Bṛhaspati—Lakṣmī and Dākṣāyaṇī. Bṛhaspati had married Dakṣiṇā (daughter of Parabrahman)—Bṛhaspati gave Laksmī to Viṣṇu and Dākṣāyaṇī to Dakṣa.

a) Here is given a description of the marriage of Lakṣmī with Viṣṇu. They exist eternally with their love of ānanda—there is no creation; they have no children.
b) Next the description of marriage of Dakṣāyaṇī with Dakṣa, who have hundred daughters (powers). All were

married to supramental Godheads. The Supramental Godheads became Creators with these Powers (Śaktis). The last daughter of Dakṣa, Satī, was given to Maheśvara and there is one child "Gaṇeśa, Brahmanaspati or Siddhidātā". On feeling her husband insulted, she destroyed her body through the sacrificial flame of Dakṣa, her own father. Again, the same power takes form through the mountains and she takes the name of Pārvatī and goes towards Maheśvara for identification. As the Gods need to enhance their military power, she gives birth to another child Kārttikeya, who becomes the Divine Commander in Chief for the three Ages (Trita, Dvita, and Kali).

c) After Dakṣa's sacrifice, the sacrifice, which was destroyed by Rudra—"the Mahākālā"; Dakṣa took the form of Hayagrīva for the change of time, from bad to good. So he manifests at the end of Kali, to help to manifest Truth upon the earth. A description of his life and actions.

d) An account of the Godhead Sarasvān (the Puruṣa part of action in the manifestation of the Divine Truth) with his power Sarasvatī.

e) Tales of the Godhead Sinibalya with his power Sinibali. This is the power, which out of the unformed nature creates the child in the mother's womb. This is his task in the divine creation of the physical form.

f) A description of the Godhead Gaṅgu with his power Gaṅgā, who provides communication between the higher and the lower level as well for the purification of the lower existence into the higher. They also participate in the divine communication between the manifested and unmanifested Truth.

g) Then there is an account of the plane of the ancestors, or fathers "Pitṛviya" through which the subtle being takes form and then proceeds to its mortal parents. There are descriptions of other Godheads in the manifestation of Truth.

28. Bhaga Maṇḍala

In this book, there are details about the awakened world soul, Viśvadeva, his actions and the power he exerts on the human mind. The establishment of his kingdom with the power of Satyadeva, the Lord of Truth, his acceptance of the Divine Dawn, Uṣā, and his identification with her.

Then there comes the description of Taraṇta, a son of Viśvadeva and Uṣā. He fights with the help of divine Truth and conquers the enemy on the vital plane. He establishes Truth on the vital plane. Then follows the influence of Bhagadevatā, who controls and guides hunger, thirst and sleep and brings joy to the suffering humanity.

Vaidadaśvi and Purumilha bring Truth to the physical plane and give strength to humanity.

29. Indra Maṇḍala

To manifest the supramental king on the earth in the form of a human figure and to prepare for a divine kingdom upon the earth, the three Supramental Godheads (Indra, Sūrya and Candra) came first upon the earth. First, a sacrificial flame was lit by the Balkhilya Ṛṣis (the wise boys, who have gathered spiritual knowledge from the time they were boys, and who then remained like innocent boys). Then through this sacrificial fire, the Supramental Godheads manifested as human figures. There are stories about their birth and how they grew up.

Then follows the description of the activities of the four Manus (They exist above humanity for creation of the new race).

The birth of Indra as Darbhya, Sūrya as Yauvanāśva and Candra as Kirtya. They were born in different parts of India, as before. With their activities, the divine royalty manifests the glory, power and unity. Then humanity merges in the divine kingdom and in turn manifests the divine kingdom upon the earth.

30. Vasu Maṇḍala

Vasukra, the son of Darbhya, takes birth as a divine man on the earth. He reigns as the Divine King and starts the Golden Age. A description of his divine birth, his early life, his boyhood with divine play. He learnt all the spiritual creeds with divine guidance. Then follows the manifestation of the divine kingdom and his knowledge. His Queen does not take a natural birth. She takes form from the ethereal water and is called Urnāvatī. There is an account of their marriage and the coronation of King Vasukra. With the reign of King Vasukra, the earth enters under the full influence of the Golden Age (Satyayuga).

There is also an account of his activities on the earth under the guidance of Truth. The effect of Truth could also be seen through the immunity that he enjoyed in his life and body. Immunity in life manifests because life continues for a thousand years. After completing a thousand years and keeping the memory of earth's nature as the only movement, he ascended to a higher plane. In this way, Vasukra transformed mortal death, by departing with his body to heaven.

After Vasukra, his son Vasukrid, came directly with his divine body to the earth. With this event, the sexual way of taking birth was changed. In this way, he brought immortality to the world. Human beings came and went from heaven to earth by stopping birth and death.

Vasukrid is then followed by Vasukarṇa, Vasurociṣa, Vasuyuva, Vasuśruta, Vasuna, and Vasumana. They all ruled over the earth for a thousand years each. In this way, the eight Vasus ruled over the earth for eight thousand years. For this period, the earth remains immortal, immune, unchanged, without birth and death. Afterwords comes a change.

31. Vriṣṇu Maṇḍala

Then follows the narration of the kingdom of Rohidaśva (not identical with King Hariścandra's son), son of Vasumana, an incarnation of Aśvadevatā who arose from the water having a human figure by the tapasyā of Vasumana. He was supreme on the earth for five hundred years. Rohidaśva is followed by Traivrişṇu, his son who takes a human form through the sacrificial flame and is an incarnation of Viṣṇu, the Preserver. He also rules for five hundred years. During his reign, the anti-divine again becomes active and the Demons start taking birth as human beings. From this time onwards, human birth again starts upon the earth.

After Traivrişṇu, comes his son, Traiaruna, an incarnation of Aruṇa, the Sun God. The Purāṇas describe him as a divine bird. He can take human form by his will power. Those who have such powers are called Kāmarūpavihaṅga. He also ruled for five hundred years. During his reign, the fight started between the Gods and the Demons. Traiaruna had hundred sons.

Purukutsya, the eldest amongst his sons, follows Traiaruna. In the time of Purukutsya's reign, also lasting for five hundred years, birth starts through the sexual way. There occurs a great battle at that time.

32. Sohana Maṇḍala

In this Maṇḍala, there are details about King Citra, son of Purukutsya, his noble character, his victory in the war against the undivine. After his victory, he starts the Aśvamedha, horse sacrifice ceremony for world peace but this was disturbed by the asuric influence. He ruled for five hundred years.

Asuric forces overwhelmed King Venya, son of Citra. He did penance for the help of Lord Viṣṇu. Through Viṣṇu's manifestation, the Demons were killed and he became again the ruler of the earth. He reconstructed his royal city called Venyapurī (later on changed to Vangapurī). He ruled for five hundred years.

King Pṛthu, his son, who was so powerful that he had no enemies, followed him. In India we still call the earth, Pṛthvī after him. Then came King Sāgara, his son, who wanted to manifest love as coming from humanity. As love does not come from this source, the whole family was destroyed by the curse of Kapila. One of his sons, Asamañja, who had been doing penance, was saved from this catastrophe. He returned to the palace to obtain an heir to the throne. On obtaining a child, Aṁśumāna, Asamañja withdrew again after thirty years to the forest to continue his penance.

King Aṁśumāna, son of Asamañja, started his austerity to bring down to the earth level love from the divine spheres. After about hundred years of efforts, he did not succeed in bringing down the divine love and he died.

King Bhagīratha, son of Aṁśumāna, started his meditation again and he brought down the love and ecstasy from the Supreme, by bringing down the Gaṅgā upon the earth. King Venya brought down the power and King Bhagīratha the love from the Supreme.

King Sohaṇa Sohanvarta, his son who was an incarnation of Hayagrīva, succeeded him. His manifestation was through sacrifice and he expressed the secret knowledge upon the earth. Again a divine human being moved upon the earth. He ruled the earth for five hundred years.

Then came the reign of King Suratha, son of King Sohanvarta and his kingdom. He was driven out of his kingdom and took shelter in the forest of Medhas Muni. With him, the Golden Age came to an end and Satyadeva the Lord of Truth disappeared from the creation. Under the influence of the dark forces, he suffered immensely in the forest. He did penance for the Divine Mother and received a boon to recover his kingdom again. An account of his return and the worship of Mother Durgā throughout his kingdom. At that time Māndhātā, son of Mucukunda, became powerful and ruled over the earth.

Subsequently, follow the descriptions of the life, reign, wars and the events in the rulers of the Sun dynasty, namely King Māndhātā, King Yauvanāśva and King Harit. King Harit is the father of King Hariścandra who was the first king of the Trita Yuga, or Silver Age.

This is the full 'AYANA'. From Satyayuga to Satyayuga that is Devāyaṇa.

From King Vasukra to King Suratha is the Satyayuga (Golden Age) about thirteen thousand years.

From King Māndhātā to King Harit—transition period of Satyayuga to Tritayuga.

From King Hariścandra to King Lava—about six thousand years, Tritayuga (Silver Age)

From King Dyumna to Queen Savītrī—transition period of Tritayuga to Dvita (Bronze Age).

From King Nahuṣa to King Parīkṣit—approximately four thousand years, Dvāparayuga (Bronze Age)

From King Janamejaya to King Bṛhadratha—Dvapara transiting to Kaliyuga (Iron Age).

From King Śiśunāga to the complete disappeance of kingdoms—nearly three thousand years, Kaliyuga (Iron Age)

In place of kings and kingdoms, there arise many 'ISMS'. To discover Truth, one scrutinises everything through the scientific eye. What cannot be proved in the laboratory is completely discounted. Matter is all supreme. Only what is available in the history books, or what the historians confirm, is considered correct.

Humanity yearns for a king to rule the whole earth, as they are increasingly disappointed by experiencing the continuous clashes between many states. They also wish for peace and unity that was unattainable by the many 'isms'.

When the laboratories and factories fail to satisfy humanity through their immense production of varied machinery, weapons, astonishing and increasing daily necessities, still the main desire of humanity to achieve unity and peace remains unfulfilled. Then appears a ray of hope in the East and the divine royalty establishes the Rule of the Gods, which brings real unity and peace.

When humanity feels tired to exist in an atmosphere where there is no belief in Gods, when many demi Gods exist and who with their egoistic consciousness and their egoistic influence, contradict each other and their isms, when humanity wishes for one simple way, in which they can depend on themselves.

When humanity wishes to surrender willingly their tired mind, life and body, to someone who is reliable, who can bear the burden of humanity, who can love the people under him as the father loves his children. When people become so helpless, they call from their innermost being for help and ask to, "manifest before us who has real love for the humanity".

At that time a voice arises, "I am here, O tired humanity, O helpless humanity, not outside. I am here inside in the depth of your heart. I am the world soul, I am the king of all, depend upon me. Give me all your worries and I will guide you all".

When these words of the world soul is heard by suffering humanity, then the aeon changes. At that time the Truth Light touches the earth, and the divine kingdom manifests in the world.

This Divine Royalty disappears when the influence of Truth wanes in humanity—It reappears with the manifestation of Truth. That is why, in ancient times in India and elsewhere, the kings were worshipped as having a Divine Personality.

CHRONOLOGY OF THE FOUR AGES

THE GOLDEN AGE / REIGN OF THE VASUS

DARBHYA – KṢETI
(INCARNATION OF INDRA)
|
THE DIVINE VASUS
|
VASUKRA – INDRASNUṢĀ (URNAVATĪ)
|
VASUKRID – VASUSAṄGA
|
VASUKARṆA – VASUPRIYA
|
VASUROCIṢA – VASUKĀNTA
|
VASUŚRUTA – VASUVARA
|
VASUYUVA – VASULATA
|
VASUNA – VASUNDHARĀ
|
VASUMANA – VASUMATĪ
|
ROHIDAŚVA
(AN INCARNATION OF AŚVADEVATĀ
BORN THROUGH A YAJÑA)
|
TRAIVRIṢNU
(BORN FROM THE
SACRIFICIAL FLAME)
|
TRAIARUNA
(ALSO FROM A YAJÑA)
MARRIED
|

100 PAURAṢAS – PURUKUTSYA, THE ELDEST

TRYASDASYU—
(FOUGHT AGAINST HIRANYĀKṢA & LOST)

CITRA
(KILLED BY HIRAṆYAKAŚIPU)

VENYA

PṚTHU

SAGARA
(FATHER OF HUNDRED SONS)

ASAMAÑJA

BHAGĪRATHA

SOHANA

SURATHA | SURATHI—MĀNDHĀTĀ

END OF GOLDEN AGE

TRANSITION FROM GOLDEN AGE

MĀNDHĀTĀ – SURATHI

YAUVANĀŚVA

HARIT

SILVER AGE BEGINS

|

SOLAR DYNASTY

|

HARIŚCANDRA

|

ROHITĀŚVA

|

IKṢVĀKU

|

DILĪPA

|

RAGHU

|

AJA

|

DAŚARATHA

|

RĀMACANDRA

|

LAVA

|

COMPLETE DESTRUCTION OF KṢATRIYAS BY BHṚGU
TRANSITION FROM SILVER AGE

|

(1) DYUMNA – FIGHT WITH ŚĀLVA & MADRA OF THE LUNAR DYNASTY

|

(2) DYUMATSENA (LOST AND WITHDREW INTO THE FOREST)

|

SATYAVĀN

|

LUNAR DYNASTY

|

RURU

|

AŚVALA

MADRA SALVA

AŚVAPATI

SĀVITRĪ – SATYAVĀN (SON OF DYUMATSENA)

BRONZE AGE

NAHUṢA

YAYĀTI

PURŪRAVĀ

DUṢYANTA

BHARATA – MĀDHAVĪ (DAUGHTER OF PRATARDANA)

KURU

HASTHI

PRATĪPA

GAṄGĀDEVĪ—SANTANU—SATYAVATĪ

BHIṢMA

VICITRAVĪRYA CITRAVĪRYA CITRĀṄGADA

DHṚTARĀṢṬRA (VYĀSA) PĀṆḌU (VYĀSA)

100 KAURAVAS – DURYODHANA etc.

YUDHIṢṬHIRA BHĪMA ARJUNA NAKULA SAHDEVA

ABHIMANYU

|

PARĪKṢIT

TRANSITION FROM BRONZE AGE

JANAMEJAYA
(CONSTRUCTED DILLINAGARA IN THE MEMORY OF DILLIKA—GREAT GRANDSON OF KṚṢṆA)

|

KUSAMBHI

|

KUMBHIKA

|

JARĀSANDHA NIKUMBHIKA

|

BṚHADRATHA (IN FAMILY OF JARĀSANDHA)

IRON AGE

ŚIŚUNĀGA

|

BIMBISĀRA

|

AJĀTAŚATRU (KUNIKA)

|

DARSAKA

|

NANDIVARDHANA

|

MAHĀNANDI

|

MAHĀPADMA

|

CANDRAGUPTA

|

BINDUSĀRA
|
AŚOKA[15]

15. Following Emperor Aśokás reign, his empire disintegrated into small states Subsequently follows the historical period

Appendix II

CANTOS 1–4 OF THE DEVĀYAṆA A CONCISE DESCRIPTION

THE DREAM AND THE VISION

Dr Hajari woke up from a profound sleep towards the end of a deep dark night. All was quiet around him. He became a witness to a magnificent vision that he saw daily. Everything he observed occurring in front of him was for the benefit of the world. He was fully convinced that this vision came directly from the supramental plane.

In his daily encounter with the Divine Truth, the Supreme Creator, Piṅgala Maheśvara and his Guru, Sri Aurobindo, inspired him. He knew that his Guru's power of tapasyā, his grace and his influence had made him an instrument through which a great Epic was to manifest.

He clearly heard the divine humming, the clear sound of *OM*, coming from the navel centre. He remained in tune with it and let the grace flow over him. It was as if ambrosia was flowing directly from heaven. He became a medium of the divine dictate and wrote down what he witnessed.

OM AND ITS SIGNIFICANCE

OM is at the root of all the creation and it enlightens the whole world. It consists of three letters—**au-ou-m = OM**— and through their play, the Akṣarabrahman, the primal universal sound is heard.

The creation begins with ***au***, is maintained with ***ou*** and is completed with ***m***. The nasal sound continues the transition again from ***m*** to ***au***.

With this movement of the nasal sound, the creation starts. In this way, ***OM*** continues with the commencing, continuing, and the dissolving of the creation.

This sound, which arose from the navel centre and manifested with a dazzling light, is the underlying basis of power and joy. Thus,—***OM***—is the lord of all Creation.

The Veda says that one should meditate on—***OM***—that is the image of Nārāyaṇa with four hands. He is the Lord of All. ***OM*** is the Supreme Being and the Absolute Reality in its universal form (*virat swarup*), august and calm.

The sound of ***OM*** upholds the creation. When in meditation, it is felt by everyone and everywhere, and is worshipped daily as the Supreme Lord.

Dr. Hajari heard the sound of ***OM*** arising from his navel centre. He woke up from his beautiful dream and became conscious of what was happening around him. He saw a divine splendour enveloping him totally.

When he awoke from this blissful dream, his heart was full of joy and his body ecstatic. He continued hearing ***Om, Om, Nārāyaṇa*** in a harmonious rhythm from his navel centre.

In the beginning, ***OM*** is the form of the Supreme Divinity that is unexpressed and unmanifested. From ***OM,*** the Divine Trinity—Brahmā, Viṣṇu and Maheśvara—manifest.

This primal sound is the Brahman and is manifested as the source of all creation. In the German philosophy it is given the name ***Das Wort*** (The creation through utterance), in Sanskrit it is called the Akṣarabrahman. This is the beginning from where the worlds of Brahmā, Viṣṇu and Maheśvara manifest—Brahmā as the creator, Viṣṇu as the protector, and Maheśvara as the destroyer of the Universe.

GODDESS GĀYATRĪ AND THE GĀYATRĪ MANTRA

When the creation began, the Vedas came out from the source of Brahman as a cosmic Truth light—called Āditya, which holds the complete memory of the creation. With the manifestation of creation from the vast light, a great power came as the metre (chanda), which had the power of realisation. This was accepted and worshipped by the Ṛṣis.

The Ṛṣis saw the movement of the original verse known as Gāyatrī, having three feet—each foot with eight letters—known as the Gāyatrī metre.

Au—is for Brahmā [the creator], **ou**—for Viṣṇu [the protector] and *m*—for Rudra [the destroyer]. The nasal sound, the Anusvāra—continues to flow even after the completion of the sound that manifests as the creation.

Creations have manifested by the light of Brahmā, continued with the power of Viṣṇu, dissolved by the power of Rudra and again arisen through the power of Piṅgala (who stands on the—Anusvāra—which is the continuation of the nasal sound).

First, there is the encircling movement of these three letters [*au, ou,* and *m*] twice. On turning the third time, it stops on the third letter—*m*—to create a foot of Gayatri (a metre of eight letters).

These eight letters make one foot, and when repeated three times, three feet are created. Gāyatrī exists on the *OM.* The Ṛṣis say that the conscious force Gāyatrī is the mother of the Vedas as she is the great power that manifests the Vedas. Thus three turns of eight letters, create the enlightened Gāyatrī chanda.

Gāyatrī is the source of the Vedas. She is supreme, omnipresent—and she is the great power that manifests all the other rhythms and metres and is known as Maheśvari.

The Ṛṣis, who always meditate on the Gāyatrī, say that to them the power behind this three feet verse of eight letters appears in three different colours and shapes at different times of the day.

Gāyatrī is first seen ablaze with the dawn—red colour—when immersed in the meditation of the creation, giving the rhyme and the rhythm. Meditating on the universe in the morning, the Goddess Gāyatrī manifests in red colour with four hands, seated on a goose. She is called Brahmāṇī, the power of Brahmā, the creator.

She awakens the universe, while holding in her hands limpid water and grass. She sprays water over the unconscious human being in sleep, and leads him to consciousness, making him aware of his own force and the power inherent in him and in this way provides movement and rhythm of poetry.

In her second form—she is dazzling in her golden colour, holding the thread of work and rhythm, manifesting with love and unity. Meditating at noon—she appears in a golden colour with four hands, seated on the Garuḍa (the eagle, the great bird). In this form, she is named Vaiṣṇavī being the power of Viṣṇu. She holds in her hands a conch (śaṅkha), a wheel (cakra), a club (gadā) and a lotus (padma). She nurtures and maintains the universe with a thread of divine love, pure joy (ānanda) and power of unity.

In the evening, she looks radiantly beautiful in a pure dusky shade and she manifests as the power of destruction. She has the power to destroy the creation and to plunge the soul into an unconscious state. Meditating in the evening, she appears to have a smoky sombre colour with four hands and is seen seated on the white bull. In this form, she is the power of Maheśvara and is called Māheśvarī.

In her hands, she holds the javelin to destroy the evil forces and the demons—by removing the world's delusion that makes humanity believe in the reality of worldly objects and in the gratification of sensual pleasures. In this way, she spreads profound peace on earth.

Such are the powers of the Goddess Gāyatrī. On that Gāyatrī Devī, who is the giver of purity, through whose power the Vedas are uttered from the mouth of Brahman—on that Gāyatrī Devī, one meditates.

With the light of Brahmā, the four Vedas came out from his four mouths. They are called the ***Ṛg, Sāma, Yajur,*** and ***Atharva Veda.*** The Ṛṣis said that the Sāma Veda came from the east, the Rig Veda from the north, the Yajur Veda from the west, and the Atharva Veda from the south.

CREATION OF OTHER METRES

The Gāyatrī exists in all four Vedas, enlightening the words of Brahmā. She is also the creatrix of the other six metres (chandas)—described as follows:

First, there is the powerful Gāyatrī with three feet, each foot consisting of eight letters, having twenty-four letters in all. The Gods worshipped another form of Gāyatrī with four feet—each foot having six letters. In this form, the metre was called the Divine Gāyatrī.

Worshipped by the Ṛṣis and Gods in these two different forms, a different metre came into being, four feet and having twenty-eight letters, named Uṣṇik. Uṣṇik has two forms. One, when it consists of three feet and another when it has four feet.

Another metre has a foot of eight letters, having four feet, and thirty-two letters in all. The Ṛṣis adored this metre and called it the Anuṣṭubh metre.

Further, there is the Bṛhatī metre of thirty-six letters, having four feet, each foot of nine letters, or having three feet, one foot of twelve letters and other two having eight letters each.

There is also the Paṅkti metre that has forty letters, consisting of four feet, each foot of ten letters—called Virāj.

Then there is the Triṣṭubh metre, with forty-four letters,—having four feet, each foot of eleven letters. Finally, there is the Jagatī metre with forty-eight letters—in all four feet, each foot of twelve letters.

From the Anuṣṭubh to the Jagatī, all the metres have four feet and they manifest in different combinations. The Ṛṣis adored these metres—the first among them being the Anuṣṭubh. The Anuṣṭubh metre, which is the most powerfully manifested new creation, is omnipresent and is most favoured by the great poets.

Now lets summarise the above. Before the creation began, Gāyatrī with six other metres [Uṣṇīk, Anuṣṭubh, Bṛhatī, Paṅkti, Triṣṭubh and Jagatī] manifested. The four Vedas came out from the four mouths of Brahmā in four different directions. OM, the letter Brahmā was ablaze in the eternal blue with omnipotent power, called by the Ṛṣis—the Āditya—Dinamaṇi (Sun).

THE EPIC DEVĀYAṆA

The supreme poet Piṅgala Maheśvara (Śiva) descended in the world to manifest a new creation in the Anuṣṭubh metre, and thus begin a new human cycle—(Kalpa) consisting of the Satya Yuga (Golden Age), Trita Yuga (Silver Age), Dvita Yuga (Bronze Age) and Kali Yuga (Iron Age), lasting 26,000 years. At the end of the Iron Age, the Golden Age recommences. Thus, this is the constant turning of the Time Wheel.

The Divine Poet—Piṅgala Maheśvara—appeared, wearing a mass of matted hair, to save humanity from the bondage of animalism. With a deep voice, he spoke to Kaśyapa the Creator of Gods, who observed him with astonished eyes.

Piṅgala said—"This is the place, O Great Creator, where I have decided that the Epic should manifest. With it, will also manifest a new creation. Please grant the power of your long tapasyā (penance) to your devotee so that he may increase his ability to bear the immense force of the stream of the flow of this Epic."

"I have decided to manifest the Epic through this young person, who is very simple in nature and who does not consider himself too intelligent, who has faith in Gods, and who always has an aspiration for Vedic knowledge. He is the medium through whom the verses of the epic Devāyaṇa will be penned."

Saying this, he roared in the rhythm of the Anuṣṭubh metre. Hearing the thundering voice of the Supreme Poet, the three worlds trembled and the vast Epic manifested.

The Supreme Poet said to the Creator Kaśyapa—"Behold, 0 Supreme Creator! The Divine Epic, Devāyaṇa, which manifests the Truth, is appearing haloed with a beautiful light."

"Look! The Time Wheel is turning—holding the secret meaning and manifestation of Gods by unfolding the divine activity."

"With the creation passing through the four ages, the divine intellect was shadowed by darkness. Now, the divine intellect is regaining its brilliance, which brightens up each day with the memory of that great encircling movement of all the creations."

"From the Golden Age, the universe is proceeding towards the Iron Age, 0 Creator! Look how all the creations darken with the passage of time. Now, once again the creation is turning towards the Golden Age."

"I name this new Epic—Devāyaṇa. It moves from one Golden Age to the next unfolding all the secrets of the creation. 0 Creator of all Gods, this Epic is the result of your efforts to manifest the Golden Age, the divine life, a supramental race upon the earth. Hence, this epic is very significant for mankind."

"It is divided in twelve volumes, each volume having a thousand pages—containing innumerable ślokas (by four feet in two lines) which is only a part of this vast Epic. Whatever has happened in the four aeons is recorded here in its entirety in the order that it occurred. Look at the Devāyaṇa in the eternal sky."

"See the four Vedas flanking its four sides, Ṛgveda in the east, Yajurveda in the west, Sāmaveda in the north, and Atharvaveda in the south."

"0 Great Creator, in the dark sky ornamented by innumerable stars and planets, the brightest are the Sun and Moon. Devāyaṇa is seen also as a bright star. In the divine blaze of light see the Solar Dynasty, with the life and glory of the Divine Incarnation Rāma (Viṣṇu), in the epic Rāmāyaṇa."

"Janārdana (Viṣṇu) descended as Śrī Rāma in a human form in the Solar Dynasty. He was a famous warrior with his incomparable and unconquerable power and became uniquely victorious in the three worlds by overpowering the demonic forces."

"On the other side, shining like the moon, you can observe the glory and life of Divine Kṛṣṇa from the Lunar Dynasty in the Mahābhārata. Descended from Janārdana (Viṣṇu) as Kṛṣṇa, he is famous for his activity through his incomparable intellect and knowledge. There are also thousands of other glorious godlike characters each glowing with divine power and knowledge."

"Additionally, there are many other divine characters described in the epic who lead pure lives. They are manifested in the Epic just like stars in the sky in this book of twelve thousand pages."

"Devāyaṇa, in the Anuṣṭubh metre, sounds as if the musical rhythms are coming straight from the beautiful Gandharva world in a low, deep and hard sound. Within this, now and then, some other metre is heard—just as the sound of lightning comes all of a sudden in the middle of the storm clouds."

"We see the four ages passing, just like day and night, in Devāyaṇa. The Golden Age is radiant like the day, where the Sun God and the Divine Mother with her children manifest. The Iron Age is pitch dark like night, with Kali influencing the demonic forces."

"In between, the time is divided further into two parts. Trita is like the evening dusk and Dvita like the second part of the night. Afterwards, comes the end of the deep dark night with the approaching Divine Dawn to awaken the consciousness of the people and the world. Then the Truth Sun manifests."

"O Divine Creator, see with your own eyes the Epic Devāyaṇa manifest in the powerful and beautiful Anuṣṭubh metre giving us all a beautiful vision." Seeing the descent of Devāyaṇa, the Divine Poet Piṅgala was happy and the Divine Creator Kaśyapa observed calmly without blinking.

METHOD OF MANIFESTING THE EPIC

On hearing this, the Creator Kaśyapa said to Piṅgala, the Supramental Poet, "This epic is so lengthy and vast that it would not be easy to manifest. Human beings these days have a very short span of life. To write such an epic, one needs at least a hundred years. How can a single life be sufficient to manifest this epic, O Poet of Poets?"

Piṅgala answered—"O Creator of Gods, listen. I have decided to compress time. Take ten pages a day from the epic and manfest it with your power. If ten pages are completed daily, then three hundred pages could be easily done in a month. Thus, in three months and ten days, one thousand pages will be manifested. Multiply this by twelve. Thus, the total time to manifest Devāyaṇa would be three years and four months, which is not long."

On hearing this plan of the Divine Poet, Kaśyapa mentioned that it still was not easy. He said that a human being could not remain three years and four months quietly at one place. He required regularly food and rest, which is a constant distraction.

Replied the poet—"O Kaśyapa, you provide support to this person through the immense power that you gained through your penance (tapasyā) for twenty-six thousand years. Surely then this mortal being will be able to receive this Epic."

"He will have no suffering; he will sit quietly as long as the work of the Epic lasts with the influence of your power. His heart will be full of joy, and the flow of the Epic will make him stronger each day."

The Creator replied, "O Lord of the Poets! For the manifestation of such a gigantic Epic, which is twelve times longer than the earlier Epics, a vast number of words will be needed."

The Divine Poet agreed that that was true. Also, many turbulences, obstacles and hostilities would be coming from the forces of darkness in the process of its manifestation.

Then Piṅgala asked Kaśyapa to invoke the elephant headed god, Gaṇeśa, who is the Lord of All and who gives accomplishment and perfection to all. He would also control opposition to this Epic and gather the immense number of words required for it. He added that by the presence of Lord Gaṇeśa all problems would be solved, all hindrances removed, as He was Brahmanaspati himself, who has manifested the creation of Brahman.

On hearing these words of Piṅgala, Kaśyapa with a melodious tone started to invoke the elephant-headed God Gaṇeśa, the remover of all obstacles. He said—"I invoke Gaṇeśa, the beloved son of Pārvatī, at the commencement of the Epic. I call upon the Giver of Perfection, 0 Vināyaka, O Brahmaṇaspati! I invoke the King of All who rides on the Rat and request him to appear amongst the people to manifest this Epic. I call on Him to awaken the Divine Truth on this earth."

"O Gaṇeśa, appear here before people who have little faith in Gods; take up the work of removing all obstacles with joy. 0 Supreme King, appear with the power of Rudra. Manifest yourself swiftly for the work on the earth."

"Your might is felt through the power of words. With them, you serve the Truth, and your intelligence provides constant felicity. To provide purity in words, and to invoke the Divine with powerful words in order to manifest the Epic, I call on you to appear swiftly."

The Divine Creator called thus upon Gaṇapati with his magnificent white elephant head, who has a golden red halo, and is attired in his wonderful apparel. He is the destroyer of obstacles and giver of perfection. He would fulfil the wish of the Poet Piṇgala to manifest Devāyaṇa in this world.

On hearing this invocation, Lord Gaṇeśa appeared sitting on the Rat. In his four hands, he held a conch, a wheel, a club, and a lotus. His three eyes were full of compassion, scattering grace and love all around. A pure light surrounded him and his smile was pure radiance. He appeared like the golden dawn, his body having a red colour. He was attired in heavenly clothes and was wearing magnificent ornaments. Around his neck was a wonderful garland.

When Dr. Hajari saw Lord Gaṇeśa's glorious white elephant

head, he felt he had witnessed the pure dawn. His whole body thrilled and started trembling with joy.

With his inner eyes, he saw the King of Poets—Piṅgala Maheśvara before him. With him was the Creator of Gods, Kaśyapa and with them Gaṇeśa, the beloved son of Pārvatī. When he heard their divine voices and their powerful conversation, he felt elevated and his entire being vibrated with joy. He was engaged to remember and to recollect the words uttered by their divine voices.

As a poor person collects gold and jewels that are very rare and precious, he started to collect and compile the divine words by penning them down every day as they came from above.

Days passed into months and years. He heard the divine voices with an increasing astonishment without any fatigue. His heart was blessed and he was swept along with the flow of the descending words. He compiled and collected this Epic with him being a medium.

—Extracts from Devāyaṇa, 1–4 cantos

Appendix III

TABLE OF CONTENTS

The subject matter of this great Epic is in the Anuṣṭubh metre, which is four feeted, each foot having eight letters. Each fifth letter is short, sixth letter long then the seventh letter is short in the second of fourth line. In the whole course of the Epic there are about two hundred and seventy five chandas (metres).

The Devāyaṇa is divided into thirty-two maṇḍalas; each maṇḍala is divided into several vargas, which are further divided into a number of saṁvargas. Additionally, in each varga, a different metre (rhythm) is used in the couplet at the end of each saṁvarga. Also different metres are used in different places in the book for hymns and prayers to the Gods.

Following are the table of contents of the great epic with the work divided among the three Kalpas – Brahmā, Viṣṇu and Rudra. The whole epic is divided into 12 volumes containing 1,000 pages each. These volumes are further divided into maṇḍalas and vargas. The names of the vargas with the numbers of saṁvargas together with the name of the different metres is given as follows:

Brahma Kalpa

Volume I

DEVA MAṆḌALA

1. Kāvya Samārambha Varga.
   (Book of Commencement)
   Four Saṁvargas

(4 Cantos)
Metre: Matta

2. Piṅgala Gaṇapati Saṁvāda Varga.
(Book of Conversation between Piṅgaḷa and Gaṇapati)
Fifteen Saṁvargas
(15 Cantos)
Metre: Rukmavatī

3. Dvandva Prabhāva Varga.
(Book on the Influence of Diversity)
Eleven Saṁvargas
(11 Cantos)
Metre: Manoramā

4. Sṛṣti Varga.
(Book of Creation)
Thirteen Saṁvargas
(13 Cantos)
Metre: Dīpakamālā

5. Abhi Varga.
(Book about Abhivarta)
Seven Saṁvargas
(7 Cantos)
Metre: Dodhaka

6. Upākhyāna Varga.
(Book of Stories)
Thirteen Saṁvargas
(13 Cantos)
Metre: Svagata

7. Dīkṣā Varga.
(Book of Spiritual Persuasion)
Nine Saṁvargas
(9 Cantos)
Metre: Rathoddhata

8. Rupayana Varga.
(Book of Transmutation)
Fourteen Saṁvargas
(14 Cantos)
Metre: Śyeni

9. Vṛṣti Varga.
(Book of Rain)
Ten Saṁvargas
(10 Cantos)
Metre: Motanaka

10. Kakṣi Varga.
(Book about Kakṣivana)
Twenty-three Saṁvargas
(23 Cantos)
Metre: Vṛtta

11. Auśija Varga.
(Book about Auśija family)
Eight Saṁvargas
(8 Cantos)
Metre: Vātormi

12. Sarasvat Varga.
(Book about Sarasvān)
Seven Saṁvargas
(7 Cantos)
Metre: Sumukhi

13. Bandhu Varga.
(Book about Bandhus)
Twenty Saṁvargas
(20 Cantos)
Metre: Indira

14. Arkṣya Varga.
(Book about Arkṣya)
Ten Saṁvargas
(10 Cantos)
Metre: Śālinī

15. Jana Varga.
(Book about Jana)
Twelve Saṁvargas
(12 Cantos)
Metre: Druta

16. Cakra Varga.
(Book about Kālacakra)

Eighteen Saṁvargas
(18 Cantos)
Metre: Upendrāvajrā

ṚṢI MAṆḌALA

17. Vasiṣṭha Varga.
(Book about Vasiṣṭha)
Eight Saṁvargas
(8 Cantos)
Metre: Anukūla
18. Nārada Varga.
(Book about Nārada)
Eleven Saṁvargas
(11 Cantos)
Metre: Śikhaṇḍita
19. Parvata Varga.
(Book about Parvata)
Nine Saṁvargas
(9 Cantos)
Metre: Indrāvajrā
20. Brahmarṣi Varga.
(Book about Brahmarṣi)
Thirteen Saṁvargas
(13 Cantos)
Metre: Upajāti

YAJÑA MAṆḌALA

21. Āgneya Varga.
(Book of Sacrificial Fire)
Thirty Saṁvargas
(30 Cantos)
Metre: Gāyatrī (three feet—each foot 8 letters)—24 letters.
Metre—Uṣṇik (three feet—8 letters each two feet and 12 letters one foot)—28 letters.
Metre—Anuṣṭubh (four feet, each eight letters)— 32 letters.

Metre—Bṛhatī (four feet, each nine letters)—36 letters.
Metre—Paṅkti (four feet, each ten letters)—40 letters.
Metre—Triṣṭubha (four feet, each eleven letters)—44 letters.
Metre—Jagatī (four feet, each twelve letters)—48 letters.

22. Deva Durjñeya Varga.
(Book about untraced Deva)
Ten Saṁvargas
(10 Cantos)
Metre: Indravaṁśa,

23. Ṛtaiṣana Varga.
(Book about Searching Truth)
Seven Saṁvargas
(7 Cantos)
Metre: Vaṁśasthabil

BITI MAṆḌALA

24. Devī Varga.
(Book of Goddess)
Ten Saṁvargas
(10 Cantos)
Metre: Candravartma

25. Īśa Varga.
(Book of gods)
Nine Saṁvargas
(9 Cantos)
Metre: Upajāti

26. Śuci Varga.
(Book of Purification)
Thirteen Saṁvargas
(13 Cantos)
Metre: Vaṁśathabil

27. Annotsava Varga.
(Book of food ceremony)
Fifteen Saṁvargas

(15 Cantos)
Metre: Jaloddhatagati

28. Satya Vyakta Varga.
(Book of Manifested Truth)
Eight Saṁvargas
(8 Cantos)
Metre: Sragbini

PRAGATHA MAṆḌALA

29. Pragathodvāha Varga.
(Book about marriage of Pragatha)
Twenty-seven Saṁvargas
(27 Cantos)
Metre: Pramitakṣara
30. Gathini Varga.
(Book about Gathini)
Ten Saṁvargas
(10 Cantos)
Metre: Vaiśvadevī
31. Duṣkrīḍā Varga.
(Book of Mischievous Play)
Seventeen Saṁvargas
(17 Cantos)
Metre: Bhujangaprayāta
32. Durmati Varga.
(Book of Mischievous Mentality)
Seventeen Saṁvargas
(17 Cantos)
Metre: Toṭaka
33. Durvidyā Varga.
(Book of Mischievous Knowledge)
Fifteen Saṁvargas
(15 Cantos)
Metre: Drutavilambita
34. Duṣkāla Varga.
(Book about Mischievous Time)
Eighteen Saṁvargas

(18 Cantos)
Metre: Kusuma Vicitra

Volume II

TRITA MAṆḌALA

35. Bharadvāja Varga.
(Book about Bharadvāja)
Thirteen Saṁvargas
(13 Cantos)
Metre: Mandākinī
36. Devarṣi Varga.
(Book about Devarṣi)
Seventeen Saṁvargas
(17 Cantos)
Metre: Tamrasa
37. Sādhana Varga.
(Book of Sādhana)
Twenty-three Saṁvargas
(23 Cantos)
Metre: Mouktikdam
38. Hariścandra Varga.
(Book about Hariścandra)
Twenty-five Saṁvargas
(25 Cantos)
Metre: Sāraṅga
39. Rohitāśva Varga.
(Book about Rohitāśva)
Twenty-three Saṁvargas
(23 Cantos)
Metre: Mālatī
40. Kakustha Varga.
(Book about Kakustha)
Eighteen Saṁvargas
(18 Cantos)
Metre: Lalita
41. Ikṣvāku Varga.
(Book about Ikṣvāku)

Fifty-five Saṁvargas
(55 Cantos)
Metre: Manimala

42. Dilīpa Varga.
(Book about Dilīpa)
Thirty-eight Saṁvargas
(38 Cantos)
Metre: Jaladharamala

43. Raghu Varga.
(Book about Raghu)
Twenty-eight Saṁvargas
(28 Cantos)
Metre: Puta

44. Aja Varga.
(Book about Aja)
Forty-five Saṁvargas
(45 Cantos)
Metre: Ujjvala

RĀMA MAṆḌALA

45. Daśaratha Varga.
(Book about Daśaratha)
Forty-one Saṁvargas
(41 Cantos)
Metre: Nava malika

46. Rāmāyaṇa Varga 1
(Book I of Rāmāyaṇa)
Bāla Kāṇḍa.
Twenty-six Sargas
(26 Cantos)
Metre: Puspitagra

47. Rāmāyaṇa Varga. 2
(Book II of Rāmāyaṇa)
Ayodhyā Kāṇḍa
Thirty Sargas
(30 Cantos)
Metre: Oupachchandasa

Volume III

48. Rāmāyaṇa Varga 3
(Book III of Rāmāyaṇa)
Araṇya Kāṇḍa
Twenty-six Sargas
(26 Cantos)
Metre: Vasantatilakā

49. Rāmāyaṇa Varga 4
(Book IV of Rāmāyaṇa)
Kiṣkindhā Kāṇḍa
Thirty Sargas
(30 Cantos)
Metre: Praharshini

50. Rāmāyaṇa Varga 5
(Book V of Rāmāyaṇa)
Sundara Kāṇḍa
Thirty Sargas
(30 Cantos)
Metre: Sundari

51. Rāmāyaṇa Varga 6
(Book VI of Rāmāyaṇa)
Laṅkā Kāṇḍa
Eighty-three Sargas
(83 Cantos)
Metre: Indra vamṣa

52. Rāmāyaṇa Varga 7
(Book VII of Rāmāyaṇa)
Uttara Kāṇḍa
Forty-one Sargas
(41 Cantos)
Metre: Aparavaktra

LAVA MAṆḌALA

53. Rāmānuja Varga.
(Book about Rāmānuja)
Twelve Saṁvargas
(12 Cantos)
Metre: Rucira

54. Janaka Varga.
(Book about Janaka)
Eighteen Saṁvargas
(18 Cantos)
Metre: Candi

55. Andan Varga.
(Book about Andan)
Eighteen Saṁvargas
(18 Cantos)
Metre: Mañjubhāṣiṇī

56. Mukti Varga.
(Book about Liberation)
Sixteen Saṁvargas
(16 Cantos)
Metre: Candrika

57. Kuśadhvaja Varga.
(Book about Kuśadhvaja)
Fifty Saṁvargas
(50 Cantos)
Metre: Kalahaṁsa

58. Mokṣa Varga.
(Book of Departure)
Twenty-four Saṁvargas
(24 Cantos)
Metre: Pravodhita

59. Kuśa Varga.
(Book about Kuśa)
Nineteen Saṁvargas
(19 Cantos)
Metre: Mṛgendramukha

60. Hanumān Varga.
(Book of Hanumān)
Thirty-eight Saṁvargas
(38 Cantos)
Metre: Mañjuhāsini

61. Aśvala Varga.
(Book about Aśvala)
Twenty-three Saṁvargas

(23 Cantos)
Metre: Kutajagati
62. Śabara Varga.
(Book about Śabara)
Twenty-three Saṁvargas
(23 Cantos)
Metre: Kanduka
63. Mantra Varga.
(Book about Mantra)
Sixteen Saṁvargas
(16 Cantos)
Metre: Mṛgendragati
64. Nartikā Varga.
(Book of Nartikā)
Forty-two Saṁvargas
(42 Cantos)
Metre: Jiva

Viṣṇu Kalpa

Volume IV

BHṚGU MAṆḌALA

65. Rita Varga.
(Book about Rita)
Twenty-seven Saṁvargas
(27 Cantos)
Metre: Aparājitā
66. Dattātreya Varga.
(Book of Dattātreya)
Twenty-two Saṁvargas
(22 Cantos)
Metre: Nandimukhī
67. Nala Varga.
(Book of Nala)
Thirty-three Saṁvargas

(33 Cantos)
Metre: Vasantatilakā

68. Dyumna Varga.
(Book about Dyumna)
Fifty-five Saṁvargas
(55 Cantos)
Metre: Nadi

69. Aśvapati Varga.
(Book of Aśvapati)
Thirty-one Saṁvargas
(31 Cantos)
Metre: Induvadana

RĀJARṢI MAṆḌALA

70. Vedānta Varga 1
(Book I of Vedānta)
Īśa Upaniṣad
One Saṁvarga
(1 Canto)
Metre: Lakṣmī
All Upaniṣads are in this metre.

71. Vedānta Varga 2
(Book II of Vedānta)
Kaṭha Upaniṣad
Nine Saṁvargas
(9 Cantos)

72. Vedānta Varga 3
(Book III of Vedānta)
Kena Upaniṣad
Four Saṁvargas
(4 Cantos)

73. Vedānta Varga 4
(Book IV of Vedānta)
Kaivalya Upaniṣad
Four Saṁvargas
(4 Cantos)

74. Vedānta Varga 5
(Book V of Vedānta)

Chāndogya Upaniṣad
Twenty-four Saṁvargas
(24 Cantos)

75. Vedānta Varga 6
(Book VI of Vedānta)
Haṁsa Upaniṣad
Four Saṁvargas
(4 Cantos)

76. Vedānta Varga 7
(Book VII of Vedānta)
Jābāla Upaniṣad
Two Saṁvargas
(2 Cantos)

77. Vedānta Varga 8
(Book VIII of Vedānta)
Mudgala Upaniṣad
One Saṁvarga
(1 Canto)

78. Vedānta Varga 9
(Book IX of Vedānta)
Śāṇḍilya Upaniṣad
Four Saṁvargas
(4 Cantos)

79. Vedānta Varga 10
(Book X of Vedānta)
Piṅgala Upaniṣad
Six Saṁvargas
(6 Cantos)

80. Vedānta Varga 11
(Book XI of Vedānta)
Bṛhadāraṇyakopaniṣad
Eighteen Saṁvargas
(18 Cantos)

81. Vedānta Varga 12
(Book XII of Vedānta)
Aitrareya Upaniṣad
Three Saṁvargas
(3 Cantos)

82. Vedānta Varga 13
(Book XIII of Vedānta)
Taittarīya Upaniṣad
Two Saṁvargas
(2 Cantos)
83. Vedānta Varga 14
(Book XIV of Vedānta)
Śvetāśvataropaniṣad
Three Saṁvargas
(3 Cantos)
84. Vedānta Varga 15
(Book XV of Vedānta)
Māṇḍūkya Upaniṣad
One Saṁvarga
(1 Canto)
85. Vedānta Varga 16
(Book XVI of Vedānta)
Māṇḍūk Upaniṣad
Three Saṁvargas
(3 Cantos)
86. Vedānta Varga 17
(Book XVII of Vedānta)
Nādavindu Upaniṣad
One Saṁvarga
(1 Canto)
87. Vedānta Varga 18
(Book XVIII of Vedānta)
Dhyānavindu Upaniṣad
One Saṁvarga
(1 Canto)
88. Vedānta Varga 19
(Book XIX of Vedānta)
Tejovindu Upaniṣad
One Saṁvarga
(1 Canto)
89. Vedānta Varga 20
(Book XX of Vedānta)

Garbha Upaniṣad
One Saṁvarga
(1 Canto)
90. Vedānta Varga 21
(Book XXI of Vedānta)
Śārirākya Upaniṣad
One Saṁvarga
(1 Canto)
91. Vedānta Varga 22
(Book XXII of Vedānta)
Sūrya Upaniṣad
One Saṁvarga
(1 Canto)
92. Vedānta Varga 23
(Book XXIII of Vedānta)
Akṣyu Upaniṣad
One Saṁvarga
(1 Canto)
93. Vedānta Varga 24
(Book XXIV of Vedānta)
Kuṇḍika Upaniṣad
One Saṁvarga
(1 Canto)
94. Vedānta Varga 25
(Book XXV of Vedānta)
Rudra Upaniṣad
One Saṁvarga
(1 Canto)
95. Vedānta Varga 26
(Book XXVI of Vedānta)
Rudra Hṛdaya Upaniṣad
Two Saṁvargas
(2 Cantos)
96. Vedānta Varga 27
(Book XXVII of Vedānta)
Varāha Upaniṣad
Five Saṁvargas
(5 Cantos)

97. Vedānta Varga 28
(Book XXVIII of Vedānta)
Nārāyaṇopaniṣad
Three Saṁvargas
(3 Cantos)
98. Vedānta Varga 29
(Book XXIX of Vedānta)
Rudra Jābālopaniṣad
One Saṁvarga
(1 Canto)
99. Vedānta Varga 30
(Book XXX of Vedānta)
Nāradopaniṣad
One Saṁvarga
(1 Canto)
100. Vedānta Varga 31
(Book XXXI of Vedānta)
Sārasvatopaniṣad
One Saṁvarga
(1 Canto)
101. Vedānta Varga 32
(Book XXXII of Vedānta)
Mārkaṇḍeya Upaniṣad
One Saṁvarga
(1 Canto)
102. Vedānta Varga 33
Devī Upaniṣad
(Book XXXIII of Vedānta)
Three Saṁvargas
(3 Cantos)
103. Vedānta Varga 34
(Book XXXIV of Vedānta)
Kālikā Upaniṣad
One Saṁvarga
(1 Canto)
104. Vedānta Varga 35
(Book XXXV of Vedanta)

Saubhāgyalakṣmi Upanishad
One Saṁvarga
(1 Canto)
105. Vedānta Varga 36.
(Book XXXVI of Vedānta)
Dakṣiṇāmūrti Upaniṣad
One Saṁvarga
(1 Canto)
106. Vedānta Varga 37
(Book XXXVII of Vedanta)
Mantrika Upaniṣad
One Saṁvarga
(1 Canto)
107. Vedānta Varga 38
(Book XXXVIII of Vedanta)
Gaṇapatya Upaniṣad
One Saṁvarga
(1 Canto)
108. Vedānta Varga 39
(Book XXXIX of Vedanta)
Sāvitrī Upaniṣad
One Saṁvarga
(1 Canto)

SĀVITRĪ MAṆḌALA

109. Śakti Varga.
Book of Divine Śakti
Twenty-five Saṁvargas
(25 Cantos)
Metre: Vipina Tilaka
110. Satya Varga.
Book about Satyavān
Twenty-seven Saṁvargas
(27 Cantos)
Metre: Mālinī
111. Dharma Varga.
Book about Death

Twenty-nine Saṁvargas
(29 Cantos)
Metre: Tunaka

112. Karma Varga.
Book of Work
Twenty-two Saṁvargas,
(22 Cantos)
Metre: Mānasahaṁsa

113. Nīti Varga
Book of Rules
Nineteen Saṁvargas
(19 Cantos)
Metre: Upamālinī

114. Sṛṣṭi Varga.
Book of Creation
Eleven Saṁvargas
(11 Cantos)
Metre: Prabhadraka

DVITA MAṆḌALA

115. Nahuṣa Varga.
Book about Nahuṣa
Sixty-four Saṁvargas
(64 Cantos)
Metre: Citrā

116. Yayāti Varga
Book about Yayāti
Seventy-three Saṁvargas
(73 Cantos)

Volume V

116. Yayāti Varga. (continued)
Twenty-two Saṁvargas
(22 Cantos)
Metre: Vanini

117. Purūravā Varga.
Book about Purūravā
Forty-nine Saṁvargas

(49 Cantos)
Metre: Pañca Cāmara
118. Duṣyanta Varga
Book about Duṣyanta
Eighty-nine Saṁvargas
(89 Cantos)
Metre: Garudaruta
119. Damanaka Varga.
Book about Damanaka
Fifty-six Saṁvargas
(56 Cantos)
Metre: Maṇikalpalatā

BHARATA MAṆḌALA

120. Madhvī Varga.
Book about Madhvī
Thirty-six Saṁvargas
(36 Cantos)
Metre: Pṛthvī
121. Ajāta Varga.
Book about Ajātaśatru
Thirty Saṁvargas
(30 Cantos)
Metre: Śikhariṇī
122. Kuru Varga.
Book about Kuru
Forty-eight Saṁvargas
(48 Cantos)
Metre: Mandākrāntā
123. Hastī Varga.
Book about Hastī
Thirty-six Saṁvargas
(36 Cantos)
Metre: Bharakranta
124. Pratīpa Varga.
Book about Pratīpa
Twenty-four Saṁvargas

(24 Cantos)
Metre: Hariṇi

125. Śantanu Varga.
Book about Śantanu,
Twenty Saṁvargas
(20 Cantos)
Metre: Hariṇi

126. Gāṅgeya Varga.
Book about son of Gaṅgā (Bhīṣma)
Twenty-seven Saṁvargas
(27 Cantos)
Metre: Narddataka

127. Vyāsa Varga.
Book of Vyāsa
Twenty-eight Saṁvargas
(28 Cantos)
Metre: Kokilaka

BHĀRATA MAṆḌALA

128. Mahābhārata Varga 1
Adi Parva
Book of Commencement,
Eighty-Seven Adhyāyas
(87 Cantos)
Metre: Upajāti

Volume VI

129. Mahābhārata Varga 2
Sabhā Parva
Ninety-eight Adhyāyas
(98 Cantos)
Book of Royal Conference,
Metre: Upajāti

130. Mahābhārata Varga 3
Vana Parva
Book in the Forest.
Ninety-five Adhyāyas

(95 Cantos)
Metre: Prahārṣiṇī
131. Mahābhārata Varga 4
Virāṭa Parva
Book in the Virāṭa
Forty-Five Adhyāyas
(45 Cantos)
Metre: Rucira
132. Mahābhārata Varga 5
Udyoga Parva
Book of arrangement
Forty-two Adhyāyas
(42 Cantos)
Metre: Rathodhata
133. Mahābhārata Varga 6
Bhīṣma Parva
Book of Bhīṣma
Forty-nine Adhyāyas
(49 Cantos)
Metre: Sālinī
134. Mahābhārata Varga 7
Droṇa Parva
Book on Drona
Fifty-one Adhyāyas
(51 Cantos)
Metre: Drutavilambita
135. Mahābhārata Varga 8.
Karṇa Parva
Book of Karṇa
Fifty-five Adhyāyas
(55 Cantos)
Metre: Śārdūlvikrīḍita
136. Mahābhārata Varga 9.
Śalya Parva
Book of Śalya
Twenty-five Adhyāyas
(25 Cantos)
Metre. Bhujaṅgaprayāta

137. Mahābhārata Varga 10.
Gadā Parva
Book on Battle of Club
Twenty-six Adhyāyas
(26 Cantos)
Metre: Rucira

Volume VII

138. Mahābhārata Varga 11.
Aiṣīka Parva
Book of Weapons
Twenty-four Adhyāyas
(24 Cantos)
Metre: Pañca Cāmara

139. Mahābhārata Varga 12
Nārī Parva
Book of Women
Twenty-five Adhyāyas
(25 Cantos)
Metre: Rathoddhata

140. Mahābhārata Varga 13
Śānti Parva
Book of Peace
Forty-eight Adhyāyas
(48 Cantos)
Metre: Puṣpitagra

141. Mahābhārata Varga 14
Anuśāsana Parva
Book of Rules
Twenty-seven Adhyāyas
(27 Cantos)
Metre: Puṣpitagra

142. Mahābhārata Varga 15
Aśvamedha Parva
Book of World Peace
Forty-eight Adhyāyas
(48 Cantos)
Metre: Praharśiṇī

143. Mahābhārata Varga 16
Āśramavāsika Parva
Book of Asylum Residence
Twenty-four Adhyāyas
(24 Cantos)
Metre: Pañca Cāmara
144. Mahābhārata Varga 17
Musala Parva
Book of Iron Rod
Twenty-four Adhyāyas
(24 Cantos)
Metre: Vaiśvadevī
145. Mahābhārata Varga 18
Svargārohaṇa Parva
Book on Ascending Heaven
Twenty-four Adhyāyas
(24 Cantos)
Metre: Rathoddhata

PARĪKṢIT MAṆḌALA

146. Kavaca Varga.
Book of Protections
Twenty-four Saṁvargas
(24 Cantos)
Metre: Nandana
147. Śuka Varga.
Book on Śukadeva
Twenty Saṁvargas
(20 Cantos)
Metre: Śarddūl Lalita
148. Yoga Varga.
Book of Yoga
Fifty-four Saṁvargas
(54 Cantos)
Metre: Harinpluta
149. Upakhyāñà Varga.
Book of Stories

Fifty-three Saṁvargas
(53 Cantos)
Metre: Candralekhā

150. Karma Varga
Book of Activities
Twenty-three Saṁvargas
(23 Cantos)
Metre: Aṣavagti

151. Pratiṣṭhā Varga.
Book of Establishment
Eighteen Saṁvargas
(18 Cantos)
Metre: Citralekhā

152. Tattva Varga
Book of Secret Knowledge
Twenty-five Saṁvargas
(25 Cantos)
Metre: Haranarttana

153. Abhisampat Varga.
Book of Curse
Twenty-two Saṁvargas
(22 Cantos)
Metre: Hiraka

Rudra Kalpa

Volume VIII

KṚṢṆA MAṆḌALA

154. Abhisantāpa Varga.
Book of Repentence
Twelve Saṁvargas
(12 Cantos)
Metre: Śardūl

155. Bhāgavata Purāṇa Varga 1
Janma Skandha
Book of Divine Birth
Twenty-five Saṁvargas

(25 Cantos)
Metre: Upajāti (Indravajrā)
Upajāti (Indravaṁśa),
Praharṣiṇī, Rucira,
Vasantatilakā, Puṣpitāgra,
Sundarī, Samanikā, Malinī,
Bhujaṅgaprayāta, Drutavilambita,
Śālini, Śārdūlavikrīḍita,
Indirā, Mandākrāntā,
Śikhariṇī, Narddataka, Svagata,
Māñjubhāṣinī, Mṛgendramukḥā,
Sragbini, Sragdharā— metres used in
Bhāgavata Purāṇa in different places.
156. Bhāgavata Purāṇa Varga 2.
Līlā Skandha
Book of Divine Play
Forty-four Saṁvargas
(44 Cantos)
157. Bhāgavata Purāṇa Varga 3
Rājya Skandha
Book of Divine Kingdom
Eighty Saṁvargas
(80 Cantos)
158. Bhāgavata Purāṇa Varga 4
Yoga Skandha
Book of Yoga
Twenty Saṁvargas
(20 Cantos)
159. Bhāgavata Purāṇa Varga 5
Nīti Skandha
Book of Divine Rules
Twenty Saṁvargas
(20 Cantos)
160. Bhāgavata Purāṇa Varga 6
Jñāna Skandha
Book of Knowledge
Eleven Saṁvargas
(11 Cantos)

161. Bhāgavata Purāṇa Varga 7
Karma Skandha
Book of Divine Activity
Twenty Saṁvargas
(20 Cantos)
162. Bhāgavata Purāṇa Varga 8
Dharma Skandha
Book of Religious Activities
Twenty-one Saṁvargas
(21 Cantos)
163. Bhāgavata Purāṇa Varga 9
Prema Skandha
Book of Divine Love
Twenty-two Saṁvargas
(22 Cantos)
164. Bhāgavata Purāṇa Varga 10.
Prayāṇa Skandha
Book of Retirement
Sixteen Saṁvargas
(16 Cantos)

AHI MAṆḌALA

165. Takṣaka Varga.
Book about Takṣaka
Fifteen Saṁvargas
(15 Cantos)
Metre: Meghavisphurjita
166. Kāla Varga.
Book about Time
Twenty-nine Saṁvargas
(29 Cantos)
Metre: Chāyā
167. Satra Varga.
Book of Snake Sacrifice
Sixteen Saṁvargas
(16 Cantos)
Metre: Surasa

168. Āstīka Varga.
Book on Āstīka
Eighteen Saṁvargas
(18 Cantos)
Metre: Fulladama
169. Dillika Varga.
Book about Dillika
Sixty-nine Saṁvargas
(69 Cantos)
Metre: Nava Pañca Cāmara
170. Janamejaya Varga.
Book of Janamejaya sacrifice
Fifty-three Saṁvargas
(53 Cantos)
Metre: Śārdūlvikṛīḍita

Volume IX

KALI MAṆḌALA

171. Santāpa Varga.
Book of Distress
Seventeen Saṁvargas
(17 Cantos)
Metre: Fulladam
172. Pāpa Mukti Varga.
Book of Release from Sin
Twenty-five Saṁvargas
(25 Cantos)
Metre: Fulladam
173. Janamejaya Karma Varga.
Book of activities of Janamejaya
Thirteen Saṁvargas
(13 Cantos)
Metre: Shova
174. Śuka-Janamejaya Saṁvāda Varga
Book of talks with Śukadeva and Janamejaya
Twenty-three Saṁvargas

(23 Cantos)
Metre: Suvadana

175. Niyati Varga
Book of Destiny
Ten Saṁvargas
(10 Cantos)
Metre: Vṛtta

176. Kuśambhi Varga.
Book about Kuśambhi
Thirty-seven Saṁvargas
(37 Cantos)
Metre: Gītikā

177. Kumbhīka Varga
Book about Kumbhīka
Thirteen Saṁvargas
(13 Cantos)
Metre: Suvansha

178. Nikumbhīka Varga
Book about Nikumbhīka
Twenty-two Saṁvargas
(22 Cantos)
Metre: Mattebhavikrīḍita

179. Sanatsuta Varga
Book about Sanatsuta
Fourteen Saṁvargas
(14 Cantos)
Metre: Bhadraka

ARBUDA MAṆḌALA

180. Bṛhadratha Varga.
Book about Bṛhadratha
Thirteen Saṁvargas
(13 Cantos)
Metre: Madira

181. Śiśunāga Varga.
Book about Śiśunāga
Twenty-one Saṁvargas

(21 Cantos)
Metre: Sragdharā
182. Bimbisāra Varga.
Book about Bimbisāra
Twenty-five Saṁvargas
(25 Cantos)
Metre: Sarasi
183. Ajātaśatru Varga.
Book about Ajātaśatru (Kunik)
Twenty-three Saṁvargas
(23 Cantos)
Metre: Lalitya
184. Darśaka Varga.
Book about Darśaka
Twenty-four Saṁvargas
(24 Cantos)
Metre: Adritanayā

LAYA MAṆḌALA

185. Khriṣṭa Varga.
Book about Jesus Christ
Forty-two Saṁvargas
(42 Cantos)
Metre: Svagata
186. Udaya Varga.
Book about Udaya
Twelve Saṁvargas
(12 Cantos)
Metre: Rathoddhatā
187. Mohammad Varga.
Book about Mohammad
Twenty-four Saṁvargas
(24 Cantos)
Metre: Dodhaka
188. Nanda Varga.
Book about Nandas
Seven Saṁvargas

(7 Cantos)
Metre: Praharṣiṇī

189. Gupta Varga.
Book about Guptas
Eighteen Saṁvargas
(18 Cantos)
Metre: Śyenī

190. Bindusāra Varga.
Book about Bindusāra
Seven Saṁvargas
(7 Cantos)
Metre: Anukūla

191. Aśoka Varga.
Book about Aśoka
Twenty Saṁvargas
(20 Cantos)
Metre: Upacitra

192. Śankara Varga.
Book about Śaṅkarācārya
Twenty Saṁvargas
(20 Cantos)
Metre: Indirā

193. Pala Varga.
Book about Pala
Thirty Saṁvargas
(30 Cantos)
Metre: Druta

194. Gaura Varga
Book about Gaurāṅga
Twenty one Saṁvargas
(21 Cantos)
Metre: Kusuma Vicitra

195. Mīrā Varga.
Book about Mīrābaī
Nine Saṁvargas
(9 Cantos)
Metre: Indra Vaṁśa

Volume X

196. Yavana Varga.
Book about Yavana
Fourteen Saṁvargas
(14 Cantos)
Metre: Kalahaṁsa
197. Mleccha Varga.
Book about Mlecchas
Thirteen Saṁvargas
(13 Cantos)
Metre: Pravodita

PRATIṢṬHĀ MAṆḌALA

198. Amara Varga
Book about immortals
Thirty-eight Saṁvargas
(38 Cantos)
Metre: Vasantatilakā,
199. Deva Sainya Saṁvāda Varga.
Book about the idea of Divine Armies
Six Saṁvargas
(6 Cantos)
Metre: Mālinī
200. Svādhikāra Varga.
Book about the Influence of Truth
Thirty-five Saṁvargas
(35 Cantos)
Metre: Mandākinī

APTYA MAṆḌALA

201. Prakāśa Varga.
Book about Manifestation
Twelve Saṁvargas
(12 Cantos)
Metre: Mandākinī
202. Rāmakṛṣṇa Varga.
Book about Rāmakṛṣṇa

Sixteen Saṁvargas
(16 Cantos)
Metre: Upajāti

203. Śāradā Varga.
Book about Sāradāmoni
Nine Saṁvargas
(9 Cantos)
Metre: Indirā

204. Vivekananda Varga.
Book about Vivekananda
Thirty-nine Saṁvargas
(39 Cantos)
Metre: Drutavilambīta

205. Ṛṣi Varga.
Book about Ṛṣis
Thirty-six Saṁvargas
(36 Cantos)
Metre: Bhāratī

KAŚYAPA MAṆḌALA

206. Svodbhava Varga.
Book of Self Revelation
Forty-six Saṁvargas
(46 Cantos)
Metre: Mandākinī

207. Bālya Varga.
Book of Boyhood
Fifty-six Saṁvargas
(56 Cantos)
Metre: Pajjhatika

208. Vidyā Varga.
Book of Education
Eleven Saṁvargas
(11 Cantos)
Metre: Pajjhatika

209. Karma Varga.
Book of Efforts
Sixteen Saṁvargas

(16 Cantos)
Metre: Oupachchhandasak
210. Sādhana Varga.
Book of Sādhana
Twelve Saṁvargas
(12 Cantos)
Metre: Upajātī
211. Tapa Varga.
Book of Tapasyā
Thirteen Saṁvargas
(13 Cantos)
Metre: Dohadika
212. Yoga Varga.
Book about Yoga
Fifteen Saṁvargas
(15 Cantos)
Metre: Arya Pathya
213. Siddhi Varga.
Book of Accomplishment
Eleven Saṁvargas
(11 Cantos)
Metre: Arya Vipula

ADITI MAṆḌALA

214. Āśrama Gaṭhana Varga.
Book of Āśrama Formation
Ten Saṁvargas
(10 Cantos)
Metre: Arya Capala
215. Dvandva Varga.
Book about Quarrel
Thirteen Saṁvargas
(13 Cantos)
Metre: Arya Mukha Capala
216. Mahas Varga.
Book about Supermind
Fourteen Saṁvargas

(14 Cantos)
Metre: Arya Jaghana Capala

217. Saṅgrāma Varga.
Book about Fight
Thirty Saṁvargas
(30 Cantos)
Metre: Ārya Gītī

218. Svarājya Varga.
Book about Independence
Twelve Saṁvargas
(12 Cantos)
Metre: Vaitaliya

219. Pāk Varga.
Book about Pāk State
Four Saṁvargas
(4 Cantos)
Metre: Oupachchhandasik

220. Prayāṇa Varga.
Book of Disappearance
Ten Saṁvargas
(10 Cantos)
Metre: Arya Vaitali

UDYAMA MAṆḌALA

221. Kavi Varga.
Book of Poet
Nineteen Saṁvargas
(19 Cantos)
Metre: Sukha Vaitali

222. Kāvyodyoga Varga.
Book of Epic arrangement
Thirty-two Saṁvargas
(32 Cantos)
Metre: Capala Vaitali

223. Saṅgaṭhana Varga.
Book of Re-construction
Six Saṁvargas

(6 Cantos)
Metre: Citra pada

Volume XI

UDYAMA MAṆḌALA

224. Udghāṭana Varga.
Book of Discovery
Sixteen Saṁvargas
(16 Cantos)
Metre: Pramanika
225. Amṛtotsava Varga.
Book about the Ceremony of Ambrosia
Twenty four Saṁvargas
(24 Cantos)
Metre: Gāyatrī, Jagatī, Triṣṭubh, Anuṣṭubh
Uṣṇīk 28, Bṛhatī 36, Paṅkti 40 letters
226. Soma Varga
Book about Drinking Nectar
Ten Saṁvargas
(10 Cantos)
Metre: Samanika
227. Saṁveda Varga.
Book of Perception
Eleven Saṁvargas
(11 Cantos)
Metre: Vitan

UṢĀ MAṆḌALA

228. Uśodbhava Varga.
Book about Birth of Uṣā (Dawn)
Thirty Saṁvargas
(30 Cantos)
Metre: Vitan

229. Uṣodvibhāsa Varga.
Book about Manifestation of Dawn
Forty-seven Saṁvargas
(47 Cantos)
Metre: Citra pada

230. Viśvacit Varga.
Book about World Consciousness
Forty-five Saṁvargas
(45 Cantos)
Metre: Anukūla

231. Viśvoshasa Varga.
Book about World Consciousness with Divine Dawn
Thirty-seven Saṁvargas
(37 Cantos)
Metre: Pajjhatika

ĀKHYĀNA MAṆḌALA

232. Bṛhaspatyākhyāna Varga.
Book of stories about Bṛhaspati
Twenty-four Saṁvargas
(24 Cantos)
Metre: Iduvadana; or Varasundarī

233. Rudrākhyāna Varga.
Book of stories about Rudra
Fifty-one Saṁvargas
(51 Cantos)
Metre: Shailashikha

234. Dakṣa Yajñakhyāna Varga.
Book of stories about Dakṣa Yajña
Ten Saṁvargas
(10 Cantos)
Metre: Lalana

235. Hayagrīvakhyāna Varga.
Book of stories about Hayagrīva
Eleven Saṁvargas
(11 Cantos)
Metre: Gaurī

236. Sarasvanākhyāna Varga.
Book of stories about Sarasvana
Twelve Saṁvargas
(12 Cantos)
Metre: Kuṭilagati
237. Sinibalyākhyāna Varga.
Book of stories about Sinibalya
Four Saṁvargas
(4 Cantos)
Metre: Vara Yuvati
238. Gaṅgu Ākhyāna Varga.
Book of stories about Gaṅgu
Four Saṁvargas
(4 Cantos)
Metre: Vara Sundarī
239. Pitrivyākhyāna Varga.
Book of stories of Pitrivyas
Fifteen Saṁvargas
(15 Cantos)
Metre: Jaladharamālā

BHAGA MAṆḌALA

240. Viśvotthāna Varga.
Book of World Awakening
Twenty-seven Saṁvargas
(27 Cantos)
Metre: Vivudhapriya
241. Prajñāna Varga.
Book about Prajñāna
Eighteen Saṁvargas
(18 Cantos)
Metre: Kokilaka
242. Taranta Varga.
Book about Taranta
Seventy Saṁvargas
(70 Cantos)
Metre: Avitatha

243. Tāranteya Varga.
Book about Son of Taranta
Twenty-two Saṁvargas
(22 Cantos)
Metre: Atiśayini

Volume XII

INDRA MAṆḌALA

244. Bālakhilya Varga.
Book of Bālakhilya
Six Saṁvargas
(6 Cantos)
Metre: Samanika

245. Manu Varga.
Book about Manu
Eight Saṁvargas
(8 Cantos)
Metre: Samanika

246. Darbhya Janma Varga.
Book about the Birth of Darbhya
Eight Saṁvargas
(8 Cantos)
Metre: Samanika

247. Darbhya Śikṣā Varga.
Book about Education of Darbhya
Eighteen Saṁvargas
(18 Cantos)
Metre: Pañca Cāmara

248. Darbhya Jñāna Varga.
Book about Knowledge of Darbhya
Thirty Saṁvargas
(30 Cantos)
Metre: Motak

249. Kirtyā Saṁmelana Varga.
Book about Meeting with Kirtyā
Nineteen Saṁvargas

(19 Cantos)
Metre: Vidyādhara
250. Youvanashwa Prāpti Varga.
Book about Meeting Youvanashwa
Thirty-six Saṁvargas
(36 Cantos)
Metre: Drutapada
251. Indratā Vyakta Varga.
Book about Manifestation of Indrahood
Thirty-nine Saṁvargas
(39 Cantos)
Metre: Lalita
252. Kṣeti Varga.
Book about Kṣeti
Sixteen Saṁvargas
(16 Cantos)
Metre: Lalana
253. Kalki Saṁvāda Varga.
Book about A Conversation with Kalki
Twenty-seven Saṁvargas
(27 Cantos)
Metre: Mañjarī
254. Kalki Prakāśa Varga.
Book about Manifestation of Kalki
Forty-two Saṁvargas
(42 Cantos)
Metre: Gāyatrī, Uṣṇik
Anuṣṭubh, Brihatī
Paṅktī, Triṣṭubh, Jagatī
255. Svayamprakaṭa Varga.
Book of Self-manifested Incarnation
Eighteen Saṁvargas
(18 Cantos)
Metre: Upajāti and Vasantatilakā

VASU MAṆḌALA

256. Arbuda Śāsana Varga.
Book about Chastisement of Arbuda

Forty Saṁvargas
(40 Cantos)
Metre: Pajjhatika, Upajāti and Gitī

257. Vasukra Varga.
Book about Vasukra
One hundred fifty-six Saṁvargas
(156 Cantos)
Metre: Upasthita, Lilakhela, Rupamali, Supavitra, Achaldhriti, Vidyunmala, and Samanika, Vasantatilaka, Upajāti, Pajjhatika etc.

258. Vasukrīḍa Varga.
Book about Vasukrīḍa
Forty Saṁvargas
(40 Cantos)
Metre: Kaumudi

259. Vasukarṇa Varga.
Book about Vasukarṇa
Twelve Saṁvargas
(12 Cantos)
Metre: Anaga Śekhara

260. Vasurociṣa Varga
Book about Vasurociṣa
Seventeen Saṁvargas
(17 Cantos)
Metre: Ṛṣabha

261. Vasuśruta Varga
Book about Vasuśruta
Five Saṁvargas
(5 Cantos)
Metre: Ela

262. Vasuyuva Varga
Book about Vasuyuva
Five Saṁvargas
(5 Cantos)
Metre: Tanumadhyā

263. Vasuna Varga.
Book about Vasuna
Eight Saṁvargas

(8 Cantos)
Metre: Ketumatī
264. Vasumāna Varga.
Book about Vasumāna
Fourteen Saṁvargas
(14 Cantos)
Metre: Candrarekhā

VṚṢṆU MAṆḌALA

265. Rohidaśva Varga.
Book about Rohidaśva
Fifteen Saṁvargas
(15 Cantos)
Metre: Daṇḍaka
266. Traivṛṣṇu Varga.
Book about Traivṛṣṇu
Ten Saṁvargas
(10 Cantos)
Metre: Drutamadhya
267. Traiaruna Varga.
Book about Traiaruna
Thirteen Saṁvargas
(13 Cantos)
Metre: Dhīra Lalita
268. Paurașa Varga.
Book about Paurașas
Fourteen Saṁvargas
(14 Cantos)
Metre: Naraca
269. Tryasadasyu Varga.
Book about Tryasadasyu
Six Saṁvargas
(6 Cantos)
Metre: Nisipalaka

SOHANA MAṆḌALA

270. Citra Varga.
Book about Citra

Five Saṁvargas
(5 Cantos)
Metre: Prabhāvatī

271. Venya Varga.
Book about Venya
Fifteen Saṁvargas
(15 Cantos)
Metre: Bhadrika

272. Pṛthu Varga.
Book about Pṛthu
Thirteen Saṁvargas
(13 Cantos)
Metre: Bhujaṅga Saṅgata

273. Sagara Varga.
Book about Sagaras
Eight Saṁvargas
(8 Cantos)
Metre: Udgata

274. Bhagīratha Varga.
Book about Bhagīratha
Six Saṁvargas
(6 Cantos)
Metre: Singha Vikrida

275. Sohana Vārga.
Book about Sohana
Thirty Saṁvargas
(30 Cantos)
Metre: Hari

Total= Vargas 275

Total= Saṁvargas 6145

GLOSSARY

A

Abhivarta	Son of Ṛṣi Aṅgirā, the King of Ṛṣis
Adharma	Ungodly, Anti-dharma (irreligious), Śani
Adharma-Śani	Manifestation of the dark force under the influence of the Sun, Opposing the Gods
Adhyāya	A chapter. A canto in the Mahābhārata
Aditi	The Divine Mother, the Mother of the Great Godheads
Āditya	The Sun
Ādityaloka	The plane of the Sun
Agni	The Lord of Fire
Agni devatā	Aspirant God, the Lord of the Aspirant Force
Ahi	Snake
Aitareya Upaniṣad	Name of an Upaniṣad
Ajātaśatru	A King, son of Bimbisāra, who committed patricide
Ākhyāna	Story of the past
Akṣarabrahman	Brahman as sound
Allah ho Akbara	Prayer of the Moslems: God is Great
Ambhrinī-Ṛṣikā	A female Seer, mother of Vāk, Dvita and Trita, wife of the Creator Aptya
Amṛta	Divine wine
Ānanda	Bliss
Angirā	One of the seven Ṛṣis, created from the mind of Parabrahman

Āṅgirasa	Sons of Aṅgirā
Animal-Śatarūpa	Śatarūpa as an animal, the evolutionary force in the form of an animal
Antarikṣa	Plane existing between the mental and the physical
Anusvāra	Nasal sound
Anuṣṭubh	A Sanskrit metre of 32 letters
Apasbaraṇa	A cover of water
Aptya	One of the seven Ṛṣis, created from the mind of Parabrahman. Also, creator of the worlds and of the two Ages, Dvita and Trita.
Apsarā	Dancing girl of heaven
Arbuda	Snake king
Arjuna	The third Pāṇḍava, the intimate friend of Divine Kṛṣṇa
Aśokavana	Garden house of Rāvaṇa
Aśvatthāmā	Son of Droṇācārya, the teacher of the Kauravas and the Pāṇḍavas, one of the immortals who reincarnated in Kaliyuga to bring spiritual awakening to mortal souls
Aśvinī devatā	Son of Sūrya (the Sun)
Astika	Son of Jaratkāru, nephew of Vāsuki
Āsura	Undivine being, Titan, Demon, hostile, opponent of the power of God
Asuraloka	Plane of the Demons
Ātmā	Soul
Atharva Veda	One of the four Vedas
Ayana	A time cycle, to come to the same point by encircling

B

Bali	Descendant of Prahlāda. By Brahmā's boon, he obtained supremacy over the three worlds. When the Gods wished for help, then Viṣṇu descended as the

	Vāmana Avatāra and expelled Bali to the nether worlds.
Bāli	Sugrīva's brother, who was killed by Rāma.
Bālakhilya	A boy Ṛṣi, who has achieved supreme knowledge
Balarāma	Brother of Kṛṣṇa
Bhaga	God of Joy, son of Pūṣan
Bhāgavata	One of the 18 Purāṇas, describing the life and works of Lord Kṛṣṇa
Bharadvāja	A Ṛṣi, one of the seven Ṛṣis, who came out from the mind of Parabrahman
Bharata	Son of Duṣyanta. He was a king of India who ruled over the whole world
Bhārata	A short name of Mahābhārata, the second epic of India
Bhāva	Source of thoughts
Bhāvana	Thoughts
Bhāvayavya	Name of the thought holders, who control and guide thoughts
Bhīma	Second Pāṇḍava
Bhīma (2)	King of Vidarbha, father of Damayantī
Bhīṣma	Grandfather of Kauravas and Pāṇḍavas, Son of Gaṅgā and Śantanu
Bhojaraja	King of Bhoja
Bhṛgu	Son of Pragatha, brother of Kali
Bhuvanas	Worlds, sons of Aptya Ṛṣi
Bhūr	The physical plane
Bhuvar	The vital plane
Bimbisāra	A famous king of India
Bird	demi-god power
Biti	A short form of Gauribiti, daughter of Śakti
Brahmā	Creator of all
Brahman	The Supreme
Brahmaṇaspati	Another name of Gaṇapati
Brahmāṇī	Power of Brahmā

Bṛhaspati	Teacher of the Gods
Bṛhatī	A metre of 36 syllables

C

Cakra	Wheel
Caṇḍī	A portion of the Mārkaṇḍeya Purāṇa, which contains the glorious description of the Divine Mother "Ambikā"
Candra	The Moon, Lord of Ecstasy
Candra-Vaṁsha	The Lunar Dynasty
Chanda	Rhythm, Metre
Chandasa	One who was born with the Vedas, Sūrya
Chāyā	Wife of Sūrya, the Sun, shadow
Caturdaśa Bhuvanas	Fourteen worlds or planes of existence
Cow-shaped Śatarūpā	Śatarūpā in the shape of a cow

D

Dakṣa	A Creator of the Goddess "Devī-Śakti", who had a hundred daughters
Dākṣāyaṇī	Daughter of Bṛhaspati—married to Putadakṣa
Dakṣiṇā	Daughter of Parabrahman—married to Bṛhaspati
Dantavakra	An enemy of Śrī Kṛṣṇa, from the snake family
Damayantī	Daughter of King Bhīma of Vidarbha
Darbhya	Incarnation of Indra to bring the Divine Kingdom on the earth
Daśaratha	King of Ayodhyā, Father of Rāma, Laksmaṇa, Bharata and Śatrughna
Devakī	Mother of Śri Kṛṣṇa, wife of King Vasudeva
Deva	Incarnation of the Supreme Truth, born as a son of Abhivarta
Devatā	God, divine being
Deva Sūrya	Deva the Truth as the Sun

Deva Yajña	Sacrificial flame kindled by Satyadeva, for the Golden Age.
Devāyaṇa	The Third Epic of India, describing the four Ages, together with the movement of the Gods towards humanity and of humanity towards the Gods for the manifestation of the Golden Age.
Devī	Goddess
Devī-Sūkta	A portion of Ṛgveda, 125th Sūkta of the tenth Maṇḍala
Dhiṣaṇā	Daughter of Agni
Dharma	Son of Sūrya (Sun)
Dharmeya	Sons of Dharma
Dhruva	On receiving the advice from his mother that for everything one has to work hard, he did such an intense meditation and austerity that he became one of the immortals. He reincarnated in Kaliyuga to bring spiritual awakening to mortal souls
Digambaras	Followers of Mahāvīra, Jainas, who do not believe in wearing any clothes
Dinamaṇi	The Sun
Dīrghatamā	A Ṛṣi
Diti	Mother of the Demons
Divya-deha	Divine body
Draupadī	Daughter of Drupada
Drobinoda	Son of Ritaba
Droṇa	Teacher of both Kauravas and Pāṇḍavas. He disclosed the secret of the divine weapons to Arjuna.
Drupada	King of Pañcāla
Durgā	Power of Śiva, wife of Śiva
Durvāsā	A Ṛṣi, who took birth under the influence of Rudra, and thus was always having a violent temper.
Duryodhana	Eldest Kaurava son of Dhṛtarāṣtra

Dvaipāyana	Another name of Vyāsa.
Dvandva	Diversity, dispute
Dvārakā	Capital of Kṛṣṇa's kingdom
Dvita	Director of the Time Wheel during the Bronze Age
Dvāpara	Bronze Age

E

Ejid	A Muslim king who issued an edict that only those who pray unitedly are the real Muslims, and others are not part of the brotherhood and should be eliminated

G

Gadādhara	An incaranation of Ṛṣi Aptya, later on known as Ramakrishna, the priest of the Dakshinesvar temple
Gaṇapati	Son of Śiva
Gaṇeśa	another name of Gaṇapati
Gandharva	Demi-Gods, celestial musicians
Gadā	Club
Gaṅgā Devī	Goddess of River Ganga
Gaṅgu	God of river, Puruṣa part of Gaṅgā
Garbha Upaniṣad	Name of an Upanisad
Garuḍa	King of birds, Viṣṇu's vehicle
Gathini	Daughter of Kuśika, wife of Pragatha, Mother of Kali, Lord of the Iron Age
Gauribiti	Daughter of Śakti, Vasiṣṭha's son
Gāyatrī	Source of all metres, Mother of all chandas or Vedas
Ghori	Muhammad Ghori who invaded India
Guṇa	Three essential properties of nature – Sattva, Rajas, Tamas
Guru	Spiritual Teacher

H

Hanumān	Monkey devotee of Śrī Rāma
Hari	A name of Viṣṇu
Hariścandra	A King of the Solar Dynasty
Hayagrīva	A Godhead with horse's head
Heramba	Son of Śiva
Hiraṇyākṣa	A Demon who dragged the earth under the waters and was then destroyed by Viṣṇu in his Varāha Avatāra
Hiraṇyakaśipu	A Demon King, brother of Hiraṇyākṣa, who due to Brahmā's boon, achieved supremacy in the three worlds. He tried repeatedly to kill his own son Prahlāda, for worshipping Viṣṇu instead of himself. Finally Viṣṇu in his Narasimha avatāra killed him.
Hindu	Aryans of India, name given by the Moslems
Himācala	The famous mountain of India
Himālaya	Biggest mountain range of India

I

Indra	The Divine King, Supreme Being
Indraprastha	Capital of the Paṇḍavas's Kingdom
Iva	Mother of mankind

J

Jagatī	A Sanskrit metre of 48 letters
Jagat-Sūrya	Sun of the three worlds
Jana	Holder of life, who controls and guides the life movement
Janaka	Rājarṣi, father of Sītā, father-in-law of Śrī Rāma
Janārdana	A name of Viṣṇu
Janamejaya	Son of Parīkṣit
Jarāsandha	King of Magadha, bitter enemy of Lord Kṛṣṇa

Jaraktkūru	Son of a Ṛṣi named Jaru
Jātaveda	Name of Agni
Jīva	A living being
Jīvātmā	Mortal soul or human soul

K

Kafir	A non-Moslem
Kāla	The Time
Kālacakra	Time Wheel, the holder of the three worlds, the Bhuvanas
Kālarātri	An inauspicious night
Kālī	The power of Rudra
Kali	The Lord of the Iron Age, Kaliyuga
Kaliyuga	Period of Time influenced by Kali
Kalpa	A day of Brahmā consisting of the four ages
Kāma	Short form of Kāmadeva, also desire, passion
Kāmadeva	Creator of the physical birth
Kāṇḍa	A section of the Rāmāyaṇa or the Veda
Kaṁsa	The evil maternal uncle of Kṛṣṇa, King of Mathurā, who was destroyed by Kṛṣṇa
Kaṇva	One of the seven Ṛṣis, who came out from the mind of Parabrahman.
Kāṇveya	Son of Ṛṣi Kaṇva
Kardama	Father of mankind
Karma-phala	The results of our actions
Karṇa	The secret son of Sūrya, born in the womb of Kuntī. Although a brother of the Pāṇḍavas, he remained their enemy and friendly to the Kauravas
Kaśyapa	Father of the Gods, who also came out from the mind of Parabrahman.
Kaśyapa-mārīca	Kaśyapa as an enlightened body
Kavi	The Seer, Poet
Kirtya	Incarnation of Candra

Kṛṣṇa	Viṣṇu's incarnation during the Bronze Age
Kṣatra	The warrior, fighter
Kurukṣetra	Battlefield of Kauravas and Pāṇḍavas
Kuśa	Second son of Śrī Rāmā

L

Lava	Eldest son of Śrī Rāmā
Laksmaṇa	Brother of Rāma
Lakṣmī	Daughter of Bṛhaspati
Laya	Universal cataclysm. At this time, the spiritual culture disappears.
Loka	Plane, world

M

Magadha	Capital of Jarāsandha
Mahābhārata	The Second Epic of India
Mahācamasya	A Ṛṣi, who discovered the supramental plane (Mahas) above the mental plane and introduced the mantra, Bhūr- Bhuvar, Svar, Mahas. He also preserved the memory of the Golden Age.
Mahākāla	The Great Time, Śiva
Mahākāla Piṅgala	A creative aspect of Śiva, a poetic form
Mahākāla-Rudra	A destructive aspect of Śiva
Mahākāli	The destructive power of Maheśvara
Mahā Kavi	A Seer who attains the consciousness of Brahman. Great poet
Mahā Kāvya	Great epic
Mahālakṣmī	Power of Viṣṇu
Mahāmāyā	Great attachment; Durgā, Māheśvarī
Mahas	The mantra Vyāhṛtis; the Supermind
Maharloka	Plane of Sun, the Supramental plane
Maha Sarasvatī	Power of Sarasvana
Maheśvara	Power of Maheśvara
Mahī	The earth

Manasā	Mother of Āstīka, Jagatgaurī
Mānava	Man; Father of Man
Mānava Cākṣuṣa	A Man born from Sūrya
Mānava-Saṁvaraṇa	A Man born from the Saṁvaraṇa Brahman
Mānavā-Śaryāti	A man born from Sarvahari, son of Indra
Mānava-Navandesthi	A man born from Somadevatā – moon
Mantra	Words which when repeated constantly help in attaining inner consciousness, power, peace, ānanda, etc.
Manu	Creator of Mānavas
Mathurā	Capital of Ugrasena, possessed by Kaṁsa and liberated by Kṛṣṇa
Marut-vāyu	Same as Vāyu
Maṇḍala	An orb; gathering of many things, persons etc. In Devāyaṇa used to divide volumes
Māṇḍūkya	Son of Maṇḍūka. a Ṛṣi who gave the Māṇḍūkya Upaniṣad.
Mārkaṇḍeya	A Ṛṣi who spoke a Purāṇa, the worshipper of Divine Śakti and the devotee of Śiva who conquered death
Māyā	Attachment
Meghapurī	High peak in the Himalayas
Mohini-maya	An attachment that charms
Mithilā	Capital of Rājarṣi Janaka
Mitra	God of life, water
Mitra-Varuṇa	God of life
Mṛdaṅga	A musical instrument
Mṛtyu	Death; daughter of the Sun from Sandhyā-Chāyā
Muṇḍaka	Paijavana, son of Parjanya—the Goḍ of rain, when cursed remains a frog (Maṇḍūka)

N

Nāda — Sound
Nakta — The dark existence
Nala — King of Niṣadha in India; Brother-in-Law of Lava
Nārada — Ṛṣi, son of Kaṇva
Naraka — Hell, Son of Saturn
Nārāyaṇa — The manifested cosmic existence, who exists throughout all creations.
Narendra — Like God Indra amongst men, King
Naṭarāja — Rudra, An aspect of Śiva at his destructive dance
Nirvāṇa — Release from the cycle of birth and death, eternal peace
Niṣadha — Capital of Nala

O

Om — The primal sound, Akṣarabrahman

P

Padma — Lotus
Pañcāla — Capital of Drupada
Paṇḍavas — Sons of Pāṇḍu-Yudhiṣṭhira, Bhīma, Arjuna, Nakula, Sahadeva
Pāṇḍaveya — Descendants of Pāṇḍavas—Pārīkṣit, Janamejaya etc.
Paṅkti — A Sanskrit metre of 40 letters
Parāśara — Son of Śakti
Parabrahman — The unmanifested eternal existence
Paramātman — Supreme Soul
Parīkṣit — Grandson of Arjuna of Mahābhārata
Parva — A section of the Mahābhārata
Parvata — Mountain
Pārvatī — Daughter of Parvata Himālaya. Wife of Śiva.

Piṇḍa	Name of an Upaniṣad
Piṅgala	The Poetic Existence, the poetic form of Maheśvara
Pīṭhasthāna	Places of religious purity, where Viṣṇu let parts of Satī's body fall down on the earth
Pitṛloka	Plane of the fathers
Pitṛviya	Guide of ancestors for creation
Pragatha	Son of Kaṇva, father of Kali, the Lord of the Iron Age
Prahlāda	Son of the Demon Hiraṇyakaṣipu, who worshipped Viṣṇu
Prakṛti	The Nature
Preta	Evil Spirit
Pṛthivī	The earth
Pṛthvīrāja	The Last Hindu Emperor of India
Pratiṣṭhā	Re-establishment
Pul	Pul King of Bengal
Purāṇa	Religious mythology
Purumilha	Son of Taranta, Ruler of the physical plane
Puruṣa	The male form
Puruṣa-Vedamaya	Who holds the Vedas, Who lives in the Vedas, Satyadeva
Pūṣa	Son of Satyadeva, the Power of Light of Truth, wars against the dark forces to manifest the dawn
Puṣkara	Nala's evil brother
Puṇya Phala	effect of virtue

R

Rājarṣi	A King who remains as a Ṛṣi, detached from worldly enjoyment
Rājasūya Yajña	Royal sacrificial ceremony
Rākṣasa	Anti-divine, Titan, Demon
Rākṣasi-force	Power of the anti-divine, hostile forces

Rāma	An incarnation of Viṣṇu, the son of Daśratha
Rāmacandra	The full name of Rāma
Rāmāyaṇa	First epic of India composed by Vālmīki
Rāvaṇa	King of Laṅkā and of the Demons, killed by Rama
Ṛbhu	Son of Ribhaba
Ṛk	Mantra
Ṛgveda	One of the four Vedas
Ṛṣi	A seer
Ṛṣikā	A female seer
Ritaba	Son of Aśvinī-devatā
Rohidaśva	Incarnation of Asvadeva. An aspect of Sūrya
Rudra	The destroyer, destructive form of Maheśvara
Rudrāṇī	The female form of Rudra

S

Sādhana	Son of Svar-bhuvana
Sādhya	Sons of Sarasvatī
Sāma Veda	One of the four Vedas
Sanatkumāra	A Ṛṣi—a Brāhmaṇa
Sanātana Dharma	The eternal religion
Saṅgana	Wife of Sūrya
Saṁvarga	Smaller form of Varga. In Devāyaṇa, it is used for a canto
Saṁnyāsin	A person who has given up normal life, and becomes a seeker of God
Saṅkalpa	Will, volition
Sarasvāna	God of words, the male part of Sarasvatī
Sarasvatī	Goddess of learning
Sarga	A canto in the Rāmāyaṇa
Sari	Clothing for women
Sarpa	Snake
Satī	Daughter of Dakṣa, married to Śiva

Satya	Truth
Satyadeva	Lord of Truth
Satya Yuga	Golden Age
Sauciki	A Ṛṣi, who kindled the sacrificial flame for the Deva
Sāvitrī	Daughter of King Aśvapati, himself the ruler of the earth
Sāvitrī–Sūrya	Power of the Sun, wife of Sūrya
Śakti	Son of Vasiṣṭha
Śakuni	Maternal uncle of Kauravas, the evil genius
Śānti	Peace; daughter of Yama
Śaṅkarācārya	A South Indian philosopher who propagated the concept of the one Brahman
Śaṅkha	Conch
Śani	Saturn
Śanti-yamayānī	Same as Śānti
Śatakratu	Indra, the King of Gods
Śāradāmoni	Sri Ramakrishnan's wife, whom he revered as mother
Śloka	A verse
Śuci-svarga	The pure heaven
Śukrācārya	The teacher of the Asuras
Śukadeva	Son of Vyāsa
Śiśupāla	King of Cedi city
Śvetāmbaras	The followers of Mahāvīra, Jains, who dressed in white
Siddhidātā	God of poetic realisation for the Truth. Other names are Heramba, Gaṇapati, Gaṇeśa, Brahmaṇaspati
Sinibali	The creator in the mother's womb
Sinibalya	The puruṣa part of Sinibali
Sītā	Daughter of Janaka and the wife of Rāma
Snake	One with undivine power

Sūkṣma-śarīra	Subtle body
Śukta	A section of Veda;
Supramental	Sri Aurobindo's name for Maharloka of the Upanisads
Suraloka	Plane of the Gods, heaven
Sūrya	Sun, lord of mental Truth
Sūrya Saṅga	Power of the Sun, wife of Sūrya also known as Sanga
Svar	Heaven
Svarga	Heaven

T

Taittarīya Upaniṣad	An Upaniṣad
Takṣaka	The snake who bit King Parīkṣit and killed him
Tapasyā	Religious austerity, penance, discipline for the achievement of power
Taranta	Son of Viśvadeva, ruler of the vital plane
Tīrthasthāna	A place of religious merit or virtue
Tittiri	Name of a bird
Trita	Director and holder of the Time Wheel. Under his guidance we have the Silver Age (Trita Yuga)
Tritayuga	The Silver Age
Triṣṭubh	A Sanskrit metre of 44 letters
Traivṛṣṇu	Incarnation of Viṣṇu
Traiaruṇa	Incarnation of the Sun God

U

Uṣṇīk	A Sanskrit metre of 28 letters
Udyama	An effort to start the work
Upaniṣad	A discussion on Vedic hymns with disciples
Uṣā	Divine Dawn, daughter of Satyadeva
Uṣā-Saṅgana	Power of the sun on the mental plane, an awakening conscious power

V

Vaidadaśvi	Son of Taranta, ruler of the physical plane
Vaiśampāyana	Ṛṣi Vyāsa's son and disciple
Vaiṣṇavī	Power of Viṣṇu
Vajra	Weapon of Indra
Vālmīkī	Poet of Rāmāyaṇa
Vanaspati	God of the Forest
Vāk	Daughter of Ambhṛṇī
Vāk-devī	Sarasvatī—Goddess of learning
Varga	Like Maṇḍala but shorter. In Devāyaṇa, it contains many Saṁvargas
Varuṇa	God of life, of water
Varṇa	Caste
Varṇāvata	House of lac made by Duryodhana to destroy the Pāṇḍavas
Vasiṣṭha	A Ṛṣi, son of Mitra-devatā
Vasu	God of riches
Vasukarṇa	The third Divine King ensures the physical transformation of the bodies into divine bodies. His power is Vasupriyā.
Vāsudeva	Another name of Kṛṣṇa
Vāsuki	The Snake King who holds the creation on his head in the subtle world
Vasukra	The first Divine King upon the earth. Commencement of the Golden Age where earth became like heaven. Death is removed from the world. Beings, if they so willed, could leave their bodies by calling upon Yamaraja. His power is Indrasnuṣā, also called Urnavatī as she came directly to the world without taking a human birth.
Vasukrīḍ	The second Divine King. Under him, souls could manifest directly upon the

	earth. Question of birth and death was solved. His power was Vasusaṅgā.
Vasuna	The seventh Vasu King who gifts to the world divine wealth and riches. Greed, passion and jealousy disappear from the earth. His power is Vasundharā.
Vasumāna	The last Vasu King, the eighth, maintains and protects all that was achieved by the Vasus. His power is Vasumati.
Vasurocisa	The fourth Vasu King from the Golden Age who gifted his people with clairvoyance. His power is Vasukanta.
Vasuśruta	The fifth Vasu King. Under him, people receive clairaudience. They can hear from vast distances. His power is Vasuvara.
Vasuyuva	The sixth Vasu King of the Golden Age. He brings down divine all-pervading love, divine rhythms, art and beauty. Misunderstanding and discord vanish from the world. His power who effects this is Vasulata.
Vāyu	Lord of the life force, Commander of the Divine Forces
Veda	The unique spiritual authority
Vibhīṣaṇa	Brother of Rāvaṇa, who gave him the right advice; one of the immortals who reincarnated in Kaliyuga to bring spiritual awakening to mortal souls
Vidarbha	Capital of King Bhīma
Vināyaka	Son of Śiva, another name of Gaṇapati
Vipāśā	Name of a river
Virāj	A Sanskrit metre having 10 letters in each foot
Viṣṇu	The Protector, who maintains and protects the world

Viśvakarmā	Son of Svar-bhuvana
Viśvāmitra	Ṛṣi, son of Gādhi Kauśika
Viśvāvasu	King of the Gandharvas, the celestial musicians
Vyādhi	Malady
Vyāhṛti	Plane in mantra
Vyāsa	The poet who wrote Mahābhārata, the second epic of India

Y

Yādava	Kṛṣṇa's family name
Yajña	A sacrifice, the flame of sacrifice
Yajur Veda	One of the four Vedas
Yama	The son of Viśvadeva, who is the Sun of the mental plane
Yamaloka	The world of Yama
Yamayani Śānti	Śanti
Yajur Veda	One of the four Vedas.
Yaūvanāśva	Incarnation of Sūrya
Yudhiṣṭhira	The eldest Pāṇḍava
Yuga	Age

MANTRAS TO BE CHANTED TO PREPARE ONESELF TO WELCOME THE GOLDEN AGE

यच्चिद्धि शश्वता तना देवं देवं यजामहे ॥
Yacchiddhi śaśvatā tanā devam devam yajāmahe—to be chanted 12 times

देवं देवं यजामहे ॥
Devaṁ devaṁ yajāmahe—to be chanted 12 times

देवं देवं ॥
Devaṁ devaṁ—to be chanted 10—100 times.
Then chant the holy word Om

आनन्दं आनन्दं केवलानन्दम ॥
Ānandam ānandam kevalānandam—to be chanted 6 times

आनन्ददेव खल्विमानि भूतानि जायन्ते ।
आनन्देन जातानि जीवन्ति ।
आनन्दं प्रयन्तं संविशंति ॥
Ānandādeva khalvimāni bhūtāni jāyante
Ānandena jātāni jīvanti
Ānandam prayantyam saṁviśanti—to be chanted 3 times.

आनन्दं आनन्दं ॥
Ānandaṁ Ānandaṁ—to be chanted 6 times

आनन्दं ब्रह्म ॥
Ānandaṁ Brahma—to be chanted 12 times

ब्रह्म सत्यं ॥
Brahma Satyaṁ—to be chanted 12 times

सत्यं देवं ॥
Satyāṁ Devaṁ—to be chanted 12 times

देवं देवं ॥

Devam devam—to be chanted from 10–100 times

तत्सवितुर्वरेण्यम् भर्गो देवस्य धीमहि ।
धियो यो नः प्रचोदयात् ॥

Tatsaviturvareṇyam bhargo devasya dhīmahi
Dhiyo yo naḥ pracodayāt—to be chanted 3 times

ॐ भुर्भुवः स्वः महः ॥

Om bhūrbhuvaḥ śvaḥ mahaḥ—to chanted 3 times

तत्सवितुर्वरेणयं भर्गो देवस्य धीमहि ।
धियो यो नः प्रचोदयात् ॥

Tatsaviturvareṇyam bhargo devasya dhīmahi
Dhiyo yo naḥ pracodayāt—to be chanted once

देवं देवं ॥

Devaṁ devaṁ—to be chanted from 10–100 times

ऋतं सत्यं अमृतं सत्यं ॥

Ṛtam satyam amṛtam satyam—to be chanted 12 times

देवं देवं ॥

Devaṁ devaṁ—to be chanted 10–100 times

अमृतं कुरु कुरु स्वाहा ॥

Amṛtaṁ kuru kuru svāhā—to be chanted 12 times

देवं देवं ॥

Devaṁ devaṁ—to be chanted 10–100 times

ॐ क्रीं क्रीं क्रीं ह्रं ह्रं श्रीं श्रीं दक्षिणे कालिके स्वाहा

Om krīṁ krīṁ krīṁ hrīṁ hrīṁ śrīṁ śrīṁ dakṣiṇe kālike svāhā—to be chanted 12 times

ॐ क्रीं क्रीं क्रीं हुं हुं श्रीं श्रीं दक्षिणे कालिके स्वाहा

Om krīṁ krīṁ krīṁ huṅ huṅ śrīṁ śrīṁ dakṣiṇe kālike svāhā—to be chanted 12 times

Then clap your hands with joy and complete the prayer by chanting devaṁ devaṁ.

END NOTES

1. Seven Kaśyapas, the sons of Kaśyapa are Avatsara, Asita-devala, Nighrubi, Bhutāṁsa, Rebha, Vivriha, Rebhasūnu and Śikhaṇḍī.
2. Forty-four Āṅgirasas, sons of Aṅgirā are Havivardhana, Abhivarta, Ayasya, Ucathya, Ūru, Ūrdhvasadma, Kutsya, Kritayaśa, Kṛṣṇa, Ghora, Tiraści, Divya, Dharuna, Dhruva, Nrimedha, Pavitra, Purumihla, Purumedha, Puruhanma, Pūtadakṣa, Praceta, Prabhuvasu, Priyamedha, Varu, Bindu, Bṛhanmati, Bhikṣu, Mūrdhavān, Rāhūgana, Virūpa, Vibhaya, Vītahavya, Vyaśavya, Śiśu, Śaunahotra, Śrutakakṣa, Saṁvanana, Saṁvarta, Saptagu, Savya, Sukakṣa, Suditi, Harimanta, Hiraṇyastupa.
3. Thirty-seven Ātreyas, the sons of Atri are Arcanana, Avasyu, Īśa, Urucakri, Evyamarut, Kumāra, Gaya, Gabiṣṭhira, Gatu, Gopabana, Dyumna, Viśva-carśani, Dvita, Mriktavaha, Pūrva, Paura, Pratiśetra, Pratiprabha, Pratibhānu, Pratiratha, Vabhru, Bahuvrikta, Buddha, Yajata, Vātahavya, Vaghri, Vasuśruta, Viśvasama, Śyāvaśva, Śrutavid, Satyaśrava, Sadaprina, Sapta-vaghri, Sasa, Sutambhra, Svasti, and Prayasvanta.
4. Twenty-eight Kāṇveyas, sons of Kaṇva are Āyu, Harinvīthi, Kusidi, Kurusuti, Kṛṣṇa, Triśobha, Nābhāka, Nārada, Parvata, Devatithi, Nipatithi, Punarvatsa, Puṣṭigu, Priśaghra, Pragatha, Praskanva, Brahmatithi, Medhātithi, Medhyatithi, Mātariśvā, Medhya, Vatsa, Śaśakarṇa, Śruṣṭigu, Sadhvaṁsa, Suparṇa, and Saubhari.
5. Three Gautamas, sons of Gautama are; Rāhūgana, Nodha, and Vāmadeva.
6. Ten Bhāradvājas, sons of Bharadvāja are: Bārhaspatya, Garga, Nara, Pāyu, Vasu, Śasa, Śrimbithi, Śunuhotra, Suhotra, and Sapratha.

7. Eleven Vaṣiṣṭhas, sons of Vasiṣṭha are: Indra-Pramati, Upamanyu, Karnaśrud, Citramaha, Dyumnaka, Pratha, Manyu, Mṛdika, Vasukra, Vṛṣagaṇa, and Vyāghrapāda.
8. Eight Maitreyas, sons of Mitra are: Gathina, Aṣṭaka, Ṛṣabha, Kaṭa, Devarāta, Pūraṇa, Madhucchandā, and Reṇu.

DEVAS

Tanūnapāt, Naraśaṁśa, Deva-hota, Pracetasa, Vanaspati, Drabina, Nirmathya, Brahmaṇaspati, Sadasaspati, Ulūkhala, Yūpa, Aryamā, Svanaya, Bhavayavya, Romaśa, Bhaga, Ilya, Barhi, Aśva, Śakadhūma, Sādhya, Arṇa, Aptrina, Raka, Gaṅgu, Apanapath, Śānkuta, Vraścana, Puriśya, Upadhyāya, Somaka, Dadhikra, Tryasdasya, Darbhya, Parjanya, Cayamāna, Vrivustākṣa, Prastoka, Pratoda, Itastran, Suda, Paijavāna, Maṇḍūka, Grabana, Vibhindou, Pakasthama, Karaṅga, Aśvikaśu, Kaśu, Tirindira, Varu, Yajña, Kanina, Pitara, Saranyu, Dhātā, Jīva, Hasta, Sāvarni, Svasti, Jñana, Manyu, Arka, Puruṣa, Hari, Drughana, Venu, Dyubhumya, Draviṇoda, Īśa, Ūrja, Saha, Sahasya, Tapa, Sraka, Ritaba....

DEVĪS

Ila, Bhāratī, Svahā, Savitā, Pṛthivī, Rātri, Sadhyā, Rati, Sinibali, Gaṅgā, Drani, Varuṇā, Ditayā, Yūpā, Nadī, Sasarparī, Rathānginī, Sītā, Rathabītī, Prasvapinī, Maṇḍukā, Dampati, Niritī, Pathyā, Urvaśī, Appadevī, Saramā, Ambhriṇī, Śraddhā, Śacī, Yajamanā, Saṅganā.

ṚṢIS

Agastya, Drihlacuta, Ajigarti, Śunaḥśepa, Atharvana, Bṛhaddiva, Bhiṣaka, Amahiyaba, Urukṣaya, Ambharīṣa, Sindhudipa, Ārbhava, Sunu, Arṣṭisena, Devāpi, Asaṅga, Playogi, Utkila, Katya, Uśana, Riṇañcaya, Nakudya, Arammada, Aravat, Jaratkarna, Aila, Pururavā, Ailuṣa, Kavaṣa, Kuśika, Aiśirathi, Ucathya, Dīrghatamā, Aurava, Aṅga, Auṣija, Kakṣīvana, Uśīnara, Śivi, Ita, Kavi, Kṛtnu, Gṛtsamada,

Śaunahotra, Cyavana, Jamadagni, Neva, Prayoga, Vena, Somahuti, Syumaraśmi, Mudgala, Bharṇyaśva, Vatsapri, Bhalandana, Sammada, Manya, Matsya, Aghamarśaṇa, Jeta Apsaba, Saṁvaraṇa, Lopāmudrā, Bandhu, Biprabandhu, Shrutabandhu, Subandhu, Bikhanasa, Bamra, Basha, Sapti, Vajambhara, Vata-raśana, Juti, Vatajuti, Viprajuti, Vṛsanaka, Ṛṣyaśṛṅga, Karikrata, Etaśa, Sumitra, Vaghyasva, Anhomuk, Bṛhaduktha, Aurddhabana, Bhṛgu, Satyaśruta, Varṣagirā, Ambarīsa, Bhayamāna, Rhijraśva, Sahadeva, Sudharā, Varṣṭihabya, Upastupa, Vītahavya, Aruna, Vaiyaśva, Viśvamāna, Vairūpa, Aṣṭadraṁṣṭa, Nabhaspravedana, Śatapravedana, Saghri, Śakkara, Ṛhishava, Śārṅga, Jarita, Droṇa, Sarisṛkka, Stambhamitra,, Śaurṣi, Suveda, Śailiśī, Kulmala, Varhihsi.

THE ṚṢIKĀS

Śāśvatī, Apalā, Viśvabarā, Ambhrinī, Indrasnuṣā, Urvaśī, Godhā, Nadī, Saramā, Sāvitrī, Asvasukti, Gosukti, Kakṣīvatī, Gauribiti, Nivavorī, Sikatā, Laukyi, Romaṣā, Rātri, Jalanaddhā, etc. etc.

FIRST FOUR CANTOS IN ORIGINAL BENGALI

দেবায়ণ

॥ ব্রহ্ম কল্প ॥

॥ দেব মণ্ডল ॥

॥ কাব্য সমারম্ভ বর্গ ॥

॥ প্রথম সংবর্গ ॥

গভীরা রজনী ঘোরে সর্ব স্তব্ধ চতুর্দ্দিকে
তৃতীয় প্রহরাতীতে নিদ্রাচ্যুত যবে স্বযং ॥
দর্শিত পরম স্বপ্ন নিত্য সাক্ষাৎ অতঃপরে
সর্ব্ব সত্য জগৎ হিতে মহর্লোক সমাগত ॥
যন্ত্র তুল্য যথাস্থলে স্রষ্টা কৃত নিরূপিত
গুরু কৃপা প্রসাদিত যৎ তপস্যা নিয়োজনে ॥
যৎ ক্ষেত্রে পরম শ্রুতি বিশ্রুত সর্ব্ব বিস্ময়ে
ওঙ্কার অক্ষর ব্রহ্ম নাভি কেন্দ্র নিনাদনে ॥
ওঙ্কার আদি কারণ সর্ব্ব সৃষ্টি প্রকাশিতে
ত্র্যক্ষর গতি কল্লোলে ধবনি ব্রহ্ম পরশ্রুতি ॥
অকারে যৎ সমুদ্ভব উকারে যৎ অবস্থিতি
মকার যৎ সমাপনে পুনর্য়োগ অনুস্বরে ॥
পুনঃ সৃষ্টি সমারম্ভ মকারন্ত পদে যথা
আবর্তে প্রণব ধবনি সৃষ্টি স্থিতি লয ক্রমে ॥
তৎ ধবনি নাভি সম্ভব মহাদ্যূতি বিভাস্বর
আনন্দ তেজ কারণ ওঙ্কার সর্ব্ব ঈশ্বর ॥

ওঙ্কার যৎ চতুর্ভুজ লোকনাথ নারায়ণ
ওঙ্কার পরমাত্মন ওঙ্কার পুরুষোত্তম ॥
ওঙ্কার সর্ব্ব ধারনে সর্ব্বব্যাপী বিরাজিত
ওঙ্কার পরমেশ্বর রূপে নিত্য উপাসিত ॥
তৎ ধবনি শ্রবণে স্বযং সচকিত সচতেন
যৎ দৃষ্ট বহিরান্তরে কহি বাক্য তদক্রমে ॥
পুণ্য স্বপ্নে পুলকিত চিত্তেনিদ্রাভঙ্গে শিহরিত অঙ্গে
নাভি ক্ষেত্রে সুবলিত ছন্দে ওঁ ওঁ নারায়ণ শুনি মন্দ্রে ॥

—ইতি শ্রীমদ্দেবায়ণ ব্রহ্মকল্প প্রথম খণ্ড দেবমণ্ডলান্তর্গত কাব্য সমারম্ভ বর্গে নাদ শ্রবণ নামঃ প্রথম সংবর্গ ॥

—☆—

॥ দ্বিতীয় সংবর্গ ॥

ওঁ তৎ বাক্য পরব্রহ্ম অব্যক্ত যৎ অনির্দ্দেশ্য
রূপ ব্যক্ত তথাস্থূলে ব্রহ্মা বিষ্ণু মহশ্বেরে ॥
ধবনি ব্রহ্ম স্বয়ংভুব ওঙ্কার সৃষ্টি কারণ
রূপোদ্ভবে জগৎচয়ে ব্রহ্মা বিষ্ণু মহেশ্বরে ॥
এতৎ সৃষ্টি সমারম্ভে বেদ সহ বহির্গত
ব্রহ্মণাস্যে মহাতেজ যৎ আদিত্য মহাস্মৃতি ॥
তৎ তেজসে মহাবেগে য়বে সৃষ্টি সমুদ্ভবে
তৎ বেগ ছন্দ বর্ণিত মহাশক্তি স্বরূপিণী ॥
তৎ গতি করি বর্ণনা ত্রিপাদ অষ্ট অক্ষরে
ঋষিবৃন্দে সুবন্দিত যৎ বর্ণ গুণ মণ্ডিত ॥
অকারে কথিত ব্রহ্ম উকারে বিষ্ণু দেবতা
মকারে রুদ্র বর্ণিত পুনর্যোগ অনুস্বরে ॥
ব্রহ্ম তেজে প্রকাশিত বিষ্ণু বীর্য্যে বিধারিত
রুদ্র বলে বিনষ্ট যৎ পুনশ্চ যুক্ত পিঙ্গলে ॥
এরূপ অক্ষর ব্রহ্মে আবর্ত্তন ত্রযাক্ষরে
বারদ্বয সমাপনে স্থিরোকারে তৃতীয়তে ॥

গায়ত্রী পাদ বর্ণিত অষ্টাক্ষরে ত্রিঘূর্ণনে
গায়ত্রী প্রণবাস্থিতা বেদমাতা সুবর্ণিতা ॥
অষ্টাক্ষরে ত্রিঘূর্ণনে তৎ প্রকার পদত্রয়ে
ভাস্বতী ছন্দ গায়ত্রী মহাশক্তি স্বরূপিণী ॥
য়ৎ বেদ আদি গায়ত্রী সর্ব্ব ব্যাপী মহেশ্বরী
তৎ গায়ত্রী মহাশক্তি সর্ব ছন্দ প্রকাশিণী ॥
অষ্টাক্ষরা পদত্রয়ে গায়ত্রী ধ্যানি সর্ব্বদা
ত্রিবর্ণা যে ত্রিমূর্ত্তিতে যথাকালে প্রকাশিতা ॥
তদ্দর্শন মনোহর বিচিত্র বর্ণ সজ্জিতা
বিচিত্র গতি বিন্যাসে সর্ব্ব সৃষ্টি প্রচালিকা ॥
প্রথমে দর্শিতা দেবী রক্ত বর্ণে সমুজ্জ্বলা
সৃষ্টি ধ্যানে সমুৎপন্না কর্ম্ম ছন্দ প্রণোদিতা ॥
প্রভাতে জগত ধ্যানে এতৎ রূপ পরিস্ফুট
ব্রহ্ম শক্তি সমাখ্যাতা ব্রাহ্মণী হংস বাহণা ॥
জাগ্রত করিতে বিশ্ব কুশ অস্ত করে ধৃত
দানি সুপ্তে চলৎশক্তি কর্ম্ম গতি সচেতনে ॥
দ্বিতীয়ে অতি ভাস্বরা দৃষ্টা দেবী হিরন্ময়ী
প্রেম ঐক্যে সমুদ্ভবা কর্ম্ম সূত্র বিধারিতা ॥
মধ্যাহ্নে জগত ধ্যানে এতৎ রূপ পরিস্ফুট
বিষ্ণু শক্তি সমাখ্যাতা বৈষ্ণবী গরুড়াসনা ॥
শঙ্খ চক্র গদা পদ্মে যথা দেবী সুশোভিতা
প্রেম সূত্রে মহানন্দে ঐক্যে জগৎ বিধারিকা ॥
তৃতীযে দর্শিতা দেবী ধৌম্রবর্ণা মনোহরা
জগৎ সৃষ্টি লয়ঙ্কর যথা শক্তি প্রকাশিতা ॥
সাযাহ্নে জগত ধ্যানে এতৎ রূপ পরিস্ফুট
মহেশ্বরী সমাখ্যাতা বৃষভ শ্বেত বাহণা ॥
ত্রিশূল কর ধারণে দ্বেষী দুষ্ট বিমর্দ্দণে
জগন্মোহে বিমোহয়া সর্ব্ব শান্তি প্রদাযিকা ॥
তৎ দেবী স্মরি গায়ত্রী সর্বব শুচিঃ প্রদায়িনী
ব্রহ্ম বাক্য যথা বেদ ব্রহ্মণাস্যে বহির্গত ॥

তৎ তেজসে পরব্রহ্মে চতুর্ব্বেদ সমুদ্ভবে
সাম যজুঃ ঋকাথর্ব্ব ব্রহ্মণাস্যে যথাক্রমে ॥
চতুরাস্যে চতুর্ব্বেদ পূর্ব্বে সাম ঋকোত্তরে
অথর্ব্ব দক্ষিণে যথা দর্শিত পশ্চিমে যজুঃ ॥
গাযত্রী বেদ সর্ব্বতে ব্রহ্ম বাক বিভাস্বরা
ষড় ছন্দ প্রকাশিণী কহি এতৎ তদক্রমে ॥
গাযত্রী অষ্ট অক্ষরে যথা উক্ত পদত্রযে
এতৎ রূপে মহাদেবী ঋষি কুলে প্রপূজিতা ॥
তদূক্ত আর্ষ্য গাযত্রী অষ্টাক্ষরা পদত্রযে
চতুর্ব্বিংশাক্ষরা দেবী সর্ব্বত্র স্মর সর্ব্বদা ॥
দেব কুলে যথা অন্য রূপে দেবী উপাসিতা
কথিত দিব্য গাযত্রী চতুষ্পাদে ষড়াক্ষরে ॥
দেব ঋষি উপাসিতা দ্বিবিধ মূর্ত্তি ধারণে
অষ্টবিংশাক্ষরা ছন্দ গাযত্রী জাত উষ্ণিক ॥
দ্বিবিধ গতি ওষ্ণিকে এতৎ হেতু সমীক্ষিত
কচিৎ অষ্টাক্ষরে পাদ ষড়াক্ষরে কচিৎ কচিৎ ॥
অষ্টাক্ষরে যথা পাদ ঋষিবৃন্দে উপাসিত
দ্বাত্রিংশ অক্ষরে ছন্দ চতুষ্পাদে অনুষ্ঠুপ ॥
তৎপরে বৃহতী ছন্দ ষড় ত্রিংশাক্ষরোদ্ভব
চত্বারিংশাক্ষরোদ্ভব পংক্তি ছন্দ তদন্তরে ॥
চতুঃ চত্বারিংশাক্ষরে ত্রিষ্ঠুপ ছন্দ বর্ণিত
কথিত জগতি ছন্দ অষ্ট চত্বারিংশাক্ষরে ॥
অনুষ্ঠুপ হতে ছন্দ জগতী যৎ সুবর্ণিত
সর্ব্ব ছন্দ চতুষ্পাদে ভিন্নাক্ষরে প্রকাশিত ॥
যথা ছন্দ চতুষ্পাদে ঋষি বৃন্দে উপাসিত
সর্ব্ব অগ্রে অনুষ্ঠুপ ব্যক্ত ছন্দ মহীতলে ॥
যৎ ছন্দ অতি তেজসে জগৎ সৃষ্টি প্রকাশক
সর্ব্ব তেজ বলান্বিত নিত্য কবি কুল প্রিয ॥
গায়ত্রী সংহতি ষড় ছন্দে পূর্ব্বে বেদোদ্ভব চতুরাস্যে
নাদ ব্রহ্মাক্ষর অতি তেজে আদিত্যাখ্যা দিনমণি দীপ্তঃ ॥

—ইতি শ্রীমদ্দেবায়ণ ব্রহ্মকল্প প্রথম খণ্ড দেবমণ্ডলান্তর্গত কাব্য সমারম্ভ বর্গে গায়ত্র্যাদি ছন্দ বর্ণনা নামঃ দ্বিতীয় সংবর্গ ॥

— ☆ —

॥ তৃতীয় সংবর্গ ॥

নব সৃষ্টি প্রকাশিতে অনুষ্টুপ বিমন্দ্রণে
উদ্বোধনে পুনঃ কল্প পিঙ্গল কবি উদ্ভব ॥
সত্য ত্রিতা দ্বিতা কলি যুগ গতি যথাক্রমে
কলি অন্তে পুনর্সত্যে কল্প গতি যবে শুন ॥
এতৎ সন্ধিক্ষণে দৃষ্ট পিঙ্গলাখ্য মহেশ্বর
জটাজুট বিমণ্ডিত পশু পাশ বিমোচক ॥
গম্ভীরে কহিতে রত লক্ষ্যি এতৎ প্রজাপতি
কশ্যপ জগত স্রজা বিস্ময়ে রত দর্শনে ॥
এতৎ ক্ষেত্র মহামতি করি কাব্য নিরূপণে
তপঃ তেজ প্রদানহ করিতে ধারণক্ষম ॥
প্রাজ্ঞ স্মন্য নহে যুবা দেব শ্রদ্ধা পরায়ণ
বেদজ্ঞানে সদা স্পৃহা করি ক্ষেত্র নিরূপণ ॥
কহি বাক্য অনুষ্টুপে মহানাদ যথাকৃত
ত্রৈলক্য সৃষ্টি কম্পনে তথা কাব্য বহির্গত ॥
কহিতে রত কশ্যপে দেব কাব্য প্রদর্শনে
অপূর্ব্ব দ্যুতি মণ্ডিত হের সত্য প্রকাশক ॥
দেবতত্ত্ব বিধারণে দেব জন্ম সমুদ্ভবে
দেবকার্য্য প্রকাশিযা যথা চক্র বিঘূর্ণিত ॥
সর্ব্ব সৃষ্টি সমাশ্রয়ে করি ব্যক্ত চতুর্যুগ
দেব বুদ্ধি সমাচ্ছন্ন যৎ প্রকারে মহান্ধতে ॥
যৎ প্রকারে প্রদীপিত দেব বুদ্ধি দিনে দিনে
তৎ বিশালায়ণ স্মর সর্ব্ব সৃষ্টি সমন্বিত ॥
দেব কাল হতে ক্রমে অন্ধকালে নিপাতিত
সর্ব্ব সৃষ্টি জগৎস্রজা কি প্রকারে নিরীক্ষহ ॥

পুনশ্চ হের তৎপরে   অন্ধকাল পরিত্যজি
দেব কালে পুনর্ব্বার   এতৎ সৃষ্টি সমুত্থিত ॥
দেব কাল হতে ক্রমে   দেব কালে পুনঃ গতি
দেবায়ণ ইহা কহি   সর্ব্ব তত্ত্ব বিধারণে ॥
যথা তব সমুদ্যম   সত্য যুগ প্রকাশিতে
একাংশে কর দর্শন   এতৎ তথ্য অবস্থিত ॥
দ্বাদশাংশে বিভাগিত   সহস্র পত্র নির্ণয়ে
দৃষ্ট লক্ষাধিক শ্লোকে   অংশেক যৎ প্রকাশিত ॥
চতুর্য্যুগে যথা সৃষ্টি   ব্যক্ত ক্রমে ক্রমান্বয়ে
অনন্ত ব্যোম সন্নিভ   দেবায়ণ সমীক্ষিত ॥
এতন্মধ্যে নিবেশিত   সর্ব্বক্রমে নিরীক্ষহ
চতুর্দ্দিকে অবস্থিত   হের বেদ চতুষ্টয় ॥
ঋগ্বেদ হের পূর্ব্বতে   পশ্চিমে যজু দর্শিত
সাম বেদ যথোত্তরে   অথর্ব্ব বেদ দক্ষিণে ॥
নভ স্থলে যথাদৃশ্য   জ্যোতিস্কাদি সুচিত্রিত
কোটি কোটি নিহারিকা   তারাগ্রহ উপগ্রহে ॥
এতন্মধ্যে বিভাস্বর   চন্দ্র সূর্য্য যথাদ্বয়
তদ্রূপ কর দর্শন   দেবায়ণ মহাত্মন ॥
সূর্য্যতুল্য বিভাস্বর   সূর্য্য বংশ সুবর্ণনে
রামায়ণ মহীতলে   রাম কীর্ত্তি সমাশ্রিত ॥
অবতীর্ণ জনার্দ্দন   রাম রূপে নরাকৃতি
অতুল্য তেজ বীর্য্যতে   কীর্ত্তি শ্রেষ্ঠ যথাস্থলে ॥
চন্দ্রতুল্য বিভাস্বত   চন্দ্র বংশ তদন্তরে
ভারত কাহিনী ধৃত   কৃষ্ণ কীর্ত্তি মহীতলে ॥
অবতীর্ণ জনার্দ্দন   কৃষ্ণ রূপে নরাকৃতি
অতুল্য বুদ্ধি কৌশলে   কীর্ত্তি শ্রেষ্ঠ প্রকাশিত ॥
এতৎ বিনা সহস্রশ   সুচরিত্র সুবর্ণিত
তেজবীর্য্যে মহৎ অতি   দেবতুল্যজনে জনে ॥
এ সর্ব্ব পূন্য জীবন   তারা তুল্য সমুজ্জ্বল
দ্বাদশ সহস্রাধিক   পত্র দলে বিমণ্ডিত ॥

দেবায়ণ অনুষ্টুপে গান্ধার গুরু গর্জ্জনে
মেঘতুল্য বিমন্দ্রিত হ্রস্ব দীর্ঘ প্লুতস্বনে ॥
এতৎ বিণা ক্ষণে ক্ষণে অন্য ছন্দ বহির্গত
বিদ্যুন্নাদ যথামত অকস্মাত সমুদ্ভবে ॥
এতৎ নভঃ সমাশ্রয়ে দিবারাত্রে যথাগতি
হের দেবায়ণে গতি এতৎ যুগ চতুষ্টয়ে ॥
সত্য যুগ দিবারূপে দেব সূর্য্য বিভাস্বর
কলি যুগ নিশারূপে অন্ধ শক্তি প্রভাবিত ॥
এতন্মধ্যে তথাদ্বয় করে ক্ষেত্র বিভাগিত
ত্রিতা সন্ধ্যা সমাখ্যাত অর্দ্ধ রাত্রি যথাদ্বিতা ॥
দিব্য উষা সুবর্ণনে রাত্রিহরা যথাপথ
জীবজগৎ প্রচেতনে দেবসূর্য্য প্রদর্শনে ॥
অত্যাদ্ভুত যথাকাল সর্ব্বাধিক মনোহর
এতৎ ক্রমে যথাব্যক্ত হরে স্বয়ং জগৎস্রজা ॥
কাব্যোন্মেষে লঘু গুরু ছন্দে মন্দ্রে দেবায়ণ নব দৃশ্যে
হৃষ্ট দ্রষ্টাবতরণ কালে দর্শে স্রষ্টা অপলক চক্ষে ॥

—ইতি শ্রীমদ্দেবায়ণ ব্রহ্মকল্প প্রথম খণ্ড দেবমণ্ডলান্তর্গত কাব্যসমারম্ভ বর্গে কাব্য প্রকাশ বার্তা নামঃ তৃতীয় সংবর্গ ॥

—☆—

॥ চতুর্থ সংবর্গ ॥

তৎ শ্রবণে কহে বাক্য কশ্যাপ পিঙ্গল প্রতি
অতি দীর্ঘ মহাকাব্য স্মরি ব্যক্ত অসম্ভব ॥
স্বল্পায়ু মানবে দৃষ্ট বর্ষ শত প্রয়োজন
কি প্রকারে অভিব্যক্তি কহ এতৎ কবীশ্বর ॥
তদূত্তরে কহে কবি যথাস্থির মম প্রতি
সংক্ষেপ করিতে কাল শুনক্রমে জগৎস্রজা ॥

দ্বাদশ সহস্রাধিক পত্র দেবায়ণে যথা
তৎ প্রকাশ যথাক্রমে স্বযং চক্ষে নিরীক্ষহ ॥
দশ পত্র দিবা প্রতি তুমি স্বযং পরিগ্রহ
তথা শক্তি প্রদানিযা কর বাক্যে প্রচালিত ॥
কর সংখ্যা নিরূপণ দশ পত্র দিবা প্রতি
প্রতিমাসে দিবা ত্রিংশে ত্রিশতক প্রকাশিবে ॥
মাসত্রয দিবাদশে হবে পত্র সহস্রশ
দ্বাদশ গুণ নির্ণযে কর কাল নিরূপণ ॥
কহে স্রজা ইথে কাল বর্ষত্রয প্রযোজন
চতুর্মাস তদূপরি দেবায়ণ প্রকাশিতে ॥
সংক্ষেপ কাল নিশ্চয এতৎ পথে কবীশ্বর
তবু প্রশ্ন বিচারহ যথা কার্য্য সুদুস্কর ॥
বর্ষ ত্রয চতুর্মাস স্থিরাসন অসম্ভব
যথা অন্নগত প্রাণ ক্ষুধাতৃষ্ণা নিপীড়নে ॥
প্রত্যুত্তরে কহে কবি স্বীয তেজ প্রদানহ
তব তপঃ যথা বর্ষ ষড় বিংশ সহস্রশ ॥
এতৎ তপঃ মহাশক্তি সমাশ্রযে রহ স্বযং
তব তেজ প্রভাবিত হবে ক্ষম প্রকাশিতে ॥
তব তেজ প্রভাবিত নহে দুঃখ কদাচন
স্থিরাসনে অবস্থানে কাব্য কার্য্য যতক্ষণ ॥
উপরন্ত প্রহর্ষিত হবে চিত্ত ক্ষণে ক্ষণে
কাব্য ধারা প্রবাহিলে হবে দৃঢ় দিনে দিনে ॥
পুনঃ প্রশ্নে কহে স্রজা স্বল্প বাক্য প্রযোজন
নহে দীর্ঘ মহাকাব্য প্রকাশিতে কবীশ্বর ॥
যথা কাব্য বৃহত্তম দ্বাদশ গুণ বর্দ্ধিত
এতন্মত প্রয়োজন বাক্যাবলী মহাত্মন ॥
কহে কবি কি সংশয় বহু বাক্য প্রয়োজন
তথা বিঘ্ন উপদ্রব বিমূঢ়ত্বে সুনিশ্চয ॥
কহি কার্য্য তথাস্থলে অবধান কর স্থিরে
বহু বাক্য সুসংগ্রহে বিঘ্নচয নিরামযে ॥

আহবানি গণনায়কে মাত্রক্ষণ অপেক্ষহ
বাকসিদ্ধি প্রদানিতে সিদ্ধি দাতা গজাননে ॥
হবে সর্ব্ব সমাধান এতৎ দেব উপস্থিতে
আখ্যাত ব্রহ্মণস্পতি ব্রহ্ম সৃষ্টি প্রকাশিতে ॥
তৎ দেবতা প্রভাবিত যথা বাক্য প্রযোজন
হবে ত্বরিত সুসংগ্রহ বিঘ্ন চিন্তা পরিত্যজ ॥
এরূপ কহি পিঙ্গল দেবস্রা কশ্যপ প্রতি
আহবানে রত সুস্বনে বিঘ্ন নাশ গজাননে ॥
স্মরি কাব্য সমারম্ভে পার্ব্বতী প্রিয় নন্দন
সিদ্ধি দাতা বিনায়ক গণেশ ব্রহ্মণস্পতি ॥
আহবানি গণ সম্রাট জন লোকে প্রকাশিতে
কাব্যেক মুষিকারূঢ় দেব সত্য প্রচেতনে ॥
দেবাস্তিত্বে অবিশ্বাস যথানিত্য নরঃ প্রতি
তৎ বিঘ্ন বারণে কার্য্য স্বয়ং হর্ষে পরিগ্রহ ॥
কবি কুল পুরোভাগে রুদ্র তেজে বিরাজিত
জ্যেষ্ঠরাজ জগৎহিতে ত্বরিৎ আত্ম প্রকাশহ ॥
বাক্ ব্রহ্ম তব তেজসে অনুভূত জগন্মনে
বাক্ শিল্প ঋত বুদ্ধিতে ব্যক্ত হর্ষে নিরন্তর ॥
দানিতে শুচিতা বাক্যে অক্ষর ব্রহ্ম দর্শনে
বাক্ চাতুর্য্য অলংকারে সুব্যক্তে স্মরি সত্তরে ॥
এরূপ কহিতে কবি তৎদেব মূষিকারূঢ়
শঙ্খ বজ্র গদা পদ্মে আবির্ভূত চতুর্ভুজ ॥
ত্রিনেত্র করুণাকর দিব্যস্নেহ বিনির্ঝর
সুজ্যোতি মণ্ডলাবৃত শুচিস্মিত গজানন ॥
প্রভাতারুণ সন্নিভ রক্ত বর্ণ কলেবর
অপূর্ব্ব ভূষণাম্বরে দিব্যমাল্যে বিভূষিত ॥
শিরঃ শ্বেত কি সুন্দর প্রভাতে পুন্য দর্শনে
হর্ষান্বিত কলেবরে শিহরিত পুনঃ পুনঃ ॥
যৎ দৃশ্যে কবি সম্রাট পিঙ্গল স-সুরস্রজা
তদগ্রে পার্ব্বতী পুত্র অন্তর্চক্ষে সমীক্ষিত ॥

তৎ বাক্য শ্রবণে স্বযং রোম হর্ষে মুহুর্মুহু
সংগ্রহে রত সর্ব্বতঃ পূন্য আস্য বিনির্গত ॥
যথা দীন পরিগ্রহে মণি রত্ন সুদুর্লভ
তৎ তুল্য লেখনীধৃত সংগ্রহি দিবস ক্রমে ॥
মাস বর্ষ দিবাক্রমে শ্রম ক্লান্তি বিবির্জ্জিত
পুন্য বার্তা যথশ্রুত বিস্ময়তর বিস্ময়ে ॥
আশ্চর্য্য কেবলাশ্চর্য্যে মমচিত্ত প্রধাবিত
তৎ বাক্য করি সংগ্রহ ব্যক্ত কাব্য মহীতলে ॥
স্রষ্টা বাক্যে কবিবরহাস্যে যুক্তাহবানে গণপতি নামে
ব্যক্ত শ্বেতানন গজ মুণ্ডে সিদ্ধি প্রাতে মধুময় দৃশ্যে ॥

—ইতি শ্রীমদ্দেবায়ণ ব্রহ্মকল্প প্রথম খণ্ড দেবমণ্ডলান্তর্গতকাব্য সমারম্ভ বর্গে সিদ্ধি প্রকাশ নামঃ চতুর্থ সংবর্গ ॥

—☆—

FIRST FOUR CANTOS IN DEVANAGARI

॥ देवायण ॥

॥ ब्रह्म कल्प ॥

॥ देव मण्डल ॥

॥ काव्य समारम्भ वर्ग ॥

प्रथम संवर्ग

गभीरा रजनी घोरे सर्व स्तब्ध चतुर्दिके ।
तृतीय प्रहरातीते निद्रा च्युत यवे स्वयं ॥
दर्शित परम स्वप्न नित्य साक्षात् अतःपरे ।
सर्व सत्य जगत्हिते महर लोक समागत ॥
यंत्र तुल्य यथास्थले स्त्रष्टा कृत निरूपित ।
गुरू कृपा प्रसादित यद् तपस्या नियोजने ॥
यद् क्षेत्रे परम श्रुति विश्रुत सर्व विस्मये ।
ॐकार अक्षर ब्रह्म नाभि केन्द्र निनादने ॥
ॐकार आदि कारण सर्व सृष्टि प्रकाशिते ।
त्र्यक्षर गति कल्लोले ध्वनि ब्रह्म परश्रुति ॥
अकारे यद् समुद्भव उकारे यद् अवस्थिति ।
मकार यद् समापने पुनर्योग अनुस्वरे ॥
पुनः सृष्टि समारम्भ मकारन्त पदे यथा ।
आवर्ते प्रणव ध्वनि सृष्टि स्थिति लयक्रमे ॥
तद् ध्वनि नाभि सम्भव महाद्युति विभास्वर ।
आनन्द तेज कारण ॐकार सर्व ईश्वर ॥

ॐकार यद् चतुर्भुज लोकनाथ नारायण ।
ॐकार परमात्मन ॐकार पुरुषोत्तम ॥
ॐकार सर्वधारणे सर्व व्यापी विराजित ।
ॐकार परमेश्वर रूपे नित्य उपासित ॥
तद् ध्वनि श्रवणे स्वयं सचकित सचेतन ।
यद् दृष्ट बहिरान्तरे कहि वाक्य तद्क्रमे ॥
पुण्य स्वप्ने पुलकित चित्ते निद्राभंगे शिहरित अंगे ।
नाभि क्षेत्रे सुबलित छन्दे ॐ ॐ नारायण शुनि मन्द्रे ॥

—इति श्रीमद्देवायण ब्रह्मकल्पे प्रथम खण्डे देव मण्डलान्तर्गतः काव्य समारम्भ वर्गे नादः श्रवण नामः प्रथम संवर्ग ॥

— ☆ —

॥ द्वितीय संवर्ग ॥

ॐ तद् वाक्य परब्रह्म अव्यक्त यद् अनिर्देश्य ।
रूप व्यक्त तथास्थले ब्रह्मा विष्णु महेश्वरे ॥
ध्वनि ब्रह्म स्वयंभुव ॐकार सृष्टि कारण ।
रूपोद्भवे जगत् चये ब्रह्मा विष्णु महेश्वरे ॥
एतद् सृष्टि समारम्भे वेद सह बहिर्गत ।
ब्रह्मणास्ये महातेज यद् आदित्य महास्मृति ॥
तद् तेजसे महावेगे यवे सृष्टि समुद्भवे ।
तद् वेग छन्द वर्णित महाशक्ति स्वरूपिणी ॥
तद् गति करि वर्णना त्रिपाद अष्ट अक्षरे ।
ऋषि वृन्दे सुवन्दित यद् वर्ण गुण मण्डित ॥
अकारे कथित ब्रह्म उकारे विष्णु देवता ।
मकारे रुद्र वर्णित पुनर्योग अनुस्वरे ॥
ब्रह्म तेजे प्रकाशित विष्णुवीर्ये विधारित ।
रुद्र बले विनष्ट यद् पुनश्च युक्त पिगंले ॥

एरूप अक्षर ब्रह्मे आवर्तन त्रयाक्षरे ।
बार द्वय समापने स्थिरोकारे तृतीयते ॥
गायत्री पाद वर्णित अष्टाक्षरे त्रिघूर्णने ।
गायत्री प्रणवास्थिता वेदमाता सुवर्णिता ॥
अष्टाक्षरे त्रिघूर्णने तद् प्रकार पदत्रये ।
भास्वती छन्द गायत्री महा शक्ति स्वरूपिणी ॥
यद् वेद आदि गायत्री सर्व व्यापी महेश्वरी ।
तद् गायत्री महाशक्ति सर्व छन्द प्रकाशिनी ॥
अष्टाक्षरा पदत्रये गायत्री ध्वनि सर्वदा ।
त्रिवर्णा ये त्रिमूर्ति ते यथाकाले प्रकाशिता ॥
तद्दर्शन मनोहर विचित्रवर्ण सज्जिता ।
विचित्र गति विन्यासे सर्व सृष्टि प्रचालिता ॥
प्रथमे दर्शिता देवी रक्त वर्णे समुज्ज्वला ।
सृष्टि ध्याने समुत्पन्ना कर्म छन्द प्रणोदिता ॥
प्रभाते जगत् ध्याने एतद् रूप परिस्फुट ।
ब्रह्म शक्ति समाख्याता ब्राह्मणी हंस वाहना ॥
जाग्रत करिते विश्व कुश अम्भ करे धृत ।
दानि सुप्ते चलत शक्ति कर्म गति सुचेतने ॥
द्वितीये अति भास्वरा दृष्टा देवी हिरण्मयी ।
प्रेम ऐक्ये समुद्भवा कर्म सूत्र विधारिता ॥
मध्याह्ने जगत् ध्याने एतद् रूप परिस्फुट ।
विष्णु शक्ति समाख्याता वैष्णवी गरुडासना ॥
शंख चक्र गदापद्मे यथा देवी सुशोभिता ।
प्रेम सूत्रे महानन्दे ऐक्ये जगत् विधारिका ॥
तृतीये दर्शिता देवी धूम्र वर्णा मनोहरा ।
जगत् सृष्टि लयंकर यथाशक्ति प्रकाशिता ॥
सायाह्ने जगत् ध्याने एतद् रूप परिस्फुट ।
महेश्वरी समाख्याता वृषभ श्वेत वाहना ॥

त्रिशूल कर धारणे द्वेषी दुष्ट विमर्दने ।
जगन्मोहे विमोहिया सर्व शान्ति प्रदायिनी ॥
तद् देवी स्मरि गायत्री सर्व शुचिः प्रदायिका ।
ब्रह्मवाक्य यथा वेद ब्रह्मणास्ये बहिर्गत ॥
तद् तेजसे परब्रह्मे चतुर्वेद समुद्भवे ।
साम यजुः ऋकाथर्व ब्रह्मणास्ये यथाक्रमे ॥
चतुरास्ये चतुर्वेद पूर्वे साम ऋकोत्तरे ।
अथर्व दक्षिणे यथा दर्शित पश्चिमे यजु ॥
गायत्री वेद सर्वते ब्रह्मवाक विभास्वरा ।
षड छन्द प्रकाशिनी कहि एतद् तदक्रमे ॥
गायत्री अष्ट अक्षरे यथा उक्त पदत्रये ।
एतद् रूपे महादेवी ऋषि कुले प्रपूजिता ॥
तदूक्त आर्ष्य गायत्री अष्याक्षरा पदत्रये ।
चतुर्विंशाक्षरा देवी सर्वत्र स्मर सर्वदा ॥
देव कुले यथा अन्य रूपे देवी उपासिता ।
कथित दिव्यगायत्री चतुष्पादे षडाक्षरे ॥
देव ऋषि उपासिता द्विविध मूर्ति धारणे ।
अष्टविंशाक्षरा छन्द गायत्री जात उष्णिक ॥
द्विविध गति उष्णिके एतद् हेतू समीक्षित ।
कच्चित् अष्टाक्षरे पाद षडाक्षरे कच्चित् कच्चित् ॥
अष्यक्षरे यथा पाद ऋषिवृन्दे उपासित ।
द्वात्रिंश अक्षरे छन्द चतुष्पादे अनुष्टुभ् ॥
तद्परे बृहती छन्द षड त्रिंशाक्षरोद्भव ।
चत्वारिंशाक्षरोद्भव पंक्ति छन्द तदन्तरे ॥
चतूः चत्वारिंशाक्षरे त्रिष्टुप छन्द वर्णित ।
कथित जगति छन्द अष्ट चत्वारिंशाक्षरे ॥
अनुष्टुभ् हते छन्द जगती यद् सुवर्णित ।
सर्व छन्द चतुष्पादे भिन्नाक्षरे प्रकाशित ॥

यथा छन्द चतुष्पादे ऋषि वृन्दे उपासित ।
सर्व अग्रे अनुष्टुभ् व्यक्त छन्द महीतले ॥
यद् छन्द अति तेजसे जगत् सृष्टि प्रकाशक ।
सर्व तेज बलान्वित नित्य कवि कुल प्रिय ॥
गायत्री संहति षड छन्द पूर्वे वेदोद्भव चतुरास्ये ।
नाद ब्रह्माक्षर अति तेजे आदित्याख्या दिनमणि दीप्त ॥

—इति श्रीमदेवायण ब्रह्मकल्पे प्रथम खण्डे देव मण्डलान्तर्गतः काव्य समारम्भ वर्गे गायत्र्यादि छन्द वर्णना नामः द्वितीय संवर्ग ॥

— ☆ —

॥ तृतीय संवर्ग ॥

नव सृष्टि प्रकाशिते अनुष्टुभ् विमन्द्रणे ।
उद्बोधने पुनः कल्प पिंगल कवि सम्भव ॥
सत्य त्रिता द्विता कलि युग गति यथाक्रमे ।
कलि अन्ते पुनर्सत्ये कल्प गति यवे शुन ॥
एतद् संधिक्षणे दृष्ट पिंगलाख्य महेश्वर ।
जटा जूट विमण्डित पशु पाश विमोचक ॥
गंभीरे कहिते रत लक्ष्ये एतद् प्रजापति ।
कश्यप जगत् स्त्रजा विस्मये रत दर्शने ॥
एतद् क्षेत्र महामति करि काव्य निरूपणे ।
तपः तेज प्रदानह करिते धारण क्षम ॥
प्राज्ञ स्मन्य नहे युवा देव श्रद्धा परायण ।
वेद ज्ञाने सदा स्पृहा करि क्षेत्र निरूपण ॥
कहि वाक्य अनुष्टुभे महानाद यथा कृत ।
त्रैलोक्य सृष्टि कम्पने तथा काव्य बहिर्गत ॥
कहिते रत कश्यपे देव काव्य प्रदर्शने ।
अपूर्व द्युति मण्डित हेर सत्य प्रकाशक ॥
देव तत्त्व विधारणे देव जन्म समुद्भवे ।

देव कार्य प्रकाशिया   यथा चक्र विघूर्णित ॥
सर्व सृष्टि समाश्रये   करि व्यक्त चतुर्युग ।
देव बुद्धि समाछन्न   यद् प्रकारे महांधते ॥
यद् प्रकारे प्रदीपित   देव बुद्धि दिने दिने ।
तद् विशालायण स्मर   सर्व सृष्टि समन्वित ॥
देव काल हते क्रमे   अंधकाले निपातित ।
सर्व सृष्टि जगत्स्त्रजा   किं प्रकारे निरीक्षह ॥
पुनश्च हेर तदःपरे   अंध काल परित्यजी ।
देव काले पुनर्वार   एतद् सृष्टि समुत्थित ॥
देवकाल हते क्रमे   देव काले पुनर्गति ।
देवायण इहा कहि   सर्व तत्त्व विधारणे ॥
यथा तव समुद्यम   सत्य युग प्रकाशिते ।
एकांशे कर दर्शन   एतद् तथ्य अवस्थित ॥
द्वादशांशे विभागित   सहस्त्र पत्र निर्णये ।
दृष्ट लक्षाधिक श्लोके   अंशेक यद् प्रकाशित ॥
चतुर्युगे यथा सृष्टि   व्यक्त क्रमे क्रमान्वये ।
अनन्त व्योम सन्निभ   देवायण समीक्षित ॥
एतद् मध्ये निवेशित   सर्व क्रमे निरीक्षह ।
चतुर्दिके अवस्थित   हेर वेद चतुष्टय ॥
ऋग्वेद हेर पूर्वते   पश्चिमे यजु दर्शित ।
साम वेद यथोत्तरे   अथर्व वेद दक्षिणे ॥
नभ स्थले यथादृश्य   ज्योतिष्कादि सुचित्रित ।
कोटि कोटि निहारिका   तारा ग्रह उपग्रह ॥
एतद् मध्य विभास्वर   चन्द्र सूर्य यथा द्वय ।
तदरूप कर दर्शन   देवायण महात्मन ॥
सूर्य तुल्य विभास्वर   सूर्य वंश सुवर्णने ।
रामायण महीतले   राम कीर्ति समाश्रित ॥

अवतीर्ण जनार्दन राम रूपे नराकृति ।
अतुल्य तेज वीर्यते कीर्ति श्रेष्ठ यथास्थले ।
चन्द्र तुल्य विभास्वर चन्द्रं वंश तदन्तरे ॥
भारत काहिनी धृत कृष्ण कीर्ति महीतले ।
अवतीर्ण जनार्दन कृष्ण रूपे नराकृति ॥
अतुल्य बुद्धि कौशले कीर्ति श्रेष्ठ प्रकाशित ।
एतद् बिना सहस्त्रश सुचरित्र सुवर्णित ।
तेज वीर्य महत् अति देवतुल्य जने जने ॥
ए सर्व पुण्य जीवन तारा तुल्य समुज्वले ।
द्वादश सहस्राधिक पत्रदले विमण्डित ॥
देवायण अनुष्टुभे गांधार गुरु गर्जने ।
मेघतुल्य विमन्द्रित ह्रस्व दीर्घ प्लुत स्वने ॥
एतद् बिना क्षणे क्षणे अन्य छन्द बहिर्गत ।
विद्युत् नाद यथामत अकस्मात समुद्भवे ॥
एतद् नभः समाश्रये दिवा रात्रे यथागति ।
हेर देवायणे गति एतद् युग चतुष्टये ॥
सत्ययुग दिवा रूपे देव सूर्य विभास्वर ।
कलि युग निशा रूपे अंध शक्ति प्रभावित ॥
एतद् मध्य तथा द्वय करे क्षेत्र विभागित ।
त्रिता संध्या समाख्यात अर्ध रात्रि यथा द्विता ॥
दिव्य ऊषा सुवर्णने रात्रिहरा यथापथ ।
जीव जगत् प्रचेतने देव सूर्य प्रदर्शने ॥
अत्याद्भुत यथा काल सर्वाधिक मनोहर ।
एतद् क्रमे यथा व्यक्त हेर स्वयं जगत् स्त्रजा ॥
काव्योन्मेषे लघु गुरु छंदे मन्द्रे देवायण नव दृश्ये ।
हृष्ट द्रष्टावतरण काले दर्शे स्त्रष्टा अपलक चक्षे ॥

—इति श्रीमद्देवायण ब्रह्मकल्पे प्रथम खण्डे देव मण्डलान्तर्गतः काव्य समारम्भ वर्गे काव्य प्रकाश वार्ता नामः तृतीय संवर्ग ॥

— ✮ —

॥ चतुर्थ संवर्ग ॥

तद् श्रवणे कहे वाक्य कश्यप पिंगल प्रति ।
अति दीर्घ महाकाव्य स्मरि व्यक्त असंभव ॥
स्वल्पायु मानवे दृष्ट वर्ष शत प्रयोजने ।
किं प्रकारे अभिव्यक्ति कहो एतद् कविश्वर ॥
तदुत्तरे कहे कवि यथा स्थिर मम प्रति ।
संक्षेप करिते काल शुनो क्रमे जगत् स्त्रजा ॥
द्वादश सहस्राधिक पत्र देवायणे यथा ।
तद् प्रकाश यथा क्रमे स्वयं चक्षे निरीक्षह ॥
दश पत्र दिवा प्रति तुमि स्वयं परिग्रह ।
तथा शक्ति प्रदानिया कर वाक्य प्रचालित ॥
कर संख्या निरूपण दश पत्र दिवाप्रति ।
प्रति मासे दिवा त्रिंशे त्रिशतक प्रकाशिवे ॥
मास त्रये दिवा दशे हवे पत्र सहस्त्रश ।
द्वादश गुण निर्णये कर काल निरूपण ॥
कहे स्त्रजा इथे काल वर्ष त्रय प्रयोजन ।
चतुर्मास तदूपरि देवायण प्रकाशिते ॥
संक्षेप काल निश्चय एतद् पथे कवीश्वर ।
तवू प्रश्न विचारह यथा कार्य सुदुष्कर ॥
वर्ष त्रय चतुर्मास स्थिरासन असम्भव ।
यथा अन्नगत प्राण क्षुधा तृष्णा निपीडने ॥
प्रत्युत्तरे कहे कवि स्वीय तेज प्रदानह ।
तव तपः यथा वर्ष षड विंश सहस्त्रशे ॥
एतद् तपः महाशक्ति समाश्रय रह स्वयं ।
तव तेज प्रभावित हवे क्षम प्रकाशिते ॥
तव तेज प्रभावित नहे दुःख कदाचने ।
स्थिरासने अवस्थाने काव्य कार्य यद्क्षण ॥
उपरन्तु प्रहर्षित हवे चित्त क्षणे क्षणे ।
काव्य धारा प्रवाहिले हवे दृढ दिने दिने ॥

पुनः प्रश्ने कहे स्त्रजा स्वल्प वाक्य प्रयोजन ।
नहे दीर्घ महाकाव्य प्रकाशिते कवीश्वर ॥
यथा काव्य बृहत्तम द्वादश गुण वर्धित ।
एतन्मत प्रयोजन वाक्यावली महात्मन ॥
कहे कवि किं संशय बहु वाक्य प्रयोजन ।
तथा विघ्न उपद्रव विमूढत्वे सुनिश्चय ॥
कहि कार्य तथा स्थले अवधान कर स्थिरे ।
बहु वाक्य सुसंग्रहे विघ्नचय निरामये ॥
आह्वानि गणनायके मात्र क्षण अपेक्षह ।
वाक् सिद्धि प्रदानिते सिद्धि दाता गजानने ॥
हवे सर्व समाधान एतद् देव उपस्थिते ।
आख्यात ब्रह्मणस्पति ब्रह्म सृष्टि प्रकाशिते ॥
तद् देवता प्रभावित यथा वाक्य प्रयोजन ।
हवे त्वरित सुसंग्रह विघ्न चिन्ता परित्यज ॥
एरूप कहि पिंगल देवस्त्रा कश्यप प्रति ।
आह्वाने रत सुस्वने विघ्न नाश गजानने ॥
स्मरि काव्य समारम्भे पार्वती प्रिय नन्दन ।
सिद्धि दाता विनायक गणेश ब्रह्मणस्पति ॥
आह्वानि गण सम्राट जन लोके प्रकाशिते ।
काव्येक मूषिका रूढ देव सत्य प्रचेतने ॥
देवास्तित्वे अविश्वास यथा नित्य नर प्रति ।
तद् विघ्न वारणे कार्य स्वयं हर्षे परिग्रह ॥
कवि कुल पुरोभागे रुद्र तेजे विराजित ।
ज्येष्ठ राज जगत्हिते त्वरित आत्म प्रकाशह ॥
वाक् ब्रह्म तव तेजसे अनुभूत जगन्मने ।
वाक् शिल्प ऋत बुद्धिते व्यक्त हर्षे निरन्तर ॥
दानिते शुचिता वाक्ये अक्षर ब्रह्म दर्शने ।
वाक् चातुर्ये अलंकारे सुव्यक्ते स्मरि सत्वरे ॥

एरूप कहिते कवि तद् देव मूषिकारूढ ।
शंख चक्र गदा पद्मे आविर्भूत चतुर्भुज ॥
त्रिनेत्र करुणाकर दिव्य स्नेह विनिर्भर ।
सुज्योति मण्डलावृत शुचि स्मित गजानन ॥
प्रभातारुण सन्निभ रक्त वर्ण कलेवर ।
अपूर्व भूषणाम्बरे दिव्य माल्ये विभूषित ॥
शिरः श्वेत किं सुन्दर प्रभाते पुण्य दर्शने ।
हर्षान्वित कलेवरे शिहरित पुनः पुनः ॥
यदः दृश्ये कवि सम्राट पिंगल स-सुर स्रजा ।
तदग्रे पार्वती सुत अन्तर चक्षे समीक्षित ॥
तदः वाक्य श्रवणे स्वयं रोम हर्षे मुहुर्मुहु ।
संग्रहे रत सर्वतः पुण्य आस्य विनिर्गत ॥
यथा दीन परिग्रहे मणि रत्न सुदुर्लभ ।
तदः तुल्य लेखनी धृत संग्रहि दिवस क्रमे ॥
मास-वर्ष-दिवा क्रमे श्रम क्लान्ति विवर्जित ।
पुण्य वार्ता यथाश्रुत विस्मयतर विस्मये ॥
आश्चर्य केवलाश्चर्ये मम चित्त प्रधावित ।
तदः वाक्य करि संग्रह व्यक्त काव्य महीतले ॥
स्रष्टा वाक्ये कविवर हास्ये युक्त आह्वाने गणपति नामे ।
व्यक्त श्वेतानन गज मुण्डे सिद्धि प्राते मधुमय दृश्ये ॥

—इति श्रीमद्देवायण ब्रह्मकल्पे प्रथम खण्डे देवमण्डलान्तर्गतः काव्य समारम्भ वर्गे सिद्धि प्रकाश नामः चतुर्थ संवर्ग ॥

— ☆ —

CHART A

THE THREE CREATIONS OF PARABRAHMAN

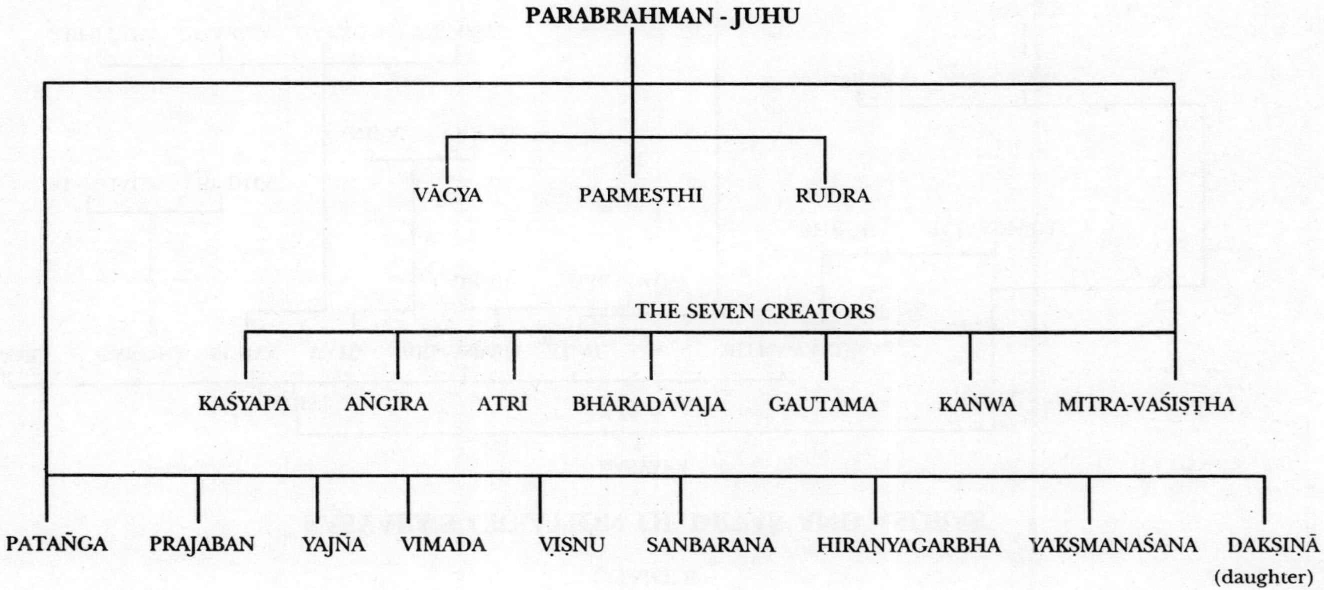

CHART B

KAŚYAPA'S CREATION OF DEVAS AND ASURAS

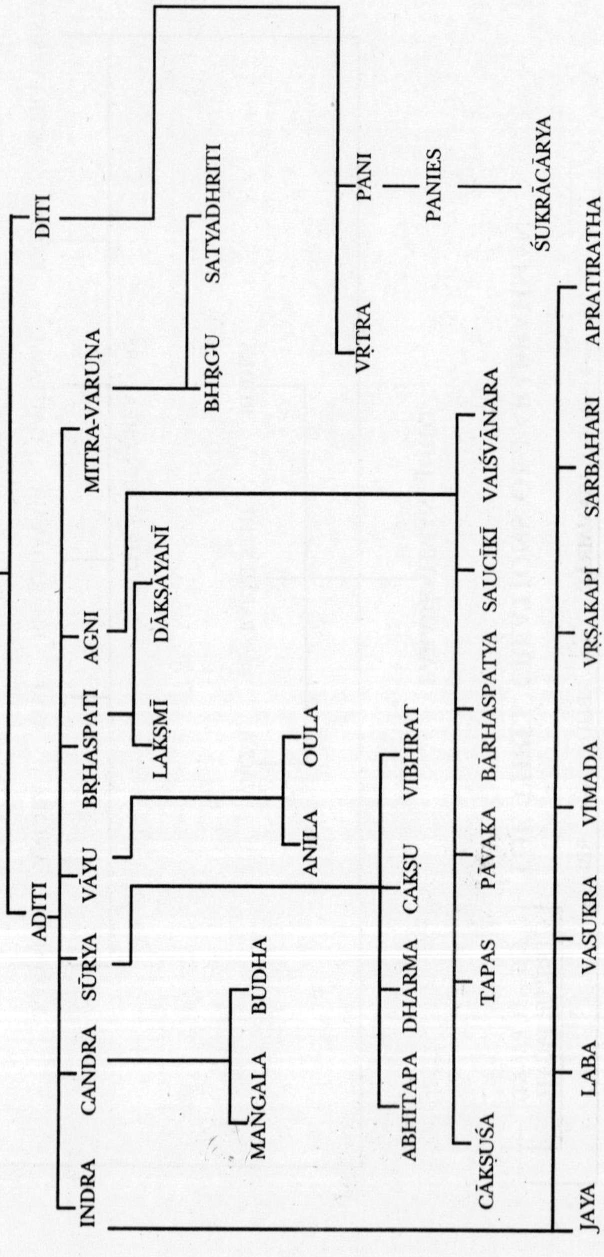

CHART C

CREATIONS OF BRAHMĀ–VIṢṆU–MAHEŚVARA

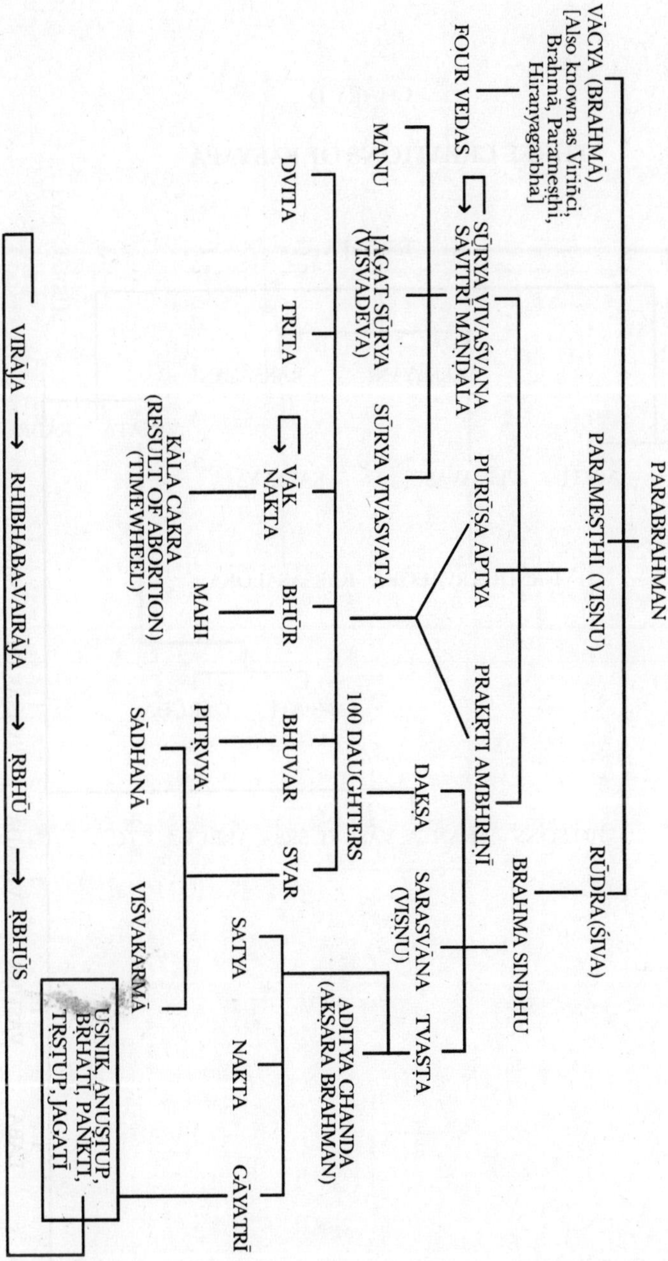

CHART D

THREE CREATIONS OF KAŚYAPA

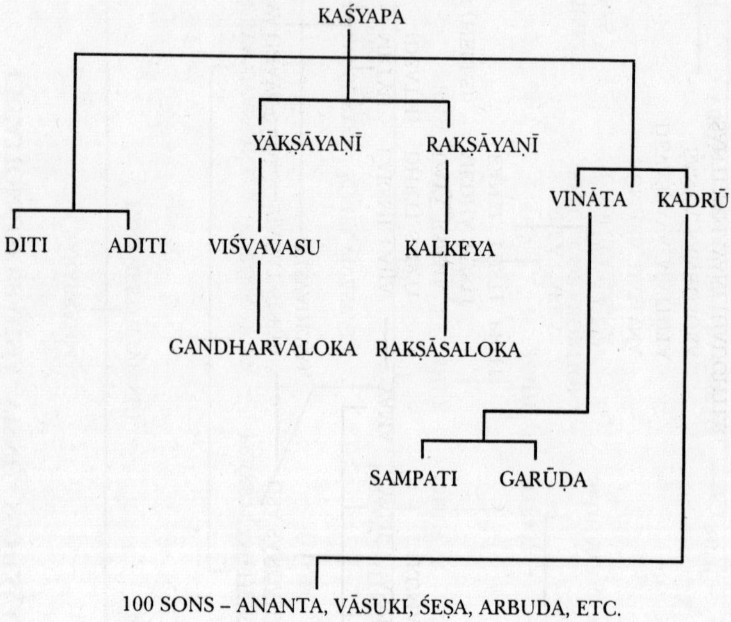

CHART E

CREATIONS OF SATYADEVA AND NAKTA

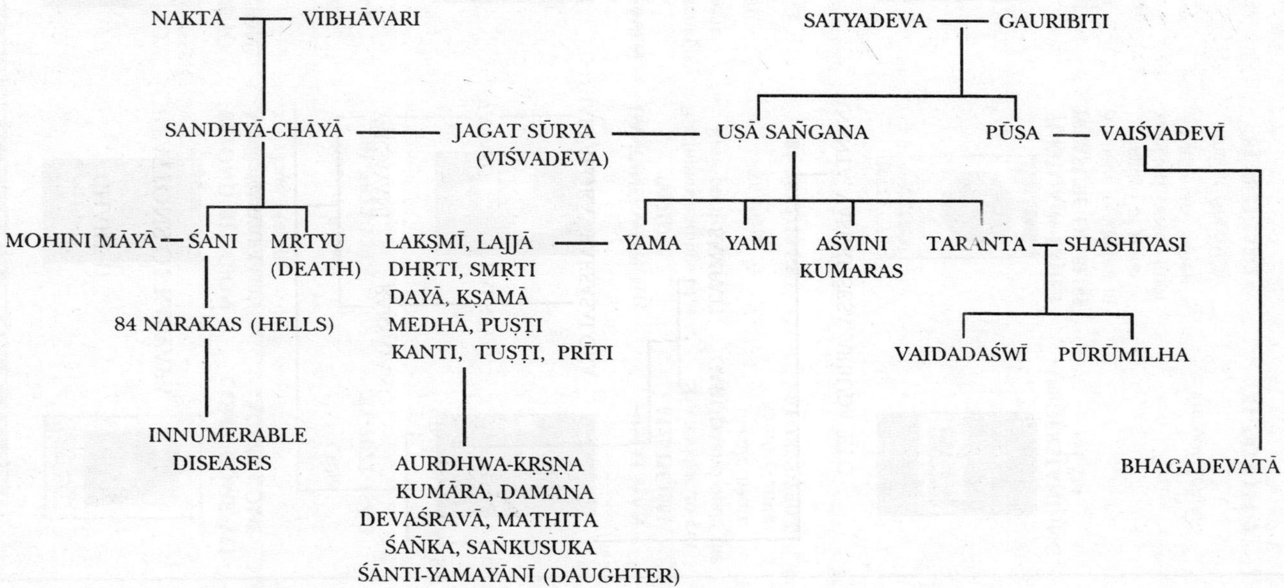

BOOKS OF RELATED INTEREST

ART AS A GUIDE TO SELF REALIZATION

J. Donald Walters

81-7822-028-8

BEYOND RELIGION
Meditations on Man's True Nature

Robert Powell

81-7822-139-x

COME, COME, YET AGAIN COME

Osho

81-7822-154-3

EMBRACING HEAVEN & EARTH
The Liberation Teachings for Enlightenment

Andrew Cohen

81-7822-218-3

DANCING WITH THE VOID
The Innerstandings of a Rare-born Mystic

Sunyata

81-7822-134-9

HIMALAYAN MYSTICISM
Shiva's disc to cut asunder and open the mystic heart
Ralph Nataraj

81-7822-290-6

ISLAM
An Historical Introduction

Gerhard Endress

81-7822-156-x

SUKHMANI SAHEB TREASURE OF BLISS
A poetic rendering in English of some selected verses from Sudhmani Saheb

Bharat Bhooshan

81-7822-258-2

UNDERSTANDING ISLAM

Frithjof Schuon

81-7822-151-9